AT THE END
OF THE
Santa Fe Trail

SISTER BLANDINA SEGALE

THE BRUCE PUBLISHING COMPANY
MILWAUKEE

Nihil obstat: VERY REV. MSGR. RAYMOND F. STOLL, S.T.D., *Censor*
Imprimatur: ✠ JOHN T. McNICHOLAS, *Archbishop of Cincinnati*
19 June 1948

Copyright, 1948
The Bruce Publishing Company
Printed in the United States of America

Sister Blandina Segale, S.C.

Original Author's Note

INTO the keeping of this Journal of my life in the Southwest, there never entered the thought of its publication. The reward for the work involved was to come if Sister Justina and myself would meet and read it together.

A short time ago, the editor of *The Santa Maria Magazine* prevailed upon me to allow its publication in that periodical. After the appearance of a few installments, requests for the Journal in book form began to come from many places in the United States, especially from New Mexico, whose Governor and Secretary of State, with the Archbishop of Santa Fe, found historic value in its record of events made by an eye-witness.

But the crowded hours that allowed no time for the leisurely writing of my Journal still prevail for me; and I realized if the urgent requests for the book were to be met, my wish to re-write it must be set aside. For the shortcomings consequently to be found in AT THE END OF THE SANTA FE TRAIL, let the busy life of a Sister of Charity offer excuse.

SISTER BLANDINA

Original Foreword

THIS simple story of the missionary work of a Sister of Charity in the Southwest of territorial days rivals in many of its pages the most thrilling romances written of that period. It is not given to many women — and especially to a religious — to take part in the upbuilding of a new country and to become familiar with the various phases of pioneer life which Sister Blandina so vividly records and which she evidently considered merely a part of her day's work.

AT THE END OF THE SANTA FE TRAIL is an inspiring record of educational and charitable work carried on for many years in Colorado and New Mexico for Indian 'and Mexican, Catholic and non-Catholic, rich and poor, the criminal and the law-abiding. Page after page bears witness to the initiative, the faith and the intrepid courage of this true daughter of Mother Seton. No work was foreign to her, provided it was God's work. One knows not which to admire the more, her instant grasp of a difficult situation or the coolness and resourcefulness with which she met it.

Humanly speaking, Sister Blandina was not fitted by birth, environment or education to meet the conditions that confronted her in the Trinidad, Santa Fe and Albuquerque of frontier times. Carefully shielded in the home of her Italian parents until she entered the novitiate of the Sisters of Charity, she was assigned after her profession to teach in the parochial schools. It was while pursuing this peaceful routine at Steubenville, Ohio, that she was informed by her Superior that she was to proceed without delay to Trinidad, Colorado — and that she was to travel alone!

Life as she had known it ceased for Sister Blandina when she arrived at the terminus of the railway at Kit Carson. Stepping into a stage-coach, with a cowboy for a fellow passenger, she entered a world immeasurably removed from the one in which she had been living. Her impressions of this new Western world, how she solved its problems, how she adjusted herself to its primitive conditions, how she met the extraordinary demands made upon her, she recorded tersely in a diary intended only for the eyes of her sister, also a religious of the Sisters of Charity of Cincinnati.

It is a story that appeals irresistibly to the imagination. The picture she sketches of life in the West in those pioneer days is one of rude and sharp contrasts, inseparable from the period of construction and conditions of the frontier.

We see her throwing the weight of her influence against lynching, which was at that time the unwritten law of the West. Never before nor since was a stranger sight witnessed in the streets of Trinidad than that of the young Sister of Charity, accompanied by the Sheriff, walking with a doomed man to the bedside of his victim to beg for forgiveness. Lynch law received its death blow that day in Trinidad.

Again she is seen fearlessly confronting the notorious outlaw, "Billy the Kid," demanding safety for the physicians of Trinidad, whose lives he had threatened, and not only winning his confidence but inspiring him with respect for every member of the religious garb. Who shall say what effect her ministrations to a neglected member of his band of outlaws may have had on the soul of this misguided youth?

On another occasion she fearlessly offers her services to quiet the Apaches who, angered by the ruthless murder of one of their tribe, are about to start on the war-path. Where in the pages of romance shall we find anything more thrilling than the graphic picture drawn of the young Sister, crucifix in hand, walking out unaccompanied to parley with the scouts and prevent the threatened uprising?

These are some of the high-lights of AT THE END OF THE SANTA FE TRAIL. There are many others of equal interest. Indeed, the book throughout is a revelation of the beauty of the life of prayer, labor and sacrifice. Only a religious woman, prompted by supernatural charity, could have found such joy and contentment in the service of God's erring or neglected children under the trying conditions she was called upon daily to meet. The book should make a wide appeal.

Contents

AT THE END
OF THE
Santa Fe Trail

Life Sketch of Sister Blandina Segale 1850—1941

"Gesu" was the first word the little Italian child, Rosa Maria Segale, learned to write at her home in the hilly village of Cicagna, Italy. Lingering over the sweetness of its sound, she smiled at her accomplishment and then laboriously added, "Madre."

Nearly a century later when she lay dying in the infirmary at the motherhouse of the Sisters of Charity near Cincinnati, Ohio, Rosa Maria Segale, now known as Sister Blandina, serenely whispered, "Gesu, Madre," smiled, turned her head, and died.

Rosa Maria Segale was born on January 23, 1850, in the northern Italian village of Cicagna which lies about fifteen miles above Genoa in the thickly populated section of the Ligurian hills. Her mother, Giovanna Malatesta, was noble and good. To her the elder Genoese women came for wise counsel in Italy and later in America. Sister Blandina wrote of her mother, "My father kept secret my mother's illustrious family name, for those were days of revolution in Italy. In the Middle Ages my mother's family had absolute control or they would know why."

Francesco, her father, was a proficient overseer and owner of two well-cultivated orchards. For generations the Segale family had lived and died in their stone houses in the rocky and rugged Ligurian hills. Known to the villagers as *Il Signorino* (The Little Lord), Francesco was quiet, refined, sensitive, and adored by his five children.

1

After the baby Rosa Maria was baptized, Giovanna took her, as was her custom, to the mountain sanctuary of Mont'Allegro, to present her to our Lady, Santa Maria. Over the high altar of the church is the Byzantine painting, *The Dormition of the Virgin*, which legend decrees was miraculously transported from Dalmatia. Offering her newly-born, Giovanna prayed, "To help mankind, *Madre mia*, to comfort the sorrowful . . . to harbor the harborless . . . to visit the sick . . . . to teach your ways to mankind."

When Rosa was four years old her father and mother gave away their stone house and their orchards, and left revolution-tossed Italy for America. Accompanied by Andrea, 11; Maria Maddelena, 8; Catalina, 6; and Rosa, they set sail from Genoa and landed at New Orleans three months later. Cincinnati was their objective. A few Genoese had preceded them there and the city appealed to them because Giovanna hoped to be able to help her countrymen there, and because the Segales had heard that Cincinnati was built upon seven hills. "It will remind us of Cicagna," Giovanna had encouraged Francesco.

The early Cincinnati days were filled with loneliness, language difficulties, dire poverty. Concerned about her children's future, Giovanna hired an English teacher and somehow managed to pay for the lessons. The Segales all lived in one room at Main and Canal Streets. There little Catalina died. An immigrant, Mr. Novello, finally prevailed upon a friend to allow Francesco to open a fruit stand on his corner, Front and Sycamore Streets. From the beginning Francesco's business thrived, and when Bartolomeo, the older boy, completed his studies in Italy and came to America, he persuaded his father to open a confectionery store. From then on Francesco was quite successful.

Little Rosa made her First Holy Communion after a year of preparation on April 21, 1861, at the Cathedral of St. Peter in Chains. She was confirmed that same afternoon by the Most Reverend Archbishop John Baptist Purcell. She attended schools conducted by the Notre Dame Sisters, the Sisters of Mercy, and

Hughes Intermediate School. Meanwhile the Segales had purchased a home at 461 West Fifth Street. There the other children were born. When Rosa completed grammar school she was allowed to attend Mt. St. Vincent Academy, Cedar Grove, a school conducted by the Sisters of Charity, in Cincinnati. Ever since she had come to Cincinnati, Rosa had observed the Sisters of Charity as they went about performing works of mercy, working among the sick, the orphans; and she loved them. She knew that during the Civil War they nursed the soldiers on the battlefields. One day she surprised her father by saying, "Father, as soon as I am old enough, I shall be a Sister of Charity." After completing her musical course at Cedar Grove, she entered the Sisters of Charity motherhouse at the age of sixteen, September 13, 1866. Her beloved sister and lifelong companion, Maria Maddelena, refused several marriage offers that same month and followed her younger sister to the Sisters of Charity motherhouse. She was known as Sister Justina.

After pronouncing their holy vows on December 8, 1868, Rosa secretly prayed to be sent to the faraway west — Santa Fe — where the Sisters of Charity had gone in 1865. Sister Blandina's desire was fulfilled, in 1872, after she had been on mission in Dayton and Steubenville, Ohio. During her twenty-one years in the west, Sister Blandina kept a journal of her experiences which were published in 1932 under the title, *At the End of the Santa Fe Trail.* The present work is a new edition of Sister Blandina's journal.

Recalled to the motherhouse, in 1894, Sister Blandina's next missions were in Ohio, at Fayetteville and Glendale. In August of 1897, Mother Mary Blanche, mother general, entrusted the care of the Italians in Cincinnati to Sister Blandina and Sister Justina. From this time on the two sisters were never separated. This work of reconverting the immigrant Italians was dear to the heart of the Archbishop of Cincinnati, William Henry Elder, who had watched anxiously as proselytism spread among the Italian people. The work of bringing their own people back into the Faith was a labor that kept Sister Blandina in the basin of the city for thirty-five busy years. Never did she slacken in her work. She herself gave instructions to 80 per cent of the Italians in the city. Her battle cry, "The Charity of Christ Urges Us," was well lived.

During that first hard year in the basin of the city, Sister Blandina wrote: "What we really need is not a school, but a center; a cheery, homey place where the immigrants can come; where the poor can receive charity and the rich bestow it. The Italian immigrants are so lonely. If we care for the children's religious life they will make good Catholics but the parents will draw within themselves and become very bitter unless we help them. . . . If this is His work it will succeed despite all opposition; if it is not His work we do not want it to succeed."

The present home of the Santa Maria Institute at 21 West Thirteenth Street is a far cry from those first cross-filled years. Their first institute for their people opened in 1899 at the old motherhouse of the Sisters of the Poor of St. Francis at Third and Lytle Streets. Through the kindness of Archbishop Elder and the Sisters, this property was placed at their disposal. From 1897–1899, Sister Blandina and Sister Justina lived with the Sisters of Charity, using the convent as headquarters for their school and social work. They opened three schools for Italians: at Springer Institute, Holy Trinity, and at Lytle Street.

It would be impossible to enumerate all the works undertaken by the Sisters at the Santa Maria Institute from 1897 to the present, because according to Sister Blandina's philosophy, individual needs are sufficient reason for the inauguration of a work. By 1905, the Sisters were able to report to the papal delegate, Archbishop Diomede Falconio, when he visited the Santa Maria, that there was no organized proselytism in Cincinnati. However, proselytism did not cease. Far from it. In 1912, it ran rampant through the city, and to combat the new menace, the Sisters moved from their second home at 534 West

Seventh Street to 640 West Eighth Street, where their property finally included four houses.

Among the undertakings of the Sisters, the following are typical: handling of juvenile court cases; Americanization centers at Walnut Hills and Fairmount; free employment bureau; reclamation of girls and women; classes for all nationality groups; day nursery; kindergarten; milk station; housing of homeless girls and women; visitation of the sick, the imprisoned, the unfortunate; distribution of food, free clothes, books; Sunday School classes; Boy and Girl Scout troops; Legion of Mary; classes in homemaking, singing, dramatics; clubs; Braille work.

When the juvenile court was organized in Cincinnati, Sister Blandina was asked to be present at the first meeting. Later the court appointed her a Cincinnati probation officer. The Santa Maria had its own juvenile court. In five years' time the Sisters had restored 157 women to normal living. In an attempt to rid the city of white slavery, Sister Blandina brought a case to court. Her action was highly commended by local attorneys, especially Mr. Ledyard Lincoln, prominent lawyer.

In September, 1916, their golden jubilee as Sisters of Charity dawned: 1866–1916. Sister Blandina briefly records the day: "Fifty years ago we made our Holy Vows on the Feast of the Immaculate Conception with a number of other Sisters. Several of them have been called Home. Today our people have given us $125.00. I am deeply moved. We shall use this money to provide books for poor children." Six years later their own Santa Maria celebrated its silver jubilee. That occasion was heralded throughout Cincinnati, and the Sisters were delighted. High Masses of Thanksgiving were sung at the convent, 640 West Eighth Street; St. Anthony Welfare Center; and Sacre Cuore Church. On December 10, there was an elaborate celebration in Memorial Hall. The night of the celebration the Sisters quietly reminisced in their convent home. Rarely were they present at the harvest. The harvest belonged to God and to whomsoever He chose.

Theirs was the laborer's part; theirs to bear the heats of the blistering sun; the ingratitude of those who did not understand. But they knew that they were indeed rich, and they wondered at the magnitude of their happiness.

The extent of Sister Blandina's dependence on Sister Justina came as a terrific blow when, on July 31, 1929, Sister Justina died at the Good Samaritan Hospital in Cincinnati. Her illness was brief; an appendectomy performed July 20, and eleven days later, at the age of 83, she was dead. Among the many letters Sister Blandina kept was the following:

August 12, 1929

My dear Sister Blandina:

May the Lord sustain you in your great loss. You have lived for God so long and so near to Him that, I am sure, you have generously given your saintly sister to heaven.

I wish with all my heart that I could have been here to pay a last tribute to Sister Justina at her funeral Mass.

I shall never forget my last conversation with Sister Justina. From her dying bed and in a weakened condition she aroused herself. She expressed her undying love for her own Italian people. She recalled in general terms the struggles that she and you faced to protect the Italian people in this Community in order that they might not lose the priceless heritage of their faith.

May Sister's great life of sacrifice in a truly missionary work prove to be an inspiration to other Sisters of Charity of Cincinnati to take up the Apostolate of Sister Justina.

Faithfully yours,
John T. McNicholas
Archbishop of Cincinnati

When she was 81, Sister Blandina went to Rome. As the news of her intended journey became known, a highly esteemed writer of the *Cincinnati Post,* Alfred Segal, wrote the following in his column, "Life as He Sees It."

"Sister Blandina starts back to Italy Sunday, after seventy-seven years. . . . Four years old she was when she left her native land; at eighty-one she returns.

"She is going to see the Pope about placing Mother Elizabeth Seton among the Saints, but people say that Sister Blandina is saint enough herself, canonized by sixty years of faithful doing.

"Trinidad, Colorado, knew her for a saint sixty years ago when she went there to teach. And if Trinidad was a rough place when she entered it, gentler it was when she departed. Rude men reverenced her walking among them as she did, unafraid; she offered a holy presence by which the power of pistols was shamed. She built a schoolhouse at Trinidad and went her way.

"She went to New Mexico and established a trade school for Indians. She made a hospital for the workmen who were building the Santa Fe Railroad and were dying in numbers from the hardships of the trail. The Apache Indians were in truculent mood; Sister Blandina went into the wilderness to meet their scouts and by gentle words made peace.

"Cincinnati became aware of Sister Blandina some thirty-five years ago. She came here with her sister, Maria Maddelena, also a nun, by name Sister Justina, and founded a social center for Italian immigrants which they called the Santa Maria Institute. . . . They offered shelter to women stranded and without work; gave food to hungry men and found them jobs; guarded the children of working women in their day nursery; visited homes, looked after erring children, visited prisons. . . . Thirty-five years of this."

One day in March, 1933, on the feast of St. Patrick, to be exact, her summons came to return to the motherhouse. She delayed not a moment, and two days later she left the Santa

Maria Institute and returned to the motherhouse of the Sisters
of Charity at Mount St. Joseph, a suburb of Cincinnati. Change
of residence did not change Sister Blandina. Her fingers were
ever busy, her correspondence enormous. People sought her sage
advice, and younger people found in her a kindred spirit; for her
interest in youth and their problems was ever of paramount
importance.

The aged Sister spent hours in the motherhouse chapel praying
for God's holy will to be done in all things. Frequently she would
plead: "Remember, my *Gesu*, to send our Community sufficient
and worthy aspirants to the religious life so that we can ade-
quately care for our work for You." And then she would smile
quickly as she added, "And don't forget the Santa Maria Institute, nor the West, my *Gesu*."

The radio she loved, and the operas, which she knew thor-
oughly, were her special delight. Political speeches she listened
to with avidity. The Rt. Rev. Fulton J. Sheen, speaking over the
Catholic Hour, held first place. The last program she listened
to was Monsignor Sheen's. Before his talk the next Sunday she
was dead.

One day before a fall, in 1937, which resulted in a broken hip
and almost a year of complete inactivity, Sister Blandina walked
across the beautiful motherhouse grounds, past the academy, the
college, and on out the tree-lined road below which the Ohio
river flows. Climbing a little hill, she paused before the delicately
wrought iron crucifix guarding the entrance to the Sisters'
cemetery. El Campo Santo, they used to call it in Santa Fe.

She made the Stations of the Cross before visiting Sister
Justina's grave, but when she did stop there to breathe a prayer,
she found that she wanted to stay always. Not because she was
afraid of life. No, life to her was Christ whose presence in the
Blessed Sacrament had become increasingly dear since Sister
Justina's death. But here in this cemetery she was among her
friends and co-laborers who had worked for the Master. And
her soul was yearning to be forever united with Him. Now she

was the oldest living member of her congregation which numbered well above twelve hundred souls. Here lay her dearest Maria Maddelena protected by the tall, straight pine trees. Below the flowering hill flowed the Ohio. How she loved that river, and now that her life was scissoring time she would soon sleep to its lulling music. She looked down the terraced rows of white crosses into the center of the valley where there was a life-size crucifix, a white corpus on black wood. No shamming in that representation. She asked to have her purgatory on earth so that death would unite her instantly to Him. She saw again in retrospect the Southwest; the hot tenements of Cincinnati where she and Sister Justina had worked, and her heart almost broke within her, so great was her desire to begin again for God.

To the Sisters who came into her room in the infirmary she would say, "Child, pray that God may give me the grace to endure, to persevere." When terrific headaches would strike her, she would smile, "From my mother I have inherited these bad headaches. My mother's name was Malatesta, which means, 'bad head.' And all my life I have had this 'bad head.'"

"How do you feel this morning, Sister?" the Sisters would ask her.

"Just as God wills," she ever replied.

In response to, "What can I do for you, Sister?" she would answer, "No, child, not for me, but for God." Then she would say, "He must be very pleased with you, child. Always keep your chin up, and your eyes on God."

The end came February 23, 1941, just a month after the celebration of her ninety-first birthday. Her Sisters in Christ and her friends watched and prayed. And throughout the city news spread that Sister Blandina was dying. Men bared their heads, went into churches, and knelt in quiet corners with bowed heads and aching hearts. The Italians of Cincinnati were grief stricken. Had she not instructed 80 per cent of them herself?

But Sister Blandina was worrying about neither past nor future. She was a little girl again in Cincinnati, sitting in a fruit wagon and looking into the faces of the first two Sisters of Charity she had ever seen. And then she was turning to *Il Signorino,* her father, and saying to him, "Father, as soon as I am old enough I shall be a Sister of Charity."

And she had been a Sister of Charity in the fullest sense for over seventy years, for "God is Charity, and they who dwell in Charity dwell in God and God in them." In great quietness she died as the Sisters prayed, "Have mercy on me, O God, according to Thy great mercy." Her last aspiration was, "My Jesus, Mercy . . . *Gesu . . . Madre.*"

The newspapers made much of her death, and to Sacre Cuore Church in Cincinnati her remains were carried with special permission, since à Sister of Charity dying in Cincinnati is always buried from the motherhouse. At Sacre Cuore a solemn requiem Mass' was sung with the auxiliary bishop, George J. Rehring giving the absolution.

Then began the journey to the motherhouse cemetery. It was difficult to believe that the vivacious Sister Blandina was being borne by others in this long procession. For so many years she had carried the burdens of countless souls. The cortege traveled the same road Sister Blandina had taken a few years before when she walked above the wide Ohio to El Campo Santo that day and found she wanted to remain there. The leaves were gone now and the ground frozen as they laid her to rest near Sister Justina where she could lovingly watch over her just as she had ever done in life.

But the sun came out just as the officiating priest blessed the grave, and her smile must have lingered as she looked again at the life-size crucifix and began to rest at the feet of her *Gesu.*

Sister Therese Martin, S.C.
Feast of the Sacred Heart
Denver, Colorado
June 13, 1947

PART

I

Trinidad

SISTER BLANDINA was stationed at Steubenville, Ohio, when she received a letter from the Motherhouse in Cincinnati, telling her to proceed at once to Trinidad for missionary work. Hastening to obey, Sister Blandina confided to her sister, Sister Justina, that she believed her happy destination to be an island off the coast of Venezuela.

Sister Blandina went alone by rail, construction train, and stagecoach to her destination, Trinidad, in the territory of Colorado, arriving there frightened yet courageous on December 9, 1872. Sister was twenty-two years old at the time.

From the outset she chose St. Francis Xavier as her patron in her new missionary surroundings. Her watchword, "May angels guard your every step," was first said to her by the Most Reverend Archbishop John Baptist Purcell, second Archbishop of Cincinnati.

Practical in each aspect of her life, she began to review her Spanish as soon as she arrived in Trinidad, and advised the other Sisters to do so. Every hovel, every needy soul knew the black capped little figure who walked right into the homes and hearts of the pioneers in the Trinidad country.

Friend to Mr. George Simpson, for whom "Simpson's Rest" above Trinidad was named; his wife, Doña Juanita; Dr. Michael Beshoar; the Circuit Court Judges; Rafael, the Indian Chief; Sister Blandina was the first person to stop lynching laws in Trinidad. Nor did she quail when she asked Billy the Kid and his gang not to scalp Trinidad's four physicians, although Billy

11

had come to Trinidad for the express purpose of killing these four men. For four years the frontier town knew her, watched her, loved her, and finally asked to assist her when, with her own hands and no resources, she built a public school for their children.

For nearly four score years her adopted townspeople have revered her name. A brief command sent her on to Santa Fe over Raton Pass in December, 1876.

§ 1

On Train from Steubenville, Ohio, to Cincinnati. Nov. 30, 1872. My Darling Sister Justina:

How interestedly you, Sister M. Louis, and myself read Eugénie de Guérin's Journal and her daily anxieties to save her brother from being a spiritual outcast! This Journal which I propose keeping for you will deal with incidents occurring on my journey to Trinidad and happenings in that far-off land to which I am consigned.

The Journal will begin with the first act. Here is Mother Josephine's letter:

> Mt. St. Vincent, O.,[1]
> Nov. 27, 1872.

Sister Blandina,
  Steubenville, O.
My Dear Child:

You are missioned to Trinidad. You will leave Cincinnati Wednesday and alone. Mother Regina will attend to your needs.

> Devotedly,
> Mother Josephine.[2]

This letter thrilled us both. I was delighted to make the sacrifice, and you were hiding your feelings that I might not lose any merit. Neither of us could find Trinidad on the map except in the island of Cuba. So we concluded that Cuba was my destination. I was to leave Steubenville quietly so that none of my obstreperous pupils might cause the incoming teacher annoyance. Hence I went to Sunday Catechetical class as usual — 2 P.M. I was to take the 3 P.M. train for Cincinnati. I said to my hopefuls, "Instead of catechism, I'm going to tell you an Indian story today." The schoolhouse roof was not disturbed, though the hurrahs were loud enough! The moral of the story was "Indian Endurance." Dismissed them at two-thirty without one word of goodby except the daily one. You remember how surprised I was to see a crowd at the station to wish me "Godspeed"; I thought I was to slip away without anyone's knowledge except our own. Mr. Tait and Mr. McCann wished to speak to me alone. Both had been in the West. "You will have a long travel on the plains," they said, "before you reach Trinidad."

"Where is Trinidad?"

"A little mining town in Southwestern Colorado." So then I knew my destination which, of course I would have been told at Mt. St. Vincent.[3] Both gentlemen said they have traveled on the plains on the Santa Fe Trail, and they seemed to have made it a matter of conscience to inform me on the subject of cowboys. This in substance was their conversation with me:

"Sister, you may be snow-bound while on the plains." I looked my assent, I knew I could not stop the snow.

"Travelers are sometimes snow-bound for two weeks, and you are alone. This, though, is not the greatest danger to you."

Mentally I was wishing both gentlemen somewhere else.

"Your real danger is from cowboys." I looked at the speakers.

"You do not seem to grasp our meaning. No virtuous woman is safe near a cowboy." Both gave up trying to make me understand what they considered danger. Why should snow or cowboys frighten me any more than others who will be traveling the same way! So you see, dearest, I'm not going to so long a distance as we thought. At three o'clock A.M. the baggage checker came through our coach. I looked to see how much the pocketbook contained — just twenty-five cents. If I used it to ride to the Good Samaritan I'd be minus the fare to Mt. St. Vincent, so I made up my mind to skirt around from the Little Miami to the Good Samaritan Hospital.

At four A.M. I rang the front doorbell — no response. I sat on the stone steps and waited till I heard the rising bell, then I waited another fifteen minutes when again I rang the doorbell. Sister Anthony[4] came.

"Why, child, where did you come from; how did you get here? I'm sure you are cold." I said I came from Steubenville.

"Oh, yes! dear Father Bigelow died there. He was good to this hospital. Last year he sent a barge of coal to us." I said he was good to anyone in need. He died possessed of three dollars and fifty cents. His hand was always open to any kind of distress.

I did not mention to Sister Anthony that I walked from the Little Miami Station.

After Mass, breakfast and miles of sympathy and "God Bless You" from the Sisters at the Good Samaritan, one of the nurses accompanied me to Fifth and Vine Streets, where I was to take "Barney's Bus" for Mt. St. Vincent. The bus was to leave at ten A.M. I waited till three P.M. then asked one of the clerks if he thought Mr. McCabe would run the bus that day.

"I fear no bus will run to-day. There is an epidemic — epizootic among the horses." I asked if Mr. Segale's place of business was anywhere near. He pointed to Wood's Theater and I started to the place indicated. Brother Henry managed to find a "hack" to send me to Mt. St. Vincent. On the way, between the first ascent of the hill and the Seminary, I met Sisters Gabriella[5] and Delphina[6] walking in the slush and cold on their way to the Orphan Asylum. I stopped to take them in. They returned with me to Cedar Grove, from there the driver was to take them to the Asylum in Cumminsville. Sister Gabriella said to me, "I would gladly go where you are going instead of shouldering this heavy burden." Sister is to be mother to three hundred orphans, taking Sister Sophia's[7] place.

The Sisters are showing great sympathy. I heard Sister Benedicta[8] say, "She does not mind going so far and alone — I've not seen her shed a tear." Nor will you, my dear Sister. The tears will flow where none but He and myself will know. Still, I'm delighted to go. I did not tell you, dearest, that one year ago last November I wrote to Mother Regina saying I envied the sacrifices the Sisters were making who were sent far away to do God's work. I've received my answer with compound interest. You know that up to date the Sisters going on distant missions were consulted and none were sent who had parents living. I am pleased that that record is broken in my case.

Mother Regina told me to spend a day at home.

Dear Lord! Give me strength. I anticipate a scene.

I spent Wednesday, December 5th, at our old homestead. Mother kept open house all day. Friends came in groups. Mr. Leverone and bride, his mother and the bride's mother, Mrs. Garibaldi, the Misses Gardelli and a host of others. Mrs. Garibaldi threatened to take off my habit. I said, "Hands off! Have you any right to detain Mary if John wishes to take her to California?"

"Oh, that is different."

"Yes, as different as heaven and earth. I have chosen my portion, Mary has chosen hers, each abides by her choice."

John Leverone's mother acted most sensibly all day. She was soothing oil to all the protests made to my going. Our dear mother kept quiet. When we were permitted a lone interview she asked, "Do you want one of your sisters to accompany you?" I answered, "I prefer to do just as my superiors have told me."

"Well, then I will give you a thousand-dollar check so that in case you desire to return you will have the wherewith."

"No, no, dear mother, I fully realize the responsibilities I assumed. As you are aware, I realized them from the first day I entered the Novitiate."

Mother replied: "And I want to tell you I never doubted your vocation. I agree to your sacrifice, my dear child, keep on serving God, I will never interfere. Now that I have your explicit answer, friends cannot urge any logical reason to prevent your going."

All day the visitors reminded me of a disturbed ant hill. When mother and I were alone she spoke the Genoese dialect. It was like hearing sketches of a favorite opera. Wednesday at 2:00 P.M. I went to visit our Ecclesiastical Superior. The Most Rev. J. B. Purcell[9] offered me several gifts. But St. Francis Xavier is my patron, so I'm not going to possess any superfluous article. I only regret I could not pass our home without going in, as St. Francis Xavier did. If I aim high I surely must reach some upper strata of detachment in His service. One thing I take with me, the impressive blessing given me by His Grace, part of which rings clear — "May angels guard your every step." He was extremely sympathetic at my having to go alone.

I went to confession to Rev. Dr. Callaghan.[10] You may recall how we enjoyed his lecture on the "School Question" delivered in Steubenville. After mother had a short interview with me, father managed to see me alone. He took hold of me and asked, "Have I ever denied you anything?"

I signified no.

"You have never disobeyed me in your life?"

I assented.

"Now I command you — you must not go on this far away mission! Are you going?"

"Yes, father." He let go the hold on my arm and walked toward the door. Not without my seeing his tears falling fast. He did not realize his hold on my arm gave me pain — not to speak of the heart-pain for him.

In the railway station at St. Louis between train time, I got off to purchase a pair of arctics. I saw several Italian women selling fruit. One of them had a daughter standing near. I asked the mother if she would permit her daughter to accompany me to the shoe store, which was in sight. The mother looked at me earnestly then said to her neighbor peddler, "How do I know who she is, she looks like a *monaca* (sister) but she might be a *strega* (witch)." I thanked the true guardian of her daughter and went to make my purchase alone. I spoke English to the peddler.

If good Sister Benedicta who thought I did not mind — because I did not cry — had seen me during the greater part of last night she would but too truly have said, "That heart is human in every fiber." That I succeeded in dignifiedly getting away from home is Thy Grace, oh, my God!

Forty-two persons accompanied me to the train, among them friends of old, but my purpose never faltered, not even in shadow. Such tactics as I executed yesterday! I see one trait strong in me, the straight service of God. Not the father whom I had never seen cry, nor the most patient, dearest mother whose heart is crushed at my being sent alone, much less the friends who used every argument to make me say I would not go — could elicit the faintest trace that I was not more pleased at my going alone than if I had had a dozen with me.

Sisters Antonia[11] and Gonzaga[12] came to the waiting room. I asked the company to permit me an interview with the Sisters. When going toward them, one of my dear old friends said, "Look, we cannot doubt she is happy." This was not intended for my hearing, the noise caused the speaker to raise her voice. Sister Antonia asked me how I had spent the day. I narrated some incidents. "I'm an ancient religious, but I could not have gone through the ordeal as creditably as you did." What if I had mentioned all the heart sighs I had witnessed! When it was time to board the train I asked that my last interview be with my mother. Cannot you picture her sad, endearing look of appreciation? I'll skip the last talk with mother — some of it was in silence.

§ 2

It is dark and lamps have been lighted. My God! if I could love my vocation more, the conversation going on round me would produce that effect. There opposite me sits a young lady giving her experience of missionary life. The elderly gentleman must be her father. He looks at me so often that the indications are he will soon turn his conversation to me. Holy Spirit, give me proper words.

"Are you a missionary, too?"

"I hope to be. Are there missionaries on the train?"

"My daughter is. Just now she is taking a rest. Where are you going?"

"To Trinidad, in the Southwest of Colorado."

"Are you going to teach the Greasers — Mexicans? Some call them 'coyotes.'"

"Oh!" How much undercurrent of thought I had in that "Oh!"

"Come here, daughter, and tell this lady some of the things you know about Gr — Mexicans." (The daughter posing affectedly and trying to be dignified at the same time.)

"I have been teaching the Mexicans for a Missionary Society."

"Do you speak Spanish?"

"A little."

"Do they speak English?"

"Not those I taught." Apparently she wanted this fact placed to her credit.

"How, then, did you teach them?"

"Religion, do you mean?"

"Anything."

"Well, I pointed to a table and they would say 'mesa.' I showed them a book and they would say 'libro' — then I would tell them the English."

"Oh, I see. Then you learned the same number of Spanish words that they learned English ones."

"Do you intend to teach by the same method?"

"No, not exactly. On the average how many words did teacher and pupil acquire in a month?" (Evaded the question.)

"I taught four months, from August to the end of November. The pupils could tell me the names of objects if I pointed to them; they could say house, sky, clouds, trees. I found the work laborious and the salary, though it is more than a public school teacher receives, ought to be raised. What salary are you going to get?"

"I made a contract to let my salary accumulate and draw interest."

"For a long time?"

"For just as long as my capitalist sees fit."

"I would not do that. You cannot tell how long the funds in these Missionary Societies will hold out."

"Never fear! My investment is more solid than the Rockies — they may crumble, but His Word will not."

"Please explain your business method."

"It is very simple to any Catholic. He or she makes application for admittance into a religious community and offers himself or herself to give service to God. The service rendered is according to the rules and constitutions of the Order for which he or she feels called. After we have tested ourselves and superiors have tested us, we, of our own will, bind ourselves by sacred promises — one of which, in our community, is not to use money for personal use — only for the good of others. Do you not think that a sure investment?"

"Do you mean you work all your life and give the money to others?"

"You are clothing my meaning with new words, but it amounts to the same."

"And will you teach Mexicans and retain no recompense?"

"Whomsoever I may teach or any amount that may come to me from teaching will be used to enlarge our facilities for the welfare of others."

"Pa, that is more than our religion requires of us."

"And, daughter, if our church required it, we would not do it."

"A religious worker or teacher in the Catholic Church, having kept the decalogue, desires to mount a little higher. The Church does not oblige any one to this life."

"I never met a Catholic before. When do you expect to return?"

"Never, as far as I know."

"But you can return if you want to?"

"That comes under another one of our promises, to go and come as we are told."

"Why did you make such promises?"

"To follow the teaching of Jesus — 'If thou wilt be perfect, go sell all thou hast, give to the poor, then come and follow Me.' This is a counsel more difficult to follow than a command — yet not of obligation."

"I would like to speak of our meeting at our next missionary conference — will you tell me your age?"

"Twenty-two."

Then followed a great commotion on the train, men running excitedly, one gentleman stopped to tell us the train ahead of us had jumped the track.

§ 3

Kansas City, Dec. 6, 1872.

Number one! Number two! Number three! I went toward omnibus number three. "Any convent in this city?" I asked. "Yes, ma'am, step in." When the bus drove on the convent avenue, I saw the whole place was lighted up. I rang the doorbell and it was answered instantly. I said to the Sisters, "Did you expect me?"

"No, Sister."

"How, then, did you respond so quickly?"

"We expected a Sister on this train. We are staying up with a dead Sister who will be buried tomorrow. In your case it is fortunate the Sister did not come — you can occupy the room prepared for her — the only spare room in the convent."

Previous to this explanation, I had quickly reasoned: Superiors at home watched the papers — saw the railroad accident — wired the convent — the result being the illumination and Sisters waiting. It did not occur to me that there might be more than one convent in Kansas City.

The next turn of affairs brought me to the reality of my position. The two Sisters who had opened the door went to report the non-appearance of the one expected and my coming. Presently the Sisters returned, but their countenances had a dejected look. I became apprehensive at once and asked:

"What is it, Sisters?"

"Our Superior wants to know if it is customary for your Sisters to travel alone?" said one.

"No, Sister, it is not."

"Have you your letter of obedience?"

"I destroyed it before starting on this journey. I have no credentials to show except the name on my wearing apparel."

"Why are you traveling alone?"

"Because I was sent alone."

With this explanation they left me to make a second report. When they returned they were more dejected than before. The elder of the two Sisters spoke:

"Sister, our Superior thinks you had better go to some hotel."

"Sisters, I have been well provided for my journey, but I cannot set people thinking by leaving the hospitality of a convent to seek shelter in some hotel. I clearly see I'm considered some sort of a fake, however, if you will kindly let me rest on that sofa, you can allay your fears by locking the door and taking the key with you."

They went to make a third report. When they returned it was a pleasure to see their cheerful faces. One spoke, "No, Sister, we are going to prepare a lunch for you."

"Please do not. This is the First Friday of the month and a Holy Communion day for me."

The last vestige of doubt and fear disappeared from their countenances. A pillow and comfort were placed on the sofa and bidding me good rest, they locked the door, taking the key with them.

At six o'clock A.M., I was shown to the chapel. After Mass I noticed some hesitancy as how to proceed with me. Would they leave me in the convent, or have me join in the funeral procession to their graveyard? Presently I felt a light thump at the left of the prie-dieu on which I knelt. I looked and saw a hand holding a candle for me to take — I understood I was to fall in line.

After the funeral, breakfast was served me in the same room in which I had rested. About ten o'clock A.M., the Superior came to interview me. I saw the handwriting on the wall, I was an impostress. Had time from interview until three o'clock to myself. During this interval I wrote. Among the jottings I wrote a letter to dear Sister Gabriella, telling her I was in a religious convent at Kansas City, but was considered some one in disguise. I told her I was glad it was I instead of Sister Justina, because her sensitiveness would make her suffer intensely. I am taking the whole incident as some of the many things that may happen to me on my journey to the Southwest.

At three o'clock P.M., I asked for a companion to accompany me to order the omnibus for the midnight train. After placing my order, I turned to the clerk and said, "Be sure to send the bus."

When I reached the exit door I returned to where the clerk was standing, and said, "It is absolutely necessary for me to take the outgoing midnight train. Under no consideration neglect to have the omnibus come for me." He assured me again the order was properly placed and would be attended to.

The train that brought me from St. Louis had been delayed two hours, owing to the accident which had occurred to the train ahead of ours. There is only one daily (nightly) train from this place to the terminus of the road. Dinner and supper were served me as breakfast had been. I am hoping that some of the Sisters will come in to relieve my mind and tell me what species of a scarecrow I am thought to be. It is seven o'clock — no one has come in so far — some one now. . . .

"You poor child! What must you think of us and the spirit of this convent?"

I did not have time to answer, for a voice called, "Sister

Martha!" Sister Martha grasped her lighted candle and briskly followed the voice.

I mentally observed that we would not carry a lighted candle through corridors and rooms. However, I have enough to think about without letting fire insurance policies annoy me. The room is dark, a reflection from a lamp-post in the street throws a small stream of light in one window. I still have fully four hours before the bus calls for me. "Angels guard your every step." I'm going to rest on the sofa. . . .

I heard a voice, "Sister?" I sat erect. "Mother wants to know if you are sure you ordered the bus?"

Was it my want of rest or injured feeling of pride which was on the verge of giving vent to my thoughts? From the gleam of light that came from the lamp-post I noticed that the speaker was a novice. "Surely, Sister Blandina, you will not scandalize an aspirant in His service!" While silently speaking thus to myself I looked at the young novice. She had a good placid face, and I said, "Sister, please say to your Superior that I surely ordered the bus." She bowed and left me.

Now, dearest Sister Justina, if by some unthinkable reason the omnibus does not come for me, I am positively certain the police will! "Angels guard your every step." How happy I am that you, dear, are not in this predicament. I am arranging my speech to the policeman. I hear him say, "The nuns sent for me to show you the way to any hotel you wish to go to!" and I shall say, "I do not wish to go to any hotel. Be kind enough to wire to the Most Rev. J. B. Purcell, of Cincinnati, Ohio, for any information you desire about me." I see a note of intelligence appear on his countenance while he critically studies me — but through it all I cannot see myself going to any hotel. Though the suspense of not knowing what may happen makes me uneasy. Twenty minutes after eleven — I hear the patter of horses' hoofs on the convent avenue. *Deo Gratias.*

When I realized the omnibus had come for me, I put on my wraps and with my traveling black basket walked toward the door. It was opened by a Sister in the hall. Then it was I noticed this Sister had performed the work of a sentinel, guarding me! My impulse was to brush by her and into the bus. But telepathy worked quicker than impulse. Right reason was on their side.

Instant remembrance recalled the fact that a few months previous I was given charge of two dressed as Franciscan Sisters and who were making a collection in Steubenville. I was to attend to them and they were not to associate with the Sisters. The day which was to be their last with us, and when they were on their way to the station to leave the town, a policeman tapped one of the two and said, "Both of you come with me." The guardian of the law had seen a big foot encased in a boot. One was a man, the other his wife, who personified Franciscan Sisters. So instead of acting by impulse, I said:

"Please, Sister, say a fervent prayer that I may reach my destination in safety." I saw a glistening tear of sympathy. Was I not reaping reward for suppressing a hasty impulse?

Nothing noticeable took place from the time the train left Kansas City until we reached the terminus of the railroad. A train was being made up of constructive material and at the end of the train I saw a very shabby coach from the windows of which a number of men were craning their necks looking at me. Gazing in every direction, I finally saw the train conductor. I went toward him and asked if I might board the made-up train. He said:

"To-morrow we will put on a day coach; this is only a construction train carrying construction material and a crowd of Irish workmen to the end of the line."

"Any objection to my going with them?"

"Not if you can put up with a working man's 'smoker.'"

I went toward the train. The conductor assisted me into the coach. The instant the Irishmen saw a Sister their hats came off and pipes were taken out of their mouths. When seated, I said to the two men in front of me:

"Please say to these good men that I am very fond of smoke

from a pipe." The men replaced their hats and resumed their smoking. I doubt which side was more pleased — they, to have me, or I to be with them. We reached the end of the line shortly after midnight.

When "End of Construction line" was called, one of the men stepped over to me and offered to carry my basket. I handed it to him; then, a gentleman bowed and gave me a letter. The one who had my basket waited to see what would happen. I read the letter and saw by its contents I was to follow the giver of the letter. Thanking the courtesy of the first man I let myself be guided by the second. This was Mr. Mullen, an agent of Otero and Sellar, the greatest commission firm of the Southwest. The loaded caravans of this firm are constantly on the Santa Fe Trail.[13]

My instructions from Mother Regina are: "Wait at the end of the line until the Sisters from Trinidad come for you." The letter handed me is from Sister Marcella, in charge of the Trinidad School Mission. It says, "Take the stage and come on to Trinidad."

Territory of Colorado, Dec. 8, 1872.

This is the feast of the Immaculate Conception, and the anniversary of making our vows. I wonder what you are doing, dear Sister Justina, while I am trying to solve the problem of either going or staying here to-day. The facts are these: Had I not been compelled to wait over twenty-two hours in Kansas City, I should have arrived here in time to take the stage that would have brought me into Trinidad on the morning of the Feast of the Immaculata. Mother Regina's instruction ceases with the new order. Only exceptionally do we travel on Sundays and feast days of obligation, so I will order the stage for to-morrow and begin a little catechetical missionary work to-day. No better feast could inaugurate my new life.

When I said Grace before breakfast, I noticed how gravely the junior Mullen looked at me; which gives me the best guarantee he hasn't been taught his prayers. I asked Mrs. Mullen if she had any objection to my taking James on the plains to watch the habits of the prairie dogs. She said, "I am glad to have him go, but prairie dogs have queer habits, they cannot be caught unless they are cornered in a place where they have no burrows."

So Jamie and myself started to watch the prairie dogs. The little midgets remained on their artificial mounds until we got quite near them, then barked their peculiar baby bark, when, with a still more singular wheezy bark, turned and bounded into their subterranean houses. Shall we ever learn the language of the animals! It was very plain we could not catch any of the creatures, so I turned my attention to my young companion.

"Can you bless yourself?"

"Like you did at breakfast?"

"Exactly."

"Daddy said I ought to know how to do what you did."

"Shall I teach you?"

"Oh! good, I will surprise daddy!"

I began with the Sign of the Cross. He learned quickly. I repeated the first part of the Lord's Prayer by periods many times. Then played catcher and tried again to run down a prairie dog. The little fellow was more anxious to learn than to play; which pleased me very much. By the time we went in to dinner, he had passably memorized the Lord's Prayer, Hail Mary and Grace before and after meals, so at dinner he silently said Grace with me.

Mrs. Mullen told me that three ladies had called to see me and would return this afternoon. We had buffalo meat for dinner. While on the train in the territory of Colorado we saw a herd of buffalo. The herd was on a stampede. The brutes did look crazy; plainly, whatever direction they made for, nothing could stop them. Someone on the train remarked that it was surprising to see a herd of buffalo, as Kit Carson[14] and Dick Wootton[15] (both frontier trappers) had declared there were no more buffalo in herds. One might see a small group here and there on the plains, but a herd of buffalo was out of the question. Yet we saw one.

The three ladies called again. They were anxious to be sympathetic at my traveling alone and so young! But they soon convinced themselves I needed no sympathy in my prospective work. . . . The stage will call for me in the morning. I was told I am the only passenger booked for to-morrow. Mrs. Mullen is having clean hay ready to put in the coach. I expected there would be others in the stagecoach with me. "Angels guard your footsteps."

§ 4

Trinidad, Dec. 10, 1872.

My dearest dear: — Here I am safe in Trinidad, Colorado Territory, instead of in the island of Cuba where we first thought I was to go. No wonder this small pebble (Trinidad, Colo.) is not on our maps. "Angels guide your footsteps." This sentence has stayed with me from the time I left the Archbishop's residence in Cincinnati, and is with me still.

I ordered the stage for the morning of the 9th. Mrs. Mullen was very attentive. She had new clean hay put in the stage to keep my feet warm, and after I got in she wrapped a large comfort around me, remarking that "traveling on the plains and in winter was not a pleasant prospect." The driver must have had strict injunctions from Otero and Sellar — they own the stage line. For the first time I had indefinable fears. The cowboys were constantly in my mind. I expected there would be a number traveling with me on the plains. "Snow-bound and cowboys" came in thought to annoy me.

At noon the driver came to the stage door and said: "We take dinner here." I thanked him and said: "I do not wish any dinner."

"But, lady, we will not have another stopping place to eat until six o'clock this evening."

I thanked him again, "but I do not wish any dinner." The jolting of the stage and my thoughts had taken all appetite away. Though I could see nothing from the stage (every flap was fastened), it seemed that the driver aimed to drive over every stone and make the wheels go into every rut. It was nothing but a jerk up and down all the way — in a stage that had no springs and traveling at the rate of twelve miles an hour!

At six o'clock we arrived at the station for supper. At every station the mules were changed. The driver came to ask me to supper. I thanked him, but said: "I do not wish any supper."

"There will not be another chance for a meal until twelve o'clock to-night, and you have not tasted anything to-day, so come now and take it if only a cup of black coffee."

"No, thank you, I have no desire for anything."

The poor man was quite distressed. He could not think I was trying to save traveling expenses, because the price of stage traveling included meals. Here is the mental attitude I was in: if the driver could surmise the vague fear that is preying on me he would know I have no appetite.

He went in to supper and presently returned. "Lady, if you do not want to eat — come in and let me have my supper. The woman who runs this station will not give me a drink of muddy water unless I fetch you in to supper — I told her how you are dressed and she goes off wild and says: 'Bring her in or you will get nothing to eat to-night, nor any other time you come.'"

I went into an adobe, log-raftered, mud-floored, mud-plastered hut. The sight of the red checkered table cloth and black coffee only added to my repugnance for food. The person who kept the station was an Irish woman of the good old stamp. I made an effort to sip some coffee, but not a drop would pass my lips. The cowboys were in my mind. I tried to ascertain if there were any in the vicinity, the answers I received were indefinite.

At midnight: "Now, lady, you will have a good meal."

"No, thank you, I desire nothing."

"What will Otero and Sellar say to me when they find out you did not take a meal during this journey? They gave me more orders about you than I ever got since I'm staging, and that's ten years."

"Say I wished for nothing. I will write the firm my thanks."

Oh, the lonely, fearful feeling! The night was dark. No passengers to allay my turbulent thoughts. Footsteps drew near the stage. My heart was thumping. The driver opened the stage door and said:

"You will have a traveling companion for some miles."

In the open door, by the light of the lantern, I saw a tall, lanky, hoosier-like man, wearing a broad brimmed hat. On one arm he had a buffalo robe. While I sat riveted, he got in — asked me if I would take part of his "kiver," and before my fright permitted me to speak, he placed part of the buffalo robe over the comfort that enwrapped me, and sat beside me on the rear seat. The driver closed the door and we were in utter darkness. By descriptions I had read I knew he was a cowboy! With crushing vividness — "No virtuous woman is safe near a cowboy" came to me. I made an act of contrition — concentrated my thoughts on the presence of God — thought of the Archbishop's blessing, "Angels guard your steps," and moved to such position as would put my heart in range with his revolver. I expected he would speak — I answer — he fire. The agony endured cannot be written. The silence and suspense unimaginable. Suddenly from out the darkness I heard:

"Madam!"

"Sir!"

"What kind of a lady be you?"

"A Sister of Charity."

"Whose sister?"

"Everyone's Sister, a person who gives her life to do good to others."

"Quaker like, I reckon?"

"No, not quite."

By this time I learned from his tone of voice that I had nothing to fear. He asked me a number of questions, all prompted by a conversation he had had with the driver before he came into the stage. In my turn I asked him why he became a cowboy. He said he had read of cowboys and ran away from home to become one.

"Is your mother still living?"

"Yes, I allow she is — leastwise she was when I left home six years ago."

"Have you written to her?"

"No, madam, and I allow that's beastly."

"It is certainly unkind to one whom you can always trust and who, I am sure, loves you as much now as she did when you were a little fellow."

His voice got husky. "What do you say I otter do?"

"Write; do so as soon as you get off this stage. Tell her you will soon make her a visit, and see to it that you keep your word."

"I will, so help me God! I was mighty feared to speak to you when I got in, because the mule driver said you was more particular than any lady he ever seen. I allow I am powerful glad I spoke to you."

To think that this lubberly, good-natured cowboy had made me undergo such mortal anguish. He got off on the outskirts of Trinidad where the driver stopped to point out to me dugouts at the side of the foothills.

"This, lady, is Trinidad."[16]

A fainting feeling came over me as I looked at what I would have thought were kennels for dogs. Then I remembered my perfect health, the many years in the order of nature, before my call would come. While these thoughts were dominating, bright and vivid came to my vision the life of St. Francis Xavier, farther away, in a more desolate country, with less companions, and yet who did more for God? Though I know the driver continued to talk, I do not recall a word he said. There on the outskirts facing the dugouts of Trinidad I took St. Francis Xavier as my model in the missionary life.

The stage stopped to throw off the mail. While so doing, a gentleman, wearing a Roman collar and having a clerical look, came to the stage door and said: "Ya, ya, Sister, come out. This is the Convent," pointing to a store, which, at a glance I could see was being used for post-office and general store. He made a motion to help me out. I put my hands in my habit sleeves and sat upright in the stage, acknowledging his proffered courtesy by "Thank you, I'll stay here." The gentleman's eyes twinkled merrily and he walked briskly away. A few minutes after the driver came out, took the reins and drove off. Another stopping place. The driver opened the door and said: "Here we are." Before making any attempt to leave the stage, I looked at the house and in the recess of the door saw two of our Sisters. I thought, this is more like it, and was helped in by Sisters Marcella and Fidelis.[17]

The gentleman who had come to the stage door is the parish priest — who wanted to see — as he expressed it "what kind of a Sister is she who was sent across the plains alone." He wanted to give an agreeable surprise by playing a joke. Before the stage reached the convent, he managed to say to the Sisters: "You cannot play jokes on her."

To-day is Mother Regina's birthday, and my first day West. I will continue this journal and some years hence send it to you, dear Sister Justina. I'm not to go in school until the 6th of January, 1873.

I began to review my Spanish. Rev. P. J. Munnecom,[18] the parish priest, is the teacher. To my surprise, the Sisters do not speak Spanish. My previous study of the language is a great help to me and has created a desire in the Sisters to study the language also.

Dec. 14, 1872.

I am sure, dearest Sister Justina, you will be interested in my viewpoint of things as I find them here. To-day I went to look at my schoolroom[19] to be; 40 ft. long; 14 ft. wide; 8 ft. high; two small windows, low-sized door, no transom; solid adobe walls on two sides, log rafters as black as ebony. Of necessity ventilation said "Goodbye" when the house was completed.

But I must add all these adobe houses were built with a view to protect the inhabitants in case of a sudden attack from the warring Indians. That does not mean that every house has these dimensions. The head of each family built to suit his taste in the matter of length, breadth, and height — but material to date is unchangeable: sunburnt mud (shaped, of course) 4x9x18 inches; the foundation the same as walls, mud roof over rafters — mud floors. There are some seventy-five of these houses on "Mexican Hill." That will be my first objective point; the second will be the jail.

The Purgatoire River — corrupted into Picatwar, but the natives kept its correct name, Purgatorio — is below the *acequia,* (artificial canal) which is the boundary line to land and house given by Don Felipe Baca,[20] one of the leading citizens here, to the Sisters for a school. The land on which the Academy is built (now in course of erection) was donated by a Mr. Heone, who lives a few miles outside of Trinidad.

This gentleman and Dr. Beshoar, our physician, have pews in the church — if you can call eight planks nailed together, pews. The Sisters use the choir loft. The church is an adobe structure[21] — with a pretense of a gable roof and a double pretense of having been shingled; mud floor, mud walls, wooden candlesticks. Previous to the Sisters coming, bottles were used for candlesticks. The only restful spot about the church are the grounds to the entrance of it.[22]

The graveyard is in the rear of the church with a street between graveyard and convent. There is a long stretch of an adobe wall from convent (academy) to public school, the only one here and taught by the Sisters. I am told there is an Academy (called "Rice") maintained by the Methodists.

We have twelve resident young ladies at the Academy, occupying the part that is built; very few in the select school. The Sisters are: Sister Marcella, in charge and music teacher; Sister Martha,[23] Housekeeper; Sister Eulalia,[24] Factotum; Sister Fidelis,[25] Select School; Sister Blandina, Public School Teacher; Sister Eulalia, Assistant.

Here is the Trinidad of today: Commercial Street, a few scattered houses the length of two blocks. Main Street, a few scattered stores occupying one side of the street about the same length as Commercial Street. Convent Street, we use to the end of the Public School grounds, where there are a few small adobe huts. So far, Mr. Baca has the only house that looks like a residence. Then there is the Mexican settlement on the hill. I am informed that very few prisoners ever come to trial. They manage to burrow out from jail before the Circuit Court convenes. The Circuit Court comes from Denver.

Here, if you have a largeness of vision, you find the opportunity to exercise it; if a cramped one, the immense expanse of the plains, the solid Rockies, the purity of the atmosphere, the faultlessness of the canopy above, will stretch the mind toward the Good. Maybe, dearest, it may please you to know my own attitude at the present writing. *Vede mio cuore.* (Look at my heart). I wish I had many hands and feet, and a world full of hearts to place at the service of the Eternal. So much one sees to be done, and so few to do it. I have adopted this plan: Do whatever presents itself, and never omit anything because of hardship or repugnance.

§ 5

Dec. 21.

Rumor is loud in predicting an attack from the Ute tribe. We have a girl at the Academy named Ida Chené, whose mother gave me a vivid account of a sudden attack from one of the roving wild Indian tribes. The purpose of the attack was to drive out all who were not Mexicans — this tribe had allied itself with the Mexicans. The outbreak took place near Taos. Mrs. Chené was in the field plowing when the machete was raised over her head and she was asked to pronounce the word *juangoche.* She did so to the satisfaction of the attacking group, who galloped away either to cleave or scalp the next who could not pronounce the word correctly. It is singular that not any of these things can cause me to fear.

We have our own chapel. Very few Catholic Americans in

Trinidad. The Church on Sunday is crowded by our native population, who come from many directions. Vehicles of every description bring the devout. Not a native woman wears any other covering on head except a mantella or shawl, and they kneel on the bare floor, and, let me add, they know how to pray and do it.

In our well-to-do churches East, to secure musical harmony, professors and trained singers are engaged; in the congregations of mediocre wealth, the best talent give their service, attend rehearsals and sing when required. Yet in both elements there is a constant friction, if not always expressed, a felt dissatisfaction, and it is frequently a subject of annoyance to the Catholic conscience as to whether or not the duty of assisting at Mass is complied with by the choir attendants. The congregation, from youth to age, is ever ready to criticise the director, organist, individual singers, and choir. In the combined action of choir and congregation, how much intrinsic honor is rendered to God! He, alone, is the Judge. Now bring your attention to a close view of a scene in this church. The performers are two grey-haired men, each holding a large violin. The instrument reclines against the left knee, which is in position to rise when the signal is given that Mass has begun; right knee bent to the ground, eyes closed and head inclined. The priest begins, *Et introibo, etc.* The violin players, with voice and instrument, strike off a half-singing, half reciting *Kyrie, etc.* The violins seldom strung to the same pitch. On great feastdays one, sometimes two, guitars are added, no two instruments tuned in unison, but who can doubt that every heart beats in harmony with that of the celebrant.

A short time after the Sisters' arrival (1870), at the request of the priest and the English speaking portion of the congregation, the music teacher took charge of choir and began gradually to train pupils to sing in church services, the congregation contenting itself by chiming in when one of its old-time hymns was sung. Even that died out, leaving Doña Juanita Simpson to lead a chorus when *Los Americanos* are not in the church.

Preparations are being made for a Christmas Tree. It is to be in the select schoolroom. I notice that two of our Italian musicians are active in seeing that the tree is well loaded, and I further remark that only the resident pupils and Sisters will share from the tree. I'm only glancing over occurrences. By another year I shall have things clear in my mind.

Some of our Eastern showmen, say Barnum of New York, or Robinson of Cincinnati, could make an addition to their curios if they so desired. Witness this feat in our unprovided gymnasium. After this, never I say "crazy as a bd — bg — ." We go to the table, seat ourselves as comfortably as the long benches will permit, begin a nice chat on the rare atmosphere, white clouds and ether blue; in lieu of having changed yesterday's menu from bread, meat and water to water, meat and bread. While our spirits clash with our wits, a number of knowing odoriferous acrobats let themselves drop from the rafter on to our midday spread. Their knowledge in mind reading is great — everything is left for them to eat! ! !

To exclude these celebrated chinches, we are going to change our dining room. Menu will be on the same lines. But our chef thinks we may soon expect a change.

Jan. 10, 1873.

I know, dear Sister Justina, you would undoubtedly be very much pleased had you my pupils. You would have abundance of material for evolution. I have always given you credit for evolving the best from any character, not only morally, but intellectually as well. I doubt if the ages of my pupils would be as satisfactory to you, the majority are older than myself, and some tower fifteen inches above my head.

To-day my capacity for controlling them was put to the test. You know I'm a companion outside of the schoolroom, and a teacher the instant the threshold of the schoolroom is crossed. Felipe Gurulé, son of a wealthy Mexican and a natural leader, said to the older pupils this morning:

"*Oigan muchachos* — listen, boys, at the 10 o'clock recess when

Sister calls class, do not file in, just to see what the little lady will do." He spoke in Spanish and thought I did not understand him.

Previous to ringing the recess bell, I called the young man and told him to remain in the room, as I wished to speak to him. When the room was vacated, I asked him to throw windows and doors open for ventilation. Having done so, he took his seat, waiting to hear what I had to say. I went to my desk, scribbled a few notes, then rang the bell for second school session; the pupils, not having a leader — "Just to see what the little lady will do" — filed in as usual. There was suppressed mirth, but nothing obstreperous. When the pupils were seated, I called Felipe and asked if he would not like a few moments' airing. He smiled and went out. At the noon dismissal, he returned and asked, "Sister, did you understand what I said to the boys this morning?" I answered that I did.

"Then you speak Spanish?"

"You may judge when a chance offers," I replied.

The afternoon session was a revelation to me, everyone was so attentive and so pleased. I wonder what the next attempt on the teacher will be — for boys will be boys all the world over.

A worried mother came to me to-day. "Sister, I have three boys — men, all of them. I heard them say they want to come to your school. I'm afraid to let 'Dwarf' come. John and Jeff are all right, but 'Dwarf' fights worse than a bulldog when you try to take meat from it."

"Send them and do not worry," I told her.

John and Jeff came to school. No teacher could desire better behaved pupils, nor any more anxious to learn. The worried mother was afraid to let "Dwarf" come. John spoke to me of "Dwarf" and said, "If he comes it will take my mind off my studies, because I will have to watch that he does not get into a fight or break some of the school rules. Yet I wish he would come. I never heard him express a wish to be with any teacher before."

"Bring him, John, and before he comes mention the few rules. 'No tobacco to be used in or around the school premises; no vulgarity in word or action.' These two rules ought not to deter anyone anxious to study from coming to school."

"Dwarf" came. John watched him as closely as an eagle does its prey.

Two weeks have passed since "Dwarf" made his appearance. Behavior good.

Feb. 5.

This day will be memorable for the pupils of Public School No. 1. Jefferson came to my desk at recess time; he wanted to speak to me.

"Well, Jefferson, what do you wish to say?" I asked.

"Sister, I want to study your religion."

"There are a number of things you would have to do which might not be to your liking," I remarked.

"Name one of the things, Sister."

"Confession."

"That means to tell everything wrong I do?"

"It means that, with a plus and plus."

"What is the first plus?"

"To be sorry you did wrong."

"And the second?"

"To resolve not to do that wrong again."

"Dwarf," standing at the schoolroom door, looked at us both, his eyes flashing anger. He came toward Jefferson, raised his fist and hit him on his left jaw. I felt certain the jaw was broken. Jefferson looked at me, my eyes said, "Keep still." "Dwarf" expected Jefferson to jump at him, and stood at defense. I broke the silence by addressing Jefferson, and said "I'll put arnica on your face, Jefferson, and meanwhile, take your seat."

A number of pupils anticipating trouble quietly gathered near the schoolroom door to witness the scene which they expected to take place. Every instant was a psychological one. The pupils intent in protecting the teacher against an infuriated human being who stood with blazing eyes and ready arms, waiting an onslaught on him from somewhere, but ready to annihilate anyone who would dare touch him. Jefferson went to his seat.

I looked at the clock and said, "Recess time is up," and rang the bell. "Dwarf" was nonplussed. He looked dejected; followed me to the door, took his place in the ranks and came in with his classmates, went to his seat and stared at me with wondering eyes. After attending to Jefferson, I took my seat at the desk and motioned to "Dwarf" to come to me. He came instantly and blurted out: "Jeff told you I was chewing tobacco, didn't he?"

"No, you were not mentioned. Jefferson was pleading with me to let him study my religion."

"Dwarf" stood amazed. The bulldog had become a lamb. I continued in low tones:

"Suppose you were speaking to me of something of interest to you, and Jefferson entered the room and hit you in the jaw with all his strength, what ought I to do to Jefferson?"

"Give him a sound thrashing to make him remember he made a fool of himself," he replied.

"I like your sense of justice," I remarked.

"Shall I get a switch?" he asked.

While he went out for something to have himself chastised, his brother John came to my desk.

"Sister, I'm afraid 'Dwarf' will do something unexpected, but I'll be at your side in one bounce."

"Thank you, but take your seat."

"Dwarf" came in with a strong branch of cottonwood tree. Without one word from me he gave me his right hand, then his left. Did he feel what I felt? I do not know. I hoped he would remain after morning session to have a little talk with me, but he did not, nor did he return this afternoon, from which I infer his school days are over, as far as this school is concerned.

I intend to follow him up at his home and help his mother as best I can to make a better boy of him. Was this not using psychic knowledge to some purpose?

Feb. 19.

This noon a number of the young men pupils came slowly into the school hall. The look on their faces puzzled me, so I walked to the front door. I ought to tell you, the road from the Convent to the end of the Public School building, one block, is used as a playground for the boys; the girls use the ground at the rear of the school. The look of the pupils made me fear some mischief was on hand. As soon as I reached the door facing the street, a man holding a child by each hand came toward me.

"Sister, I want to tell you, your pupils are not kind to my boys. I brought them here to play, and your pupils walked away."

I felt sorry for the two poor innocent lads, so only said, "Put at least a small shirt on each of them and bring them at playtime."

The man's eyes and mouth opened wide, then he said, "Ah, I see, I will put a *camisa* on them."

Feb. 23.

Organized a Vigilant Club among the most earnest pupils. The object of this club is to report to me any case of distress in families or individuals. We are to have fun, too, but all leading to self-improvement. Clubs must have some object. This club is to meet conditions as we find them here, and improve them when possible.

Oh, the immense field of work there is in this place! I've not mentioned the location of Trinidad and its consequent results. It is the rendezvous for the outlawed, who take to the Santa Fe Trail, and an equal protector for those who use the "Statute of Limitation" from the Territory of New Mexico. The boundary line between Colorado and New Mexico is just twelve miles from Trinidad. The spot is marked by a large stone, a few rods from which is the toll-gate kept by Mr. Dick Wootton, one of the first trappers of these regions. Mr. Wootton's home is a refuge for all sorts of characters who can hold themselves in check while under his roof.

§ 6

March 1, 1873.

My Dear Sister Justina:

It is some time since I jotted down anything in my journal. The fact is, so many incidents followed one another that it is difficult for me to note even the ones most out of the ordinary. To-day Sister Marcella and myself were at choir rehearsal when one of our native boys came in to say — quite enthusiastically for a Mexican: *Hay muchas hermanas y* (There are many Sisters and people). And he added in English: "And Bishop Salpointe,[26] and priests, and mules, and wagons, all in the corral!" This from the speaker who was anxious to have courtesy shown the travelers. Let me remark that every Spaniard or Mexican I've met has an innate refinement.

Sister Marcella sent me to see to the travelers — for, so we surmised, they were. When I got to the corral, I saw a medley crowd sure enough of holy men and women, and a very unholy sight of wagons, mules, and shabbily appareled, dusty and tired travelers. I took in the situation at a glance. Among the groups waiting some recognition I noticed a number of Sisters toward whom I made my way, and only succeeded in saying, "You are welcome, Sisters," when one of them fairly lifted me off my feet. When she let me down, I raised my eyes to look at her — she is quite tall — wondering if I knew her. At first glance my wonder ceased. It was Sister Martha from the convent of my Kansas City adventure!

The travelers remained with us five days. They were on their way to Arizona. Our Sisters here are, as elsewhere, most hospitable. What time I could give from my school work, I gave to our visitors. Three of these Sisters were at the Kansas City Convent, where, it will be recalled, by an accident to the train ahead of us, I had been obliged to stop off, and I had gone to their convent to await the arrival of the next train. From these Sisters I learned why I was suspected of being an impostor. A few weeks before my arrival, two men had made a wager. One man asserted that he could gain admittance to the convent after closing hour, the other positively denying that he could do so. The former, to prove his assertion, dressed in woman's clothes, applied to the convent for a night's lodging, "I have no money, I am hungry, please give me something to eat and shelter for the night." The pseudo-woman was served supper, at which time the preconcerted signal was given in proof that he had gained entrance. He gave a shrill whistle and rushed from the Convent. The Sisters hardly had had time to get over their fright when I made my appearance. This accounts for the many questions put to me. Yet the unique part of the whole proceeding was that every question I answered was my own condemnation.

"Do your Sisters travel alone?"

"No, Sister."

"Why are you alone?"

"Because I was sent alone."

"Your letter of Obedience?"

"I destroyed it before starting on this journey."

Under these conditions, who would not have been suspicious of me, and who would not have taken the precaution to watch my every act? Sister Martha then told me that, with all appearances against me, the Sisters had been sympathetic. They had felt an uneasiness of mind during all the hours I was compelled to wait for the outgoing train.

Good Friday, 1873. — Sisters Marcella, Fidelis, and myself went up the mountainside — to see the *Penitentes* make the "Way to Calvary." About one hundred took part in it. They walked in twos, faces covered, backs bared. Each had several branches of long bruised cacti, with which they lashed their backs as they slowly ascended the spur. At each lash they said, "*Yo penitente pecador*" (I, a repentant sinner). When the one dragging the cross reached the summit of the spur, some of the *penitentes* helped to raise the cross he alone had dragged. It seemed impossible for any one man to have accomplished such an act, but we saw him do it. We were several miles from Trinidad and wanted to reach our convent home before the lighter of our globe threw his golden rays to warn us that he soon would retire.

Easter Sunday, 1873. — I must tell you what information I received concerning the *Penitentes*. The Way of the Cross, of course, was taught the natives by the good Franciscans; so also penance was preached to them. When the Franciscans were obliged to leave the Southwest, it naturally fell to the stronger-minded and piously inclined to perpetuate what had been taught them, but in this teaching each leader followed his own idea; hence, we find that whilst the members of some lodges are perfectly docile to the teachings of the Church, other lodges have not the least conception of the correct spirit of Catholicity, though they consider themselves good Catholics.

The *Penitentes* in this vicinity do not even make their Easter duty. They do not scruple to abstract cattle from another man's ranch on the Easter Monday, after having scourged themselves on Good Friday and called themselves "Repentant sinners." This reminds one of the private interpretation of the Bible. The *Penitentes* interpret the teaching of the Franciscans in their own way. The initiation to these lodges varies also. Here is one form: — Ridges are made from neck to waist-line with sharp stones. By privilege I was allowed to visit one of their lodges — it was literally bespattered with blood — side, walls, and ceiling, too — yet the members of the lodge I visited are adroit pilferers of any branded domestic animals seen on the plains. These same members never approach the Sacraments.

Easter week — Here is a tragedy which took place this week. An elderly lady and gentleman — Americans — residing a few miles from Trinidad, were found murdered in their home. Suspicion at once pointed to the natives as the perpetrators of the horrible deed. Small groups of men were sent out to capture the murderers. One posse trailed four Mexicans, and because they would not acknowledge the deed, were hanged on the first tree to which they came. Afterwards the corpses were huddled into a wagon, brought to Trinidad in triumph and thrown into an old vacant adobe hut, twelve feet from the graveyard near the Convent. Can you imagine how we felt! Two days later the real murderers were captured and confessed the crime. They were outlawed Americans!

Rafael, Indian Chief of the Utes, is on the warpath because the government agents have repeatedly made his tribe "move on." Poor Indians! Will they ever understand that the conquerors claim the land? How quickly the Indian detects true sympathy from the counterfeit!

Feast of St. Aloysius, 1873. The resident students were to have a free day and enjoy it on the mountains. The pastor's new white maria (a white covered wagon) and traveling horses had been put at the Sisters' disposal. The driver that was to take the reins came at the last moment — 9 o'clock A.M., to say he found it impossible to go to the mountains for the day.

The young ladies were woefully disappointed. Singularly for me, I did not offer to drive.

Sister Marcella said: "Sister Blandina, unless you take the young ladies to the mountains, they will have a second disappointment. Sister Eulalia can remain with them while you come back for the second load." So I started with the first load. The horses had been resting for two weeks and stable-fed during that time. They were horses accustomed to traveling forty or fifty miles a day to and from the various mission posts, consequently use horse sense when they start on their mission journey by not tiring themselves out at the start. When I had driven about six miles, we came to an enticing place to camp for the day. The young girls in great glee jumped to the ground. Keeping the youngest pupil to return with me, I reined the horses' heads toward Trinidad, when lo! I saw at once we had a runaway team. I recalled many horse traits so managed to guide and keep them on the road. Presently I saw our way lay through a very rough road where I had all I could do when driving out to keep clear of large boulders. So I tried my strength against the runaway horses. The reins were new and cut my hands to the bone. The atmosphere here is so clear one can see a great distance ahead, and I saw death if I kept on the road, so I gathered strength by will power and turned the horses to the left of the road on to level ground followed by a ravine.

What happened I do not know, but when I awoke I saw the bus turned over, the horses grazing at a distance, the top of the bus about five rods from it, and no sign of my companion. I felt no pain, so I tried to raise the bus — one ton — needless to say, it did not budge. I began to search for my companion. I could see her nowhere. I went toward the white canopy of the wagon and there, under its shade, was Miss Chené, blood oozing from her nose and no sign of life. I raised her in my arms and said: "Blessed Mother, you know I had no desire to come out here to-day. I did so through obedience. So, please, see to the life of this child, while I go for the horses." When I got to where the horses were grazing I picked up the reins, but horselike they understood they had the best of me, and though I said, "Get up," they did not move; so I changed my system with all the energy I could and repeated, "Get up!" They trotted to the place of the upset bus where I tied them to one of the wheels and returned to where I had left my companion in apparent death. She was sitting up and greeted me by saying, "Oh, Sister, there is blood all over your neck." Remember there was not a house in sight, nor any water. Guided by her voice, I wiped my neck and asked her if she could walk. She attempted to get up, but could not. I tried to raise her in order to carry her, but she was as heavy to me as a mountain. So we talked for a while, then attempted to walk to Trinidad.

We had walked about half a mile when we saw a country wagon advancing toward us. We knew at once that whoever was in the wagon was coming to our relief. I felt no pain until I knew help was near. The instant I realized the situation, and that the burden would be shared by others, I simply collapsed. It was sheer exercise of will which prevented me from fainting.

We were assisted into the wagon and started for Trinidad. On the last descent we met one of the best horsemen in these parts. He said he could see from his ranch that some accident had taken place, so he came with rope and hammer, etc., to be of some service. I remarked, "As good a horseman as you are, you cannot trust that team." He smiled incredulously, but he had a runaway when he attempted to drive to town. He took a jockey's precaution — tired the horses before he again turned their heads toward Trinidad.

When the pastor met me, he remarked: "I did not anticipate any trouble with you at the reins." I responded: "Were I to drive that team again, I would surely tire it in sand before trusting it on any road." Within the next week, when the Rev. gentleman was answering a sick call, the horses started on a gallop which he could not check. When the horses recognized they were the masters, they started at full speed. He was thrown out and was picked up wounded, and had to be brought into Trinidad in someone else's vehicle, leaving his own for repairs. When he came to the convent to have his wounds dressed, he remarked, "Those horses gave me the surprise of my life — no wonder, Sister, you could not hold them in."

So St. Aloysius day, 1873, will not soon be forgotten by me.

§ 7

Dear Sister Justina: —   July, 1873.

The last time I wrote in this journal I gave you an account of what occurred on St. Aloysius day. All intervals of this journal are overcrowded with events not of daily occurrence in the United States. I will note incidents which intimately concern our life work. I've discovered that the wild lemetes make a nice syrup jelly, so we shall have syrup jelly next year added to our ordinary menu. Nearly every housewife in Trinidad has come to the convent to verify the syrup fact.

August: Sister Eulalia and myself strolled up the Purgatoire River looking for wild flowers. We found plenty, and also a cluster of wild plum trees — plums as delicious as any cultivated plums. The land is "virgin" and can be made to yield fruits and vegetables pleasing to the best of agriculturists.

Another Indian scare is on. This will stop land-grabbers for a while. Here any dishonest man can become possessor of the acres he covets. It has repeatedly happened that when a land-grabber nails a small house on land acquired by spurious methods, and a grabber more greedy than himself claims this theft, the result is a fight — whoever kills the other, holds possession. Such disturbances are of frequent occurrence; they cause a sensation for a few days, then all is forgotten. But the Mexican cannot forget that all his earthly possessions have gone into the hands of strangers. Woe to the poor native if he attempts to retaliate! He has no rights that the invading fortune hunters feel obliged to respect.

Many of our Mexicans hold lands by traditional possession of *Mercedes* (Grants) and believe they are secure. The land-sharper comes in and proves their claim is not legal. No matter that they have lived on the land for years, the Mexicans must "vamoos," as these corrupters of the Spanish language say. Upon a less legal tenure than the one the Mexican was made to move, the grabber takes possession. The crisis comes when one despoiler is overreached by another artful shark who, during the dark hours of the night, removes the hastily constructed lumber shanty and replaces it by one of his own — having previously torn out any county records which could prove possession. At the dawn of the next day appear on the coveted land the violators of "Thou shalt not steal," ready for what may happen. The usual outcome is that one rogue recognizes the other, and each knows he has but one chance for life — who will shoot first.

The last of this series of crimes is: a disappointed, dejected, would-be-rich-quick man trying to drown his disappointment in *aqua fortis*. Just such a man straggling along the street saw one of our quiet, honest men coming toward him. Was it the sight of goodness that aroused his infernal hatred? Without a word he drew his revolver and shot him. The victim could only say, "Lord, have mercy on me," and expired.

This murder aroused the indignation of every citizen. Several men who witnessed the deed caught the murderer and held him till the sheriff came. A mob gathered, and in short time the murderer was condemned to be hanged to a tree near the river, in sight of my schoolroom! The sheriff sent a messenger to ask if I wished to speak to the criminal, with the hope of making him realize the gravity of his crime and that in a few minutes he was to answer to Almighty God for the life of an innocent man. I could not see that my going to the place of retribution would bring good results, consequently, I sent a member of our Vigilant Club to try to induce the criminal to make an act of contrition, but the poor man did not comprehend, or possibly did not wish to, for he said: "I die game! This is not the first man I made eat the earth. I die game!" No one except those that have witnessed such a scene can imagine its horror. The hanging was done in broad daylight and as orderly as a funeral train!

I mentioned in the first pages of this journal that any prisoner can burrow out of our adobe jail, and since the circuit court comes only at long intervals, it happens that no criminals are ever put on the docket. I visit the jail regularly. And here is how I am able to do it: I offer to be chaperon to the young ladies of the Academy, as most of them love open air and take horse rides on the plains, and so it requires more than ordinary sights to shock or unnerve them. Hence, in our walks, I invariably visit the prisoners. It does both the prisoners and the young ladies good.

Among the group that is very fond of fresh air is a Miss C——. She has read books of the ex-nun type and the horrors of what they say takes place in Convents. Consequently, she is suspicious and watches the nuns closely. Last Sunday Miss C—— was so homesick she actually cried out loud. Sister Eulalia was "Angel" at the time, and came to ask me if I could not devise something to make Miss Annie forget her homesickness. I went at once to the recreation hall and found the girl sobbing. I said: "Come, young ladies, let us take a stroll to Simpson's Rest." The seniors in my class have made a trail to the top of the "Rest." Miss Annie brightened up at once and said: "Yes, girls, let's go."

We started. After crossing the little stream called a river, we had everything to ourselves. The canopy above — the plain below, leading to the base of Simpson's Rest. Miss C—— asked why this spur of the Rockies was named Simpson's Rest. I was glad of anything that would divert her mind, so I narrated what Mr. Simpson himself had told me.

"I went up the mountain," Mr. Simpson said, "to get away from an attack of Indians. I wanted to draw their attention to me so that the few men and women in Trinidad would have time to make preparation for defense. The ruse succeeded, the squad of Indians followed me. I knew every inch of the land, and the shortest cut to the vantage spot, where I could snap off anyone coming to the top of the spur. Two Indians tried to come, and I shot each one in turn. The others of the group — so I surmised — would make me die of thirst. My provisions were giving out, but the Indians held to their purpose — possibly thinking if they got rid of me, they could make a raid on Trinidad. Meanwhile, the inhabitants had brought as much water as they could store, killed two steers and dried the meat in the sun. In fact, were prepared for a siege. But, apparently, I was the one wanted. Day after day passed. The besiegers did not attempt to ascend to the place of my captivity. I had to hoard my ammunition. I was getting unbearably thirsty when suddenly I recalled a natural cut on the left of the spur where the snow never disappears. Under cover of night I cautiously crawled to the place and found plenty of snow. I ate all I needed and took a lump with me to my hiding place. I repeated my visit to the cut for more snow. Having something to drink, I knew I could hold out indefinitely.

"At the end of a week the Indians gave the war whoop, no doubt, thinking I was dead. I felt they would climb the mountain for my scalp. Two of the most agile ran ahead of the others. I shot

one and reloaded for the other, but he ran out of sight. I was
worn out, for I only napped during the day and kept wide awake
at night, knowing the warfare methods of the Indians. At the end
of the second week I saw my besiegers gallop away, but I did
not trust myself to go down to Trinidad. The watchers in
Trinidad saw them depart and knew I was alive, because the
Indians gave no war whoop, nor showed any scalp. So they dis-
patched three runners to bring me something to eat and some
strong coffee. I saw them coming, and began to descend. When
we met, they told me the Indians had made one raid, but were
met with such a volley of shots that they did not attempt a
second attack."

George Simpson was a young man from the East. He came
West as an adventurer, and became a pioneer hunter and trapper.
He married a beautiful Mexican girl, Juanita, and made his home
near Trinidad.

The following poem written by himself some time after this
adventure with the Indians, refers to her as "one mourner":

SIMPSON'S REST

Lay me to rest on yon towering height,
Where the silent cloud-shadows glide,
Where solitude holds its slumbrous reign,
Far away from the human tide.

I fain would sleep near the old pine tree,
That looks down on the valley below,
Like a soldier guarding a comrade's grave,
Or a sentinel watching a foe.

'Twas a refuge once in the bygone time,
When a pitiful fate was near,
When my days were young and full of love
For a life I held too dear.

Thro' all the long years that have passed away
Since those nights of storm and dread,
I've prayed that the boughs that sheltered me then
Might wave o'er my breast when dead.

Delve deep my grave in the stern gray rock
In its rigid embrace let me rest,
With naught but my name on the stone
And the symbol of Faith on my breast.

One mourner perhaps may remember where sleeps
In the rock-ribbed tomb, the lone dead,
May breathe for the loved one to Heaven, a prayer,
A tear to his memory shed.

By the time I had narrated what had been told me, we had ascended one-half of the spur. Then Miss Annie and another girl sprang to the front and were following the trail, telling us they were not afraid of mountain cats or any other animal. "We are ready for any adventure," they said. They continued following the trail until they came to a curved projection which hid me from the view of anyone coming in the opposite direction. We had been walking briskly, so no one felt like talking. The two young ladies stopped at the projection. When we reached the curve we heard men's voices. By this time I could see the quizzically amused expression on the faces of the young ladies. Meanwhile the men were saying all sorts of things to the girls while walking toward them, not suspecting the presence of anyone else. As they neared them the girls stepped backward toward us and I went in front of all my protégées.

What followed was so comical, that Miss C—— and her companion had to sit down on the trail to get over their convulsive laughter. The instant the two (what shall I name them?) saw me, they both gave one spring toward the descent, which on their side had no trail. Realizing the law of gravity, I hid my

Sister Justinia Segale, S.C.

View from a corner of the Plaza, Santa Fe, 1870

MUSEUM OF NEW MEXICO PHOTO

face, believing I would have to notify their friends of their sudden death in their attempt to descend the steep side of Simpson's Rest. The laughter of the girls made me look to where the men had gone down. They had reached the bottom without injury. As soon as Miss C—— could speak, she changed laughter into seriousness and said: "I want a catechism, and I want to become a Catholic. Maria Monk and Edith O'Gorman may talk and have books published against Convents — but what I saw this afternoon has counteracted all I have ever read derogatory to convents and Sisters."

Shall I add the two men came early the next day to make an apology? What does this signify? They were afraid to lose the trade of the Convent!

§ 8

Sept., 1873.

Dearest Sister Justina: —

Our schools opened with a good attendance. During the vacation months, a native carpenter reduced the eight feet sitting desks to four feet. In his opinion, space and lumber were wasted. However, he got a job which I helped him to finish, fearing that in his great interest he might drop his rusty tools, in which case the pupils would still have to climb over one another to reach the recitation bench. By some means, the public school superintendent heard of the carpenter work and came to the Convent. He said to me: "Sister, if you will make a sketch, or some sort of drawing of a desk that you would like for School No. 1, I will propose having desks made at our next board meeting." I want to remark that we have neither sawmill nor planingmill, nor is Trinidad as yet on the map of the United States. But surely our dear Lord has made a survey of these regions. He will not forget us forever!

This noon Rafael, chief of the Ute Indians, came to tell me that his son is dead. "Shall I throw him away like a dog?" meaning without Christian burial, "or will you take him? The white men call us dogs!"

Poor creature! There are crimes which cry for vengeance. Surely our treatment of these unevolved minds comes in line. Generations to come will blush for the deeds of this, toward the rightful possessors of the soil. Our government, which poses with upraised finger of scorn on any act which savors of tyranny, lowers that finger to crush out of existence a race whose right to the land we call America is unquestioned. Has custom made might right? Rafael continued: *"Nana, tu hijo está muerto"* (Mother, your son is dead), Rafael made the motion of pouring water on the head, wanting me to understand that his son had been baptized. He continued: "When one of us dies, we move camp. Will you bury him?" The missionaries called the members of a tribe "children," hence, Rafael said: *"Tu hijo"* (your son) is dead.

Three from the Vigilant Committee were selected to go to the Utes' camp to bring in the corpse. They procured a ranch wagon, taking Rafael and companion to camp with them. Meanwhile, Sister Eulalia and myself prepared a catafalque with the crucifix and candles, and placed it in the Seniors' schoolroom. Allowing the Committee four hours to go and return (the distance to camp was three miles) we calculated the corpse would arrive the very latest at 5 P.M. Six, seven, eight, and nine o'clock came, and no sign of either Committee or a message from the Indian camp. The town folks got an inkling of what was being done at Public School No. 1. Some came to suggest sending out a posse of men, fearing the Utes had acted treacherously, others with more feeling and common sense brought us a nice lunch (which we did not touch).

At 10:30 we began to hear lamentations. When the wind blew in our direction the somber sounds were like the wind on the prairies, which had met an obstruction in its race, and agonized because it could not gather more strength to continue. Suddenly the obstruction was conquered and the weird sounds began again. All I write cannot possibly describe the natural dirge. Had the town people here not known that a corpse from the

Utes' camp was expected, not one but would have been prepared for any disaster.

Ahead of this funeral cortege came William Adamson, one of the three who went for the dead Indian. He left the procession and hastily came into the temporary mortuary chapel and said:

"Sister, you have been imposed upon. The young Eagle lives."

I responded: "Surely, William, there is a misinterpretation of words somewhere."

He continued: "No, Sister, he is sick, but not dead. We brought him in because we thought that is what you would want us to do."

"Did you bring the tribe, too?" I asked.

"No, Sister, just Rafael and the relatives are coming."

"Please ask Rafael to come to me." I questioned Chief Rafael.

"Did you not say to me, '*Tu hijo está muerto*'?" (Your son is dead.)

"*Sí, Nana.*" (Yes, mother.)

"But this gentleman says he is ill, not dead."

"Oh, Nana, he is dead. I tell you he is dead. I will carry him in to let you see he is dead."

Rafael carried the young man into the room and stood him before me. The agonizing patient could not stand, and the father caught him before he fell. We took the pillows that had formed part of the catafalque, made a bed on the floor, and attended the poor creature during the night. Next morning a room was provided through the hospitality of a Mexican family. The young man died in the afternoon and was buried as became one who had been regenerated by the waters of holy baptism.

Still, I was anxious to know why Rafael called his son's condition death, so I asked him, "When do you say an Indian is dead?" "When he has no heart. You saw, Nana, he had no heart when I carried him in to let you see him." Meaning, his son had given up hopes of living and had no pulse, which he called heart. He knew no other way of expressing his meaning, "no heart," means death.

Dec., 1873.

We are preparing for Christmas. The Vigilant Committee now composed of ten in the senior class is making secret preparations to supply a Christmas surprise for certain families and children who only know of Santa Claus by hearsay. In my turn, I suggested to the pupils not on the Committee to surprise the Seniors. Clothes and shoes are put in new dress suit cases. Candy boxes are hung on the Christmas tree. The young ladies of the Academy gave their last season's dresses, which are almost new. These will be sent to some families that have been reported as "Needy." Two of the convent girls each received diamond clustered rings and, because the diamonds were not set to their liking, they discarded them. I could not refrain from saying, "I hope I will never see the day you would be glad to possess them."

After the Vigilant Committee has distributed the prepared boxes to the different families, all our pupils will assemble in the Christmas tree room and receive their surprise. Then those who have to go to confession will do so. Those who remain will contribute Yuletide facts or legends.

Then preparations for midnight Mass. The choir will render Mozart's 12th Mass; organ, harp, and first violin will accompany. Quite a change from the time of an untuned instrument and nasal singing. As you will notice, we are progressing rapidly, though Trinidad is not yet on the map.

What came to my mind just now is: "Will the frontier missionaries in the South and West, Franciscans and Jesuits, fare any better in public records than did the first missionaries who staked all to bring the knowledge of God to those who inhabited the newly discovered lands?" True, Mr. Bancroft did narrate in his History of the United States some of the hardships and heroic sacrifices made by the first Jesuits, but I have been told on excellent authority that bigots are determined to have Mr. Bancroft omit the praise given the first Indian missionaries when he issues the next edition. If he does so, I predict that he, with his history, will sink in the estimation of every honest reader of history, and the result will be a change of Bancroft's U. S. History in many of the schools now using it.

How much is there made of Lord Baltimore giving freedom of conscience to those who lived where he controlled! Yet look at the stream of articles constantly given to the public about Plymouth Rock and the Pilgrim Fathers! "Oh, Justice, where art thou!"

Jan. 6, 1874.

Our Christmas was a wonderful event. The whole program was a surprise. The needy and bashful were made happy by the Seniors. The Juniors surprised the Seniors, and all surprised their teachers. Now, when we visit the jail, our hands will not be empty, because our baskets are full. Was not the whole proceeding a beautiful tribute to our new-born King?

We are beginning the exercises for the close of school the latter part of June.

To-day, while acting as moderator on the playgrounds, a woman came staggering on her way to me. She asked: "Do you know me, Sister?"

"I do not remember having met you before."

She stammered: "I'm Crazy Ann." ·

I looked at her kindly. She continued: "Why can't I be like you?"

"You are the only one that can answer the question," I replied.

Meanwhile, she seemed to be regaining her equilibrium and she resumed: "Sister, I was a good girl. My father compelled me to marry a man I did not love. I married him and sailed the same day for America. This happened in Ireland. I landed in New York. Now I am here, an outcast."

"Poor, poor Ann! Why not start life over again?" Ignoring what I said, she straightened herself and soliloquized: "I'm coming to church Sunday."

Encouragingly I said: "Do, Ann, but wear something on your head and drink only water Sunday morning." Sunday came, and so did Ann come to church. She made sure to look up to the choir loft to let me see she had kept her word. Only once have I seen the unfortunate woman since our first meeting. At the second encounter, she was surrounded by a crowd of men enjoying whatever she was saying to them. Suddenly she saw me. She made a rush through the crowd and disappeared. Her audience turned to discover what had caused her sudden departure and saw only two Sisters of Charity wending their way to the post-office.

Next to our public school playground, with only a pretense of a street between, there lives a widow, one of the best in the world. She takes care of a scrofulous girl and a poor cripple. This cripple, at one time, was the best horseman in this part of the country, but having lost his balance in a cock pit fight, injured his spine.

This cock pit fight may not mean anything to you, so I will explain. Some natives take pleasure in raising a special breed of cocks, and train them to become fighters. The training begins as soon as the cocks can find their own feeding, and is continued until they become bloody fighters, which means until one of the couple trained will kill the other. The survivor is then kept until the day for the pit fight, when the poor fowl is buried in an artificial hole, leaving only the head exposed. A number of swift riders will start a race about half a mile from the buried fowl. The horsemen spur their broncos to swiftness, and when passing the buried cock stoop to catch it by its head. The one who succeeds in pulling it out of the pit is followed by the rest of the riders, until someone can snatch it from him. If it is still alive, it is buried again; if dead, someone else who has trained a fowl for the occasion, puts it into the pit and the race is continued. This seems savage cruelty, but there are other things committed by intelligent beings against intelligent beings, which are still more shockingly cruel.

§ 9

Dear Sister Justina: —

It is nearly one year since I wrote anything in the Journal I'm keeping for you. The reason is simply that the things I could write are so ghastly that they had better be left untold. Keep in mind that the only three aims I can read in the minds of those who, at present, live in Trinidad, and its surroundings are:

1. Health for invalids.
2. Strenuous efforts in money making.
3. Jesuits[27] and Sisters of Charity trying to stem undesirable conditions. For the last named, their effort is like attempting to stop an avalanche.

Fearing you may consider me ambiguous, I will narrate one instance I would prefer not to write. One of the most thoughtful members of our Young Men's Vigilant Club came cautiously to see me and related the following:

"Sister, you know Mr. —— and Mr. —— ?" I bowed my knowledge of the men. Intuitively I felt a revelation was coming. He continued: "These men covet a coal mine that is now being worked. The mine shows prospects of making its owner a millionaire in the very near future. To-day a number of posts were placed in the first excavation. These can be shifted to such positions that when the boss and miners begin work to-morrow morning all the props will suddenly collapse. That diabolical act has been accomplished. The two men who did this are desperadoes and will stop at nothing if they find out we have had a hand in preventing the slaughter. The premeditated deaths not taking place would be ignored by them, but not getting possession of the coal mine would make them furious. What do you suggest?"

Realizing the deep significance of what he disclosed, I needed to reflect seriously. The two desperadoes — especially one of them, and this one controlled the mind of the other — were well known to me. The coal mine is located at some distance from Trinidad. Should I absent myself from school, it would be noticed. To go out to the mine would cause a sensation. So I revolved the matter over in my mind, while my informant waited for some suggestion. There was no time to lose.

Among my former pupils is a level-headed Indian. Mentally I had already sent for him. Continuing the conversation, I said: "Leave this affair to me; rumor is often unjust. Only assure yourself of this: if there is truth in what you were told, the supports in that mine will not collapse to-morrow."

To keep everything under cover, a small Mexican boy carried this message to the Indian: "I have some work for you, come." The Indian arrived some time before the return of the boy who took the message. When the messenger came back, the Indian was cleaning the windows in my schoolroom.

After the boy left, the Indian and myself got to work. His first question was, "*Qué, hay, Hermana?*" (What is it, Sister?) I answered: "A big one this time. Working men are wanted at the mine — go to the boss and hire yourself this evening. Be the first at the mine in the morning. Bring your miner's light with you. Inspect the supports and call the attention of the boss to anything that looks dangerous to you. You understand?"

"*Sí, Hermana.*" (Yes, Sister.)

"Remain working at the mine, and instruct the natives how to detect danger in wrongly put-up supports and tell them to inspect the posts every time they resume work. Watch for powder and fuses. Instruct those most capable to carry out what you say."

"*Sí, Hermana, yo voy.*" (Yes, Sister, I go.)

This Indian has the instinct of silence: to this, add that of loyalty to goodness, and you have the character of the one intrusted to frustrate the murderous design of the desperadoes. No long explanation was needed. I give you the conversation as we had it.

The mine remained in possession of its rightful owner, and no one was injured by the infernal plot to kill boss and miners. In my estimation, a good Indian is the best ally in an emergency.

The Jesuits are going to open a novitiate in Albuquerque. The present indication is that several of my seniors will be their first subjects.

§ 10

Nov. 14.

Three of my senior pupils have gone to Albuquerque to be among the first subjects of the Jesuit Novitiate in these parts. The good Fathers are also to publish a Spanish paper — *The Revista Católica* — Rest assured, I'm working for subscriptions. I have twelve already. The paper, I know, will be a medium of instruction for our native population. . . .

One of my oldest pupils came to ask to have his sister excused from school. He looked so deathly pale that I inquired, "What has happened?" He answered, "Haven't you heard?"

"Nothing that should make you look as you do."

"Sister, dad shot a man! He's in jail. A mob has gathered and placed men about forty feet apart from the jail to Mr. Mc-Caferty's room. The instant he breathes his last, the signal of his death will be given, and the mob will go to the jail and drag dad out and hang him."

"Have you thought of anything that might save him?" I asked.

"Nothing, Sister; nothing can be done."

"Is there no hope that the wounded man may recover?"

"No hope whatever; the gun was loaded with tin shot."

"John, go to the jail and ask your father if he will take a chance at not being hanged by a mob."

"What do you propose doing, Sister?"

"First to visit the wounded man and ask if he will receive your father and forgive him, with the understanding that the full force of the law be carried out."

"Sister, the mob would tear him to pieces before he was ten feet from the jail."

"I believe he will not be touched if I accompany him," I said.

"I'm afraid he will not have the courage to do as you propose."

"That is the only thing I can see that will save him from the mob law. Ask your father to decide. This is Friday. I'll visit the sick man after school this afternoon. Let me know if he will consent to go with me to the sick man's room."

Immediately after school, with a companion, I went to see the wounded man. Sister Fidelis had preceded me. She was writing a letter to his mother bidding her good-bye until they would meet where the Judge was just, and their tears would be dried forever.

I looked at the young man, a fine specimen of honesty and manliness. My heart ached for the mother who expected frequent word from her son, then to receive such news! To be shot unjustly, to die in a strange land, among strangers, so young!

As soon as Sister Fidelis and companion took leave of the sick man, the subject of the present visit was broached. The young man was consistent. He said, "I forgive him, as I hope to be forgiven, but I want the law to take its course."

Fully agreeing with him, he was asked: "Will you tell Mr. —— this if he comes to beg your pardon?"

"Yes, Sister," he answered.

Friday evening the prisoner's son came to say his father was very much afraid to attempt to walk to Mr. McCaferty's room, but if Sister would walk with him, he would take the chance of having the court pronounce sentence on him.

Early Saturday morning we presented ourselves to the Sheriff in his office.

"Good morning, Sister!" was the Sheriff's pleasant greeting.

"Good morning, Mr. Sheriff. Needless to ask if you know what is taking place on our two principal streets."

"You mean the men ready to lynch the prisoner who so unjustly shot the young Irishman?"

"Yes. What are you going to do to prevent the lynching?"

"Do! What has any sheriff here ever been able to do to prevent a mob from carrying out its intent?"

"Be the first sheriff to make the attempt!"

"How, Sister?" Standing to his full height — he must be six feet four — he reminded me of a person with plenty of reserve strength, and on the *qui vive* to use a portion of it.

"The prisoner was asked if he would be willing to walk between the sheriff and Sister to the victim's sick bed and ask his pardon." The sheriff interrupted: — "Sister, have you ever seen the working of a mob?"

"A few, Mr. Sheriff."

"And would you take the chance of having the prisoner snatched from between us and hanged to the nearest cottonwood?"

"In my opinion, there is nothing to fear." He straightened himself and looked at me, shrugged his shoulders and said, "If you are not afraid, neither am I."

We — the sheriff, my companion and myself — started to walk to the jail. All along the main street and leading to the jail were men at about a distance of a rod apart. These were the men who were to signal Mr. McCaferty's death by three taps of our school bell, in order that the mob might proceed to the jail, take the prisoner and hang him. Our group arrived at the jail, where we encountered the greatest discouragement. The prisoner saw us coming. When we got near enough to speak to him, he was trembling like an aspen. We saw his courage had failed him. We paused while we assured him he was safe in going with us.

He hesitated, then said: "I'll go with you." All along the road we kept silence, and no one spoke to us. When we got within a block of the sick man's room, we saw a crowd of men outside his door. It was at this juncture that my fears for the prisoner began. Intent upon saving our protégé from mob law, we hastened to the sick man's door. The crowd made way. Intense fear took possession of me. "Will the prisoner be jerked away when he attempts to enter his victim's room?"

The Sheriff and I remained at the foot of the few steps which led into the room. Meanwhile, I quietly said to the prisoner: "Go in," which he did, myself and companion following. The sheriff remained outside. The door was left wide open that those standing outside might hear the conversation taking place within.

The culprit stood before his victim with bowed head. Fearing a prolonged silence, I addressed the prisoner: "Have you nothing to say?"

He looked at the man in bed and said: "My boy, I did not know what I was doing. Forgive me."

The sick man removed the blanket which covered his tin-shot leg, revealing a sight to unnerve the stoutest heart. The whole leg was mortified and swollen out of proportion, showing where the poisonous tin had lodged and the mortification creeping toward the heart.

"See what you have done!" said the wounded man.

"I'm sorry, my boy, forgive me."

"I forgive you, as I hope to be forgiven, but the law must take its course."

I added, "Yes, the law must take its course — not mob law." Those outside the door with craned necks distinctly heard the conversation.

We returned to the jail where the prisoner was to remain until the Circuit Court convened.

From the time Judge Hallet became judge of the Circuit Court, he and his court members have regularly made a visit to the Convent.

§ 11

June, 1876.

Dear Sister Justina:

To-day I asked Sister Eulalia if, in her opinion, we did not need a new school building, which would contain a hall and stage for all school purposes. She said: "Just what we need, Sister. Do you want to build it?" I answered, "Yes, I do." She added, "We have not enough cash to pay interest on our indebtedness. Have you a plan by which you can build without money? If so, I say build."

"Here is my plan, Sister. Borrow a crowbar, get on the roof of the schoolhouse and begin to detach the adobes. The first good Mexican who sees me will ask, "What are you doing, Sister?" I will answer, "Tumbling down this structure to rebuild it before the opening of the fall term of school.""

You should have seen Sister Eulalia laugh! It did me good. After three days' pondering how to get rid of low ceilings, poor ventilation, acrobats from log-rafters introducing themselves without notice, and now here is an opportunity to carry out a test on the good in human nature, so I took it. I borrowed a crowbar and went on the roof, detached some adobes and began throwing them down. The school building is only one story high.

The first person who came towards the schoolhouse was Doña Juanita Simpson, wife of the noted hero of Simpson's Rest. When she saw me at work, she exclaimed, *"Por amor de Dios, Hermana, qué está Vd. haciendo?"* (For the love of God, Sister, what are you doing?)

I answered, "We need a schoolhouse that will a little resemble those we have in the United States, so I am demolishing this one in order to rebuild."

"How many men do you need, Sister?"

"We need not only men, but also straw, moulds, hods, shovels — everything it takes to build a house with a shingle roof. Our assets are good-will and energy."

Earnestly Mrs. Simpson said: "I go to get what you need."

The crowbar was kept at its work. In less than an hour, Mrs. Simpson returned with six men. One carried a mould, another straw, etc. The mould carrier informed me at once that women only know how to *encalar* (whitewash), the men had the trades and they would continue what I began. In a few days the old building was thrown down, the adobes made and sun-burnt. In two weeks all the rubbish was hauled away. The trouble began when we were ready for the foundation. Keep in mind it was only by condescension I was permitted to look on. At this juncture I remarked to the moulder:

"Of course, we will have a stone foundation."

"Oh, no!" he answered, "we use adobes laid in mud."

"Do you think if we laid a foundation with stone laid in mortar, the combination would resist the rainy season better than adobes laid in mud?"

"No, no, Sister, we never use stone for any of our houses," he replied.

I was at the mercy of those good natives and my best move was to let them have their way. Moreover, I recalled the fact that in the Far East there are mud structures centuries old in a good state of preservation. No mistake would be made by not changing their mode of building in that one point. We got the necessary lumber, sashes and shingles from Chené's mill, sixty miles from Trinidad. Wagons hauled the material. As the Chené family has a daughter at our boarding school, there will be no difficulty in meeting our bill. Mr. Hermann's daughter is a resident student, and Mr. Hermann is a carpenter and will pay his bill by work.

When the schoolhouse was ready for roofing, a number of the town carpenters offered to help. The merchants gave nails, paints, brushes, lime, hair, etc.

But now came the big obstacle. There is but one man who calls himself a plasterer, and his method is to plaster with mud. It is impossible to get a smooth surface with mud. I remarked to the plasterer: "You will use lime, sand and hair to plaster the schoolrooms."

His look plainly said: "What do women know of men's work?" Yet he condescended to explain: "I am the plasterer of this part of the country; if I should use any material but mud, my reputation would be lost."

I said to him, "But if lime, sand and hair made a better job, your reputation would gain."

He made answer, "Sister, I'll make a bargain with you. I will do as you suggest, but I will tell my people I carried out your American idea of plastering."

We both agreed to this. Meanwhile, the other men had shouldered their implements and were on their way home. The plasterer had to mix the sand, lime and hair following my directions. All that was done satisfactorily to me, at least. But there was not a man to carry the mortar to the plasterer, so I got a bucket and supplied a man's place. The comedy follows:

Rev. Charles Pinto, S.J., pastor, took pleasure in telling his co-religionists that the study of human nature, combined with good will and tactfulness, were building a schoolhouse.

On this day of my hod-carrying, the Rt. Rev. Bishop Machebeuf[28] of Denver, Colorado, arrived on his visitation. The first place to which he was taken was the schoolhouse being built without money. Bishop and Pastor had just turned the kitchen corner when the three of us came face to face. Both gentlemen stood amazed. I rested my hod-bucket. Father Pinto looked puzzled. The Bishop remarked:

"I see how you manage to build without money." I laughed and explained the situation.

They took the bucket, and the three of us went to where the plasterer was working. After the welcome to the Bishop, the plasterer said:

"Your Reverence, look at me, the only Mexican plasterer, and I am putting aside my knowledge to follow American ways of doing my trade; but I told Sister the failure will not be pointed at me." The Rt. Rev. Bishop analyzed the material at a glance, then said: "Juan, if this method of plastering is better than yours, come again to help Sister when she needs you. If it fails, report to me and between us we shall give her the biggest penance she ever received."

The schoolroom walls turned out smooth, the plaster adhesive, and the plasterer will now make a lucrative living at his American method of plastering. . . .

We have not had any mob to hang delinquents since the

Sheriff and some members of the Vigilant Committee asserted the rights of courts instead of unauthorized groups to carry out the interest of the laws.

The Circuit Court came to Trinidad. At its sitting it sentenced the prisoner to ten years in the penitentiary. Mr. McCaferty had lived three days after being shot, hence the deed is called manslaughter, minimum, one year, maximum, ten years.

Shall I prophesy? The prisoner will be at large in less than two years. Yet this small unmapped town is making strides in the right direction.

To-day we went to visit our cripple — spinal invalid — who was once the best horseman of the Southwest. His eyes are hungry for someone to speak to, and his appetite craves a change of diet. Among the edibles we brought him was a baked custard, which he literally devoured. During the time he was eating, his look was frequently directed to one particular part of the room.

When we turned to leave, my attention was arrested by a crouching figure. The object looked like a huddled dressed-up skeleton, head bald, eyes as if they had been placed in the sockets. The only indication of life was a terrified expression from the orbs that looked from the hollow sockets. I walked toward the bundle and said:

"Poor child, what can we do for you?"

"You do not recognize me, Sister? I am Crazy Ann! They told me you come to see this cripple, and I came to see you. I have no place where I can go to die."

"We shall find a place for you, Ann. You are one of God's children, but forgot you once loved Him, yet He still loves you."

Her sobs were sincere. We found a room and bed for her yesterday, to-day we went to see her. Her first request was for the scapulars. Oh! the feeling of repugnance that came over me to put the image of the purest of creatures on this all but God-forsaken, shriveled creature! But she was a "Prodigal Son." She told us she had cast off the scapulars when she began her downward career. She had but a few days to live. Her repentance is sincere, not because she now cannot sin, but because the faith instilled in early years has revived and prevented self-destruction.

Three days later, "Crazy Ann" — we knew her by no other name — was buried. The corpse was carried on a sort of stretcher covered with a sheet. She was lowered into a hole 3x6 ft. May her soul rest in peace, for surely peace left her from the moment her downward course began, and only returned when she came back to God.

§ 12

Sept. 1876.

The pupils and myself will have to be introduced daily to our schoolroom. It will take some time to wear off the novelty of entering a well-lighted, well-ventilated room, flowers in blossom on window sills, blackboard built into the walls, modern desks, and a stage for Friday exercises. I think one of my ambitions has been reached, viz.: to walk into my schoolroom and feel that it is "up-to-date" and I, "Mistress of all I survey," particularly of the minds to be taught.

My scattered notes on "Billy the Kid's Gang" are condensed, and some day you will be thrilled by their perusal.

The Trinidad Enterprise — the only paper published here — in its last issue gave an exciting description of how a member of "Bill's Gang" painted red the town of Cimarron by mounting his stallion and holding two six-shooters aloft while shouting his commands, which everyone obeyed, not knowing when the trigger on either weapon would be lowered. This event has been the town talk, excluding every other subject, for the past week.

Yesterday one of the Vigilant Committee came to where I was on our grounds — acting as umpire for a future ball game — and said: "Sister, please come to the front yard. I want you to see one of 'Billy's gang,' the one who caused such fright in Cimarron week before last." My informant passed the news to the Nine and their admirers, so that it became my duty to go with the pupils, not knowing what might take place.

When we reached the front yard, the object of our curiosity was still many rods from us. The air here is very rarefied, and we all are eagle-eyed in this atmosphere. We stood in our front yard, everyone trying to look indifferent, while Billy's accomplice headed toward us.

He was mounted on a spirited stallion of unusually large proportions, and was dressed as the *Toreadores* (Bull-Fighters) dress in old Mexico. Cowboy's sombrero, fantastically trimmed, red velvet knee breeches, green velvet short coat, long sharp spurs, gold and green saddle cover. A figure of six feet three, on a beautiful animal, made restless by a tight bit — you need not wonder, the rider drew attention. His intention was to impress you with the idea "I belong to the gang." The impression made on me was one of intense loathing, and I will candidly acknowledge, of fear also.

The figure passed from our sight. I tried to forget it, but it was not to be. Our Vigilant Club, at all times, is on the alert to be of service. William Adamson, a member of the Club, came excitedly, to say — "We have work on hand!"

"What kind of work?" I asked.

"You remember the man who frightened the people in Cimarron, and who passed our schoolhouse some weeks ago?"

"Yes, William."

"Well, he and Happy Jack, his partner, got into a quarrel, and each got the drop on the other. They kept eyeing and following each other for three days, eating at the same table, weapon in right hand, conveying food to their mouth with left hand.

"The tragedy took place when they were eating dinner. Each thought the other off guard, both fired simultaneously. Happy Jack was shot through the breast. He was put in a dug-out 3 x 6 ft. Schneider received a bullet in his thigh, and has been brought into Trinidad, thrown into an unused adobe hut, and left there to die. He has a very poor chance of living."

"Well, William, we shall do all we can for him. Where did this all take place?"

"At Dick Wootton's tollgate — the dividing line between Colorado and New Mexico."

At the noon hour we carried nourishing food, water, castile soap and linens to the sick and neglected man. After placing on a table what we had brought, my two companions, William Adamson and Laura Menger, withdrew. I walked towards the bed and, looking at the sick man, I exclaimed, "I see that nothing but a bullet through your brain will finish you!"

I saw a quivering smile pass over his face, and his tiger eyes gleamed. My words seemed heartless. I had gone to make up for the inhuman treatment given by others, and instead, I had added to the inhumanity by my words.

After a few days of retrospection, I concluded it was not I who had spoken, but Fear, so psychologists say.

At our first visit I offered to dress the wound, but to my great relief the desperado said, "I am glad to get the nourishment and the wherewith to dress my wound, but I shall attend to it myself." Then he asked: "What shall I call you?"

"Sister," I answered.

"Well, Sister, I am very glad you came to see me. Will you come again?"

"Yes, two and three times a day. Good-bye."

We continued these visits for about two months, then one day the sick man asked: "Sister, why is it you never speak to me about your religion or anything else?"

I looked and smiled.

He continued: "I want to tell you something. I allude to the first day you came. Had you spoken to me of repentance, honesty, morals, or anything pertaining to religion, I would have ordered you out. 'I see that nothing but a bullet through your brain will finish you.' Sister, you have no idea what strength and courage those words put into me. I said to myself, 'no shamming here, but the right stuff.'"

Dear Sister Justina, imagine what a load was lifted, to know for a certainty I had not added pain to the downtrodden culprit, for so he is at present. The patient seemed to wish to talk. He asked:

"Sister, do you think God would forgive me?"

I repeated the words of Holy Scripture as they then came to my mind. "If your sins were as scarlet, or as numerous as the sands on the seashore, turn to Me, saith the Lord, and I will forgive."

"Sister, I would like to tell you some things I have done — then, I will ask you, if you think God can forgive me."

Seating myself, I waited, as he continued:

"I have done all that a bad man can do. I have been a decoy on the Santa Fe Trail."

He saw I did not grasp his meaning, so he explained:

"I dressed in my best when I expected to see horsemen or private conveyance take to the Trail. Addressing them politely, I would ask, 'Do you know the road to where you are going?' If they hesitated, I knew they were greenies. I would offer to escort them, as the Trail was familiar to me, and I was on my way to visit a friend. We would travel together, talking pleasantly, but all the while my aim was to find out if the company had enough in its possession to warrant me carrying out my purpose.

"If I discovered they did not have money or valuables I would direct the travelers how to reach the next fort. If they possessed money or jewelry, I managed to lose the trail at sunset and make for a camping place. When they slept, I murdered them and took all valuables. The fact of being off the Trail made it next to impossible for the deed to be discovered.

"Another thing I took pleasure in doing was to shoot cows and steers for their hides. I remember one time I shot several cows that belonged to a man from Kansas. I left the carcasses for the coyotes. The old man had a great deal of spunk in him, so he and his herders trailed and caught me with the hides.

"They had a rope with them which they threw over the limb of a tree and placed me under the rope. Before going any farther the old man said to me, 'Say your prayers, young man; you know the law of the plains, a thief is hanged.' I said, 'I'm not a thief, I shot at random. When I saw my shots had taken effect, I took the hides of the animals I had shot. What would you have done?'

" 'I would not have shot at random into a bunch of cows,' he answered. I saw some of the fellows felt sorry for me, and I added: 'Did none of you ever make a mistake? I acknowledged I did wrong.' All but the old man said, 'Let the fellow go,' and waited for the old man to speak. 'Well, if you all think he ought to be let go, I don't say anything against it,' he said. So they let me go. As soon as I got where my pals were, I told them how near I came to being strung up. They all laughed and said I had the young ones to thank that I was able to tell the tale. I added, 'I'll wager ten cents I'll scalp the old man and throw the scalp on this counter.' They laughed and took up my wager.

"The next day I went to find in what direction the cattle I had fired into had gone. I soon discovered the herd trail and followed it, and at noon I saw the cattle. The old man was sitting on a stump with his back to me. I slipped up quietly behind him, passed my sharp knife round his head while holding his hair, and carried his scalp on a double run to where I had left my bronco; then, whirled to where my pals were. They each had told some of the deeds he had done, and Happy Jack had just finished telling an act which I will not tell you, but I added: 'Here is my last achievement. Scalped a man on a wager of ten cents.' While saying this I threw the scalp on the counter. 'Give me my dime.'

"Sister, now do you think God can forgive me?"

I answered: "Turn to Me in sorrow of heart and I will forgive, saith the Lord."

"Sister, I do not doubt that you believe that God will forgive me: I'm going to tell you what I think God would do. Through you, God is leading me to ask pardon for my many devilish acts.

"He is enticing me, as I enticed those who had valuables; then, when He gets me, He will hurl me into hell, more swiftly than I sent my victims to Eternity. Now what do you think about that, Sister?"

"I will answer you by asking you a question. Who was the sinner who asked Christ to remember him when He came into His kingdom?"

"I don't know, Sister."

"It was the malefactor dying at the side of Christ on the cross who called for mercy at the last moment. He was told by the very Christ-God — 'This day, thou shalt be with Me in Paradise.'"

"That sounds fine, Sister; but what will my pals think of me? Me, to show a yellow streak! I would rather go to the burning flames. Anyhow, when I get there, I will have to stay chained."

"Experience is a great teacher."

"You bet it is, Sister."

"I'm going to give you an experience." I got the fire shovel and placing two burning coals on it, brought it to the bedside of the patient. "Now place one finger over these coals, or let me tie your hand, so that one finger will burn for ten seconds, then tell me if, in either case, the pain will be diminished."

"Say, Sister, let me think this thing over."

At our next visit the patient did not allude to our last conversation. I do not speak on religious subjects to him unless questioned. This routine work of taking him nourishment, linens, etc., continues. We had been doing it for about four months when this particular incident took place.

On a Saturday morning we arrived at our patient's adobe house when, for the first time, we heard voices in his room. Rapping at the door, the patient in a loud irritated voice called out: "Come in, Sister, and look at these hypocrites and whited sepulchres. Do you know what brought them here? Shame! You shamed them, you, a Catholic Sister, who has been visiting me for over four months and bringing wherewith to keep me alive. You never once asked me whether I was a Jew, Indian, or devil. You shamed them into coming. They say I belong to their church!"

Not noticing the aggressive language, I remarked: "I'm so glad your friends have found you. Should you need us in the future, we will be at your service."

Then one of the ladies of the company said: "It was only yesterday that a member of our Methodist congregation was told that the sick man was a Methodist. She went at once to our minister and he appointed this committee, and we are here, ready and willing, to attend to the sick man."

I told her that it made me happy to know the patient will have his own visiting him.

With a pleasant good-bye, we took our leave. On returning to the Convent, while making our program for sick calls, I remarked: "Billy the Kid's partner has found friends. Rather they have found him, and they intend to give him all the aid he needs. So we will withdraw, but be on the alert, in case we should have to continue our visits." This was said to a member of the Vigilant Club, who always accompanied my companion and myself to this particular patient.

Two weeks had elapsed when our protector of the Vigilant Committee came to the schoolhouse to say: "Sister, Billy's pal needs us again. I visited him several times during the past two days. He told me that no one has been to see him for a week."

So this noon we visited the desperado, the same as we had done at first. His being neglected by those who had promised to attend to him made me think that the ladies we met in his room are perhaps mothers of families, and cannot spare the time from their home. Again, some of the ladies maybe were as much afraid of him, as I had been, so it is easy to see why they could not keep their promise, but it would have been more just to let me know they were going to discontinue aiding him. Perhaps their husbands did not approve of their visiting a bandit. The general sentiment is, "Let the desperado die."

To-day when we got to the adobe, everything was deathly quiet and the door was ajar. I noiselessly walked in. This is the scene that met me. The patient stretched full length, his eyes glazed and focused on the ceiling; his six-shooter in his right hand with the muzzle pointing to his temple. Quick as a flash I took in the situation and as quickly reached the bedside. Placing my hand on the revolver and lowering the trigger while putting the weapon out of his reach, I remarked: "The bed is not a good place from which to practice target shooting."

He said, "Just in the nick of time, Sister," as though we had not been absent a day. I named the different edibles we had brought him. The subject of the act he was about to commit was never mentioned. By intuition he understood he was not to speak against those who had promised to attend him and did not do so.

Another month passed by and the patient was visibly losing strength. I managed to get his mother's address. She lives in California.

After a week we resumed our visits. At the noon call our patient was quite hilarious. I surmised something unusual had taken place. He lost no time in telling me that Billy and the "gang" are to be here, Saturday at 2 P.M., and I am going to tell you why they are coming.

"Do you know the four physicians who live here in Trinidad?"

"I know three of them," I answered.

"Well, the 'gang' is going to scalp the four of them" (and his tiger eyes gleamed with satisfaction) "because not one of them would extract the bullet from my thigh."

Can you imagine, Sister Justina, the feeling that came over me? One of the gentlemen is our Convent physician!

I looked at the sick man for a few seconds, then said: "Do you believe that with this knowledge I'm going to keep still?"

"What are you going to do about it?"

"Meet your gang at 2 P.M. next Saturday."

He laughed as heartily as a sick man could laugh and said, "Why, Sister, Billy and the gang will be pleased to meet you. I've told them about you and the others, too, who call themselves my church people," but seeing the conversation did not please, he said no more.

In the interval between this visit and the Saturday 2 P.M., which was to be such a memorable day for me, I wrote to his mother not in an alarming strain, but enough to give her to understand he might not recover. Fourteen days later, she arrived. That was quick time, for she depended on mules and horses for conveyance. I cannot give you any idea of the anxiety of the days previous to the coming ordeal of meeting the gang.

Saturday, 2 P.M., came, and I went to meet Billy and his gang. When I got to the patient's room, the men were around his bed. The introduction was given. I can only remember, "Billy, our Captain, and Chism."

I was not prepared to see the men that met me, which must account for my not being able to recall their names.

The leader, Billy, has steel-blue eyes, peach complexion, is young, one would take him to be seventeen — innocent-looking, save for the corners of his eyes, which tell a set purpose, good or bad. Mr. Chism, of course this is not his real name — has a most bashful appearance. I judge he has sisters. The others, all fine looking young men. My glance took this description in while "Billy" was saying: "We are all glad to see you, Sister, and I want to say, it would give me pleasure to be able to do you any favor."

I answered, "Yes, there is a favor you can grant me." He reached his hand toward me with the words: "The favor is granted."

I took the hand, saying: "I understand you have come to scalp our Trinidad physicians, which act I ask you to cancel." Billy looked down at the sick man who remarked: "She is game."[29]

What he meant by that I am yet at a loss to understand. Billy then said: "I granted the favor before I knew what it was, and it stands. Not only that, Sister, but at any time my pals and I can serve you, you will find us ready."

I thanked him and left the room. How much of this conversation was heard by my companion who waited in the corridor, I do not know. Here are the names of the physicians who were doomed to be scalped:

Dr. Michael Beshoar, our Convent and Academy physician;

the two Menger brothers. The elder has a large family, the younger is a bachelor. The fourth is Dr. Palmer, whom I know only by reputation. They will never know from me what might have happened.

Life is a mystery. What of the human heart? A compound of goodness and wickedness. Who has ever solved the secret of its working? I thought: One moment diabolical, the next angelical.

The patient's mother is going to have her son removed to a private family. I am unable to judge how much the mother knows of the life of her boy. His tiger expression must have developed since he left her side, and she is too happy to be with him to notice anything except that life is losing all attractions for him. From a number of conversations we have had, I judge she has a high opinion of herself and every member of her family, including the patient. She is a Methodist. Hereafter, our visits will be friendly ones, no relief, whatever. The mother has taken full responsibility.

Please do not suppose that my outside service infringes on my schoolwork. I do not know what fatigue feels like.

The Seniors have the privilege of free Friday afternoon, provided their average reached 90% for the week. All recitations are filed. I take this method of originating ideas in the minds of the pupils.

When they know they have Friday afternoon off, some come with horses, others with burros and jolt wagons – anything the pupils can ride. The plan of how or where to go is first arranged among themselves. I seldom have reason to make any change in the program. One point is insisted on: to go some place known to the oldest resident, and that the place be of note, made so by warring tribes, whose history still is fresh in the minds of our ancients here, or given us by tradition, or yet more interesting, the pupils narrating what their fathers have seen or were actual participators in the scenes described.

At this time every conceivable place that had Indian or Mexican tradition, or personal experience, had been visited by the class, and it also had exhausted every part of the Raton Mountains and Simpson's Rest. Somehow, the pupils arranged to climb the face of Simpson's Rest by ropes.

"Why do you go to all this trouble," I asked, "when you can so easily scramble up the mountain side?" But before the attempt was made to use ropes, we were to visit the Sulphur Cave. We were on our way to the cave, having still to round a projection, when we heard shot after shot. The class made a rush towards me. The action did not impress me as that of fear, but of acting. Some said: "Let's go back!" Others, "Who is afraid? Let us go on." I led, and turned the projection, and there at the spot that would first catch our sight was a figure with a rope around its neck dangling from a tree! Standing still and eyeing it a few seconds I remarked: "Why did you go to all this trouble?"

"On a bet, Sister. All the pupils said nothing could frighten you. Philip Gurule declared he could manage something that would frighten you. So now, we shall have a fine treat."

"Claim your treat," I said.

Philip is the son of a rich rancher. This is the second time the pupils of my room were treated. The former treat was won in this way: A well dressed young man came with his books to attend Public School No. 1. He claimed to be the nephew of a Senator just now in the public gaze. Whether he relied on his uncle's reputation, or possibly that he has no particular love for higher mathematics, whatever the cause may be, he failed in several recitations. At the last failure he turned quite suddenly to the desk and said:

"I'll place a problem on the board and if anyone in the room can solve it, I'll stand a treat for the school."

"Very well, leave your puzzle on the board, and I believe that when you return to-morrow the answer to it will meet you."

A number of enthusiastic pupils copied the figures and some remained after school. It was a puzzle problem. The point was to find the key to it, which was found. Well, the school got its treat.

There are no amusements for the young folks, nor for old ones either, so the school frequently gives entertainments. Having our own assembly hall, the fun is enjoyed by all, especially by the parents and friends of the pupils.

The pupils have experimented on impromptu dramatics. The class and teacher were so pleased with the success of the effort that they were told they may be called on at any time without notice to give us an entertainment.

Feast of All Saints, 1876.

Our poor desperado is fast approaching the shores of eternity.

He has become more thoughtful, even his tiger eyes are softening. The mother is all attention and goodness to her son, but neither will hear to our discontinuing our visits. This is the ninth month of our work with this patient who now never mentions "the Gang," though Trinidad often hears of the atrocities committed by it — only say "Billy the Kid" and every individual is at attention.

Dear Sister Justina, were I to write many of the incidents of daily occurrence, this journal kept for you instead of giving you a little diversion, and perhaps a wee bit of knowledge, might bring you only sadness and weariness.

Billy and his gang are terrorizing the country between this place and La Glorieta, the historic battleground of Texans and Mexicans.

Our school is rehearsing for a concert to be given during the Christmas holidays. We are not depending upon outside talent for our vocal numbers, but we will be assisted by two Italian musicians — violin and harp.

Our desperado patient has the comfort of his mother's presence, yet neither her love nor sacrifice can stay his fast dissolution. December 2. This morning I felt quite uneasy about him, so made an early visit to be on time for the morning school session. When we entered the patient's room we saw plainly he could not survive many hours. Kneeling, we said prayers, which included an act of contrition, he repeated them, then said "good-bye." We felt this was the end of our services to the tiger desperado. We left him to the mercy of God.

The sick man's mother came to the Convent after the funeral and told me some minister had come to see her son shortly after our last visit. He said to the minister: "Do not disturb me. I want to keep in mind the prayers said by the Sisters." *Miserere mei Deus, secundum magnam misericordiam tuam.* He is in God's just, yet merciful, hands.

§ 13

December 16. Just received a startling message: "As soon as Sisters Theodosia and Ann Mary arrive in Trinidad, you and Sister Martha will go to Santa Fe."

Both of us are ready when the conveyance comes to the Convent door. So this pioneer will still be in advance of the railroad. The present railroad terminus is at El Moro, five miles from Trinidad. Protests from friends come in at every hour in effort to prevent our leaving. How useless! The conveyance will be at the door Tuesday morning. . . .

Tiptonville, New Mexico.

We have seen what there is to be seen in this place, so shall narrate what occurred after we stepped in the conveyance at Trinidad. The Rev. Pastor, Father Pinto, S.J., said: "The citizens headed by Mr. Gerrardi want to wire Mother Superior to have you remain in Trinidad. I think you better consider it, Sister."

"What about St. Joseph receiving the order to go into Egypt, which is always stressed in our retreats?"

"Well, Sister, if that is your attitude, word will go to the promoter to have him stop his efforts to detain you." The Rev. gentleman, having business in Las Vegas, accompanied us to that city. In my opinion, the Las Vegas business was a secondary consideration. "Billy's Gang" is quite active on the plains. The conveyance makes a good showing. The Rev. gentleman wants to be helpful in case of attack. I say nothing.

When we arrived at Aqua Dulce — Sweetwater — all at the place were prepared to fight the Gang and leader, if attacked. Possibly my silence was construed as being ignorant of what the gang is capable of doing. Whatever may have been the thoughts of those prepared to defend their lives, we were not molested.

We had reached Aqua Dulce at sunset and started on our journey early next morning. Before reaching Tiptonville, Father Pinto said to us, "At our next stopping place we will meet one of our Fathers who is considered one of the best mathematicians in the Order. He is also a linguist."[30]

When nearing the place I sized it up by counting three American habitations and a dozen low mud-thatched adobe houses, a church and parish residence. My curiosity was raised many degrees to see who the man might be who was consigned, with his knowledge of mathematics and languages, to a map-forgotten place. We stopped at the schoolroom door. A boy about eight years old heard the footsteps and at once opened the door. This is the scene my glance took in: 20 pupils from the ages of 7 to 13 years, in their seats, and the man of high attainments demonstrating that 2 plus 3 equals 5 plus 5 equals 10! The introduction took place, which gave me time to look at the teacher. "Do you like teaching, Father?" I asked.

"It is all the same, Sister. Whatever road is pointed out to us leads to Home." This is the spirit that animates every Jesuit I've met. We arrived at Las Vegas, dismissed the private conveyance and took the stage. We are to go soon after Mass and breakfast.

First change of mules. We stop here one-half hour. When the stage came to the Jesuit College for us, in Las Vegas, the faculty, minus the "Scalper" (the critic writer on the *Revista*[31]) came to the stage to see us off. Presently he too, came, gave me one disdainful, more correct, sarcastic look, which I read, "Why so much attention to such an insignificant being?" I admired his candor, and the look was a good subject on which to meditate.

Santa Fe, City of Holy Faith. We arrived on time. Whatever my assignment may be, "Here's a heart for every fate."

PART

II

Santa Fe

SANTA FE. The City of Holy Faith. How Sister Blandina loved
her new home with its surrounding mountains so similar to her
childhood Cicagna mountains in far-away Italy. Her heart found
its home in Santa Fe. She loved its ancient churches, its narrow
streets, still holy with the blood of Franciscan martyrs. She
listened intently to Archbishop Lamy when he told the Sisters of
his solitary journey to Durango, Mexico, in 1851, where he
verified his credentials as the newly appointed Bishop of Santa Fe
with the Bishop of Durango. She thrilled to the Archbishop's
account of his journey across the plains in 1867. Her own Sisters
of Charity and the Sisters of Loretto were with him then when
they were attacked by Indians. From his lips she heard of the
bravery of Sister Augustine Barron, Sister of Charity, who forgot
her own safety and went to the aid of a young man, the Bishop's
Major Domo, who was dying of cholera during the Indian attack.
During that same Indian attack, Archbishop Lamy told them, a
very young Loretto Sister, Sister Alphonsa Thompson, died and
was buried out there on the plains. Her grave has never been
found.

Sister Blandina loved the legend of the famed statue of Our
Lady, *La Conquistadora*, brought by de Vargas to Santa Fe, in
1692, when he retook the City of Holy Faith from the Indians
after the Rebellion of 1680. On De Vargas' journey northward to
Santa Fe, she was told, the diminutive statue of the Virgin grew
so heavy that even his strongest soldiers could not lift her. Riding
to the head of his band, the leader alighted from his horse, and

81

tried unsuccessfully to lift the statue. Then he made a vow. If he could wrest Santa Fe from the Indians he would build a chapel on that exact spot. He promised that each year a procession would march to the chapel from the church in Santa Fe where the statue of the Virgin was to be kept. When the vow was made, the statue could be lifted.

Sister Blandina watched the new Cathedral of St. Francis of Assisi, "so long a building," take on the harmonious lines of beauty. Begun in 1869, at Bishop Lamy's request, the Cathedral dated back to 1711–1714, and even before that time the Franciscan Custodian, Fray Alonso Benavides had built a church on this spot. It was destroyed in the Indian Rebellion of 1680.

Sister refreshed her soul in the deeply rooted Catholicity of Santa Fe while endless problems outwardly confronted her. She knew and understood Santa Fe's extreme need for Christ's workers there.

In Trinidad she had built a one story schoolhouse with no funds; in Santa Fe she would build a three story building from empty pockets. She begged funds for the hospital from the miners and railroad workers. She made caskets and buried the dead; wrote letters to the bereaved families. She distributed alms, visited Billy the Kid and other prisoners in the Santa Fe jail. In December, 1880, she saw with satisfaction the Sisters' Hospital lighted with gas for the first time. She established an excellent school for the orphans and gave them a mother's love.

Sister Blandina's submission to the will of God in grave misunderstandings, disappointments, and tragedies is a remarkable feature of her life. Failure never claimed her; discouragement never daunted the flashing, dark eyed, little figure. In spite of the flagrant spread of evil in the Territory, she carried on courageously, even gaily.

§ 1

Santa Fe, Jan., 1877.

Dear Sister Justina:

There is some history to this place, other than church history.

MUSEUM OF NEW MEXICO PHOTO

Parroquia (parish church) on site of present cathedral, Santa Fe

Old adobe church near Santa Fe

MUSEUM OF NEW MEXICO PHOTO

Archbishop J. B. Lamy

First: Santa Fe contains a military post, which is the stopping place of renowned generals of the United States, especially protecting the interest of the Southwest. Generals Pope, Carleton, Kearney, Hatch.

General Carleton sent a little papoose, which was found on a battlefield, to the Orphan Asylum. The Sisters named her Mary Carleton. Werè I to guess to what tribe she belongs I would say, "Navajo." She is a "Chato" (Flat Nose). Fort Marcy is north of the hospital. The Governor's palace faces the Santa Fe Plaza. It is a one story adobe, and has been the scene of much strife and contention. The last governor made himself obnoxious to the native population; many think he is a Mormon. His successor, Lew Wallace, is above reproach, a man of strong principles, and a student of humanity. Such characters are seldom left where they can accomplish most good. Whatever the cause, this fact is apparent.

Jan. 28, 1877.

Now, dear Sister Justina, what can I say of this nested (am I coining a word?) town! "Antique" to the first degree, is uppermost in my mind. There is a small brick dwelling northeast of the hospital, the rest are all made of adobe laid in mud. This includes the Archbishop's home, the Governor's Palace, San Miguel College,[1] Sisters of Loretto Academy,[2] and last and least as well, the buildings belonging to the Sisters of Charity.

Later our Most Rev. Archbishop J. B. Lamy[3] imported an architect and stonemason. The architect, Antoine Mouly, was an expert stonecarver as well. He became stone blind, and had to return to France, leaving his son, Projectus Mouly in charge of building the proposed Cathedral and a chapel for the Sisters of Loretto. The chapel was begun and well under way when persons in authority criticized his work. They would have him make changes which would spoil the architectural beauty of the buildings. A lover of art, he could not submit to work on an inferior plan; he resigned.

Disappointed in his artistic aspirations, and discouraged, he fell a prey to bad company. That is the last I have heard of the talented young architect.

To date, February 3, 1877, not having any special duty assigned me, I asked Sister Catherine[4] to recount anything of note which took place on the journey of our first Sisters from Cincinnati, Ohio, to Santa Fe, New Mexico. Sister's narrative follows:

The first band, viz.: Sister Vincent,[5] superior; Sisters Pauline,[6] Theodosia[7] and myself, left the Motherhouse, Mt. St. Vincent, August 21, 1865. All are still living, and often recall the many acts of contrition made during the journey. Rail and boat were the means of locomotion from Cincinnati to Omaha. In Omaha we were hospitably entertained by the Sisters of Mercy. The Creighton family did everything possible to lessen the hardships of traveling, which would begin at Omaha and last until Santa Fe would be reached.

In a stage built for four passengers, and in which six could be seated by crowding, eight had to ride. Two gentleman managed, with the aid of two small boxes, to sit between the passengers of front and rear seat of the stage by leaning back to back, hanging their legs outside the stage doors. When this position could no longer be endured, the other two gentlemen passengers relieved them. Those seated suffered greatly from overcrowding, and all endured great heat and thirst. All these tortures combined were in a great measure lost sight of in the constant fear of being attacked by the Indians. The jolting, thumping and bumping in stage-coach days was worse than rides in runaway freight trains.

For the luxury, twenty-five cents a mile was paid, with an allowance of forty pounds of baggage. We made a stop in Denver, going directly to Planter's Hotel.[8] The Rt. Rev. J. P. Machebeuf was soon informed of our arrival, and he sent his carriage to have us conveyed to the Convent of the Sisters of Loretto, where, through the kindness of the Sisters, we soon forgot our past fatigues, and made preparations to continue our route to our destination. The stage from Denver to Santa Fe had no occupants but the Sisters. This was one comfort, but the fear of Indians kept us in misery.

When we reached Fort Union, New Mexico, no one recognized the costume of the American Sisters of Charity, and as the Mormons were around recruiting, our travelers overheard the remark made about them, "An addition for the Mormons!"

Maxwell's ranch in New Mexico was reached in the evening of September 11, and we were only to stop long enough to change horses. But the relay had broken lariat and was roaming over the ranch miles away. The driver did not return from his hunt till morning.

Meanwhile we sat in the coach wondering if the driver had fallen into the hands of Indians, and momentarily expected to hear the war whoop for ourselves. What cannot fright imagine!

At daybreak we took a survey of the place. Our fears were only confirmed. There, in the open air, singly and in groups, lay a number of Indians sleeping! Early rising among a certain industrial class of natives was proverbial, and Mrs. Maxwell belonged to that class. Whilst we Sisters were in fear and suspense as to what would happen, Mrs. Maxwell made her appearance. She was inconsolable to find the Sisters had been in the coach during the night, more especially when she learned of their fright. The Maxwell family is noted for its hospitality. There, the American, the native, the Indian, are all made to feel at home. The feeling of "live and let live" permeates the very atmosphere of the Maxwell ranch, hence, the Indians as they were seen by our Sisters, were guests on the ranch.

We reached Santa Fe at nightfall, September 13, 1865,[9] and we were received with open arms by Mother Magdalen[10] and her pious community, the Sisters of Loretto.[11] The next day, September 14, feast of the Exaltation of the Holy Cross, the truly good Mother escorted the Sisters of Charity to the quarters that had been provided for them.

Imagine the surprise of persons coming from places where houses are built with every convenience and sanitary device, suddenly to find themselves introduced into several oblong walls of adobes, looking like piled brick ready to burn, to enter which, instead of stepping up, you step down onto a mud floor; rafters supporting roof made of trunks of trees, the roof itself of earth which they were told had to be carefully attended, else the rain would pour in; door openings covered with blankets; the whole giving you a prison feeling; a few chairs, handmade and painted red; a large quantity of wool which they were assured was clean and for their use; no stoves, square openings in corners where fires could be built — all those things were to constitute their future home. Where the bare necessities of life were to come from was an enigma to them. Strangers to the country, the customs, and the language, do you wonder that a lonesome feeling as of lingering death came over them? Can you doubt that it would have required the presence of an angel to convince them that the preparations made for them were princely? Yes, so they were, for the time and country. This had been the Bishop's Palace, which he was giving up, so that the Sisters might have easy access to the Cathedral!

In 1863 the Rev. Stephen Avel had left $3,000, and his dying request was to have the amount go towards establishing a hospital in Santa Fe. During the interim of Father Avel's death and the arrival of the Sisters of Charity, the Most Rev. J. B. Lamy had secured a large property near San Miguel College, with the intention of having the Sisters locate there. But on reconsideration, the Bishop judged it was not so desirable as a site near the Cathedral where the services of a priest, when needed, could be had at a few minutes' notice. Hence, he sold the first purchase and transferred his rights of the present location to the Sisters of Charity, to be used for the purpose of hospital and orphan asylum. The first $2,000 possessed by the Sisters was made over to Archbishop Lamy to pay for the house and land which had been his. The Bishop retained two rooms until such time as he could make provision for himself on the adjoining land. "The Bishop's Garden," it was called.

Mother Magdalen made it a practice for the first six months to reserve a portion of what her Sisters had for their table and sent it to the Sisters of Charity. The Bishop sent meat, flour, and wood, in consideration of which he, the students and servants had their meals served at St. Vincent's.[12]

For the first six months no money was seen. The first patient received was Mrs. Mary Herbert, the first orphan, Mary Carleton. This Mary Carleton was a Navajo Indian baby, found on the battlefield and brought to the Sisters by General Carleton himself. The General proved a friend to the Sisters in every possible way.

General Carleton, with General Sherman and Colonel Meline, assigned rations for eighteen orphan children at the Asylum, with privilege of purchasing provisions from the United States "Commissary." The better to understand what this meant to the Sisters, here is the price of edibles at the time: Butter, $1.25 per lb.; Flour, $15.00 to $18.00 per hundred lbs.; Eggs, seventy-five cents per dozen; Potatoes, $12.00 to $15.00 per bushel, or twenty-five cents per lb., scarce at that. Sugar and corn, almost incredible to believe, were known to be sold at forty cents per pound. Price of everything else in proportion.

There was a fund called the "California Fund," from which General Carleton could draw for those left destitute by his fight on the Navajo Indians. From this fund he gave our Sisters $1,000.

Col. Meline, speaking of the Sisters of Charity on his visit to Santa Fe, said: "The Sisters of Charity, four of them from Cincinnati, also have a hospital, orphan asylum, and free school, and are of the same good and devoted class of women so well known to the wounded soldiers of the Army of the Cumberland, and the sick strangers in all our large cities. Their hospital here, I am told, is not likely to be a sinecure. New Mexico is too healthy for its success. But the Sisters have their hands full with orphans, aged and infirm, and poor scholars. When we think of those heroic women, taking up their line of march like a soldier's forlorn hope, crossing desert, facing every danger, falling in the ranks, or dying at their posts, with no aim but for the sake of God and suffering humanity, I must confess that I, for one, became impatient at the exaggerated praise some of us received."

§ 2

Spring of 1877.

My dear Sister Justina:

The last entry made in the journal I'm keeping for you gave a brief description of the journey of the first band of our Sisters from Cincinnati to Santa Fe Territory, New Mexico. They traveled by rail, water and stage. The second band of our Sisters, traveling by caravan, had some stirring encounters as novel and dangerous as any experienced by Kit Carson, or Uncle Dick Wootton.

Both these men have been intelligent guides to avoid warring with the roving Indian tribes. Kit Carson was, for a time, General Fremont's "Power behind the throne" in scouting and guiding over trails, and places where foot of civilized man had never trod. He acted in the spirit of a Free Lance. Military discipline must have been galling to him. Carson saved the life of General Fremont on two occasions, and the General saved Kit Carson's life at least once. Is that not cementing friendship for life? Mr. Wootton (Uncle Dick) is an entirely different character from Mr. Carson. Mr. Carson is astute and daring; Mr. Wootton is kindhearted and depends much on "Luck," as he terms it. I am acquainted with all his children, and have often met Uncle Dick. His life at present is very quiet. His present occupation is keeping the tollgate near the dividing line between Colorado and New Mexico. He still has enough excitement to live on. "Wootton's Place," as it is called, is a refuge for many outlawed characters. Not that he wants it so, but it is the inevitable consequence of present conditions.

The second band of our Sisters left Mt. St. Vincent May 10, 1867. They were Sister Augustine Barron and her sister, Sister

Louise Barron.[13] At the time Sister Augustine was missioned to Santa Fe, she was assistant-Mother of the Community. Previous to this time, she had had charge of two of our largest establishments, so you can at once surmise the middle post of life had been passed. Sister Louise is two years younger.

In the fall of 1866, the beloved Bishop Lamy stopped at Mt. St. Vincent and pleaded for an addition to our Sisters already doing mission work in Santa Fe. He wanted to establish some industry by which the native girls might, in time, make a living for themselves. He strongly emphasized "Industry for the Native Girls." He was then on his way to France, where he hoped to find recruits from the seminaries and financial aid from friends. He returned in the spring of 1867 with a reinforcement to help him carry out plans approved by the Holy See for the betterment of the inhabitants of his vast diocese. Twenty-six souls accompanied him.

When, at some future day, the Church in New Mexico will find a historian, no greater names will be written than the heroes of this pioneer band: Rt. Rev. J. B. Lamy, Rev. D. M. Gasparri, S.J.; Rev. M. Bianchi, S.J., and Rev. M. Leone, S.J. The life of each of these pioneers was made up of self-oblation and heroism so sublime by the side of which the most notable characters in Tasso pale as meteors before the sun.

Rt. Rev. Bishop Lamy wrote from France to have the Sisters meet him in St. Louis. Three Loretto Sisters and our two Sisters proceeded in company with the Rt. Rev. Bishop Lamy and his twenty-six recruits to Leavenworth, Kansas. In Leavenworth, the Rt. Rev. Bishop manned a caravan of about one hundred covered wagons and started on his famous journey on the Santa Fe trail on the 14th of June. On the 18th, the caravan reached St. Mary's of the Potawatomis. The Jesuit Fathers and students came several miles to meet the travelers. Sunday was spent at St. Mary's, from which the caravan left June 24th.

On the 29th, the Feast of St. Peter and St. Paul, the caravan camped a few miles from Junction City. At noon four Indians

visited the camp. This did not portend any good. After a consultation with some of the experienced drivers, the Bishop gave
orders to return to Leavenworth at which place all the mules
attached to the caravan were sold and replaced by oxen, as having more endurance.

From Leavenworth the Bishop ordered a detour from the
Santa Fe Trail. The Kiowas — the most rapacious Indian tribe
of the plains — had sent scouts to visit our travelers when camping near Junction City. The Bishop who understood Indian tactics
and Indian warfare, changed the animals and the route, in hopes
that the Kiowas would be thrown off the scent. The caravan
continued its slow travel until the latter part of July. The eagle
eye of the Bishop was constantly on the watch for any sign
which might indicate the near approach of Indians. The
Comanches and Apaches had also free scope on the plains, but
the Kiowas were feared the most. When victorious in their attack
on white men, they were most ferocious. The men were first
scalped, then killed, the children were also killed; the women
were made prisoners — a fate far worse than death.

On the 30th day of July, without any apparent reason, the
Bishop ordered a corral to be made. Every wagon in the caravan
was arranged to form a circle; the oxen were driven inside the
circle. The travelers and teamsters ran inside the circle none
too soon, for the Kiowas' death whoop preceded the sling
of hundreds of arrows which fell harmlessly for some time.
This was kept up until sunset, when the Indians retired. The
order from inside the circle was: "Be on the alert, hands on guns,
no fires to be lighted."

The day's travel had been arduous for want of water. All were
suffering from thirst, and, though the water of a river could be
seen distinctly not more than a few rods from their improvised
corral, to attempt to satisfy their thirst, or to water the oxen,
would be certain destruction to all. The Sisters prayed their
beads and the men kept a vigilant watch, not to be surprised by
a night attack from the fierce Kiowas. At daybreak it was dis-

covered that cholera had broken out in the caravan! Soon after the Indians renewed their attack! Word was circulated that one of the Sisters of Loretto had the cholera![14] Whether it was cholera or fright the victim gave up her soul to God. Meanwhile, the Indians flung their arrows in quick succession. The travelers were well protected by the circle of wagons, from which vantage ground their guns carried death to some of the attacking Indians.

Some kind-hearted messenger came to Sister Augustine and said: "A young man under a wagon on the opposite side of the circle has the cholera and is pitifully calling for his mother." The words were scarcely uttered when Sister Augustine said, "I'll go at once to render what help I can."

Sister Augustine crawled under from one wagon to the next, while arrows were thickly showering above her, and some arrows fell near her, but lost their force by striking either wagon hub or cogs. When speaking of this to me, she said, "I could only compare the flying of arrows around me to a disturbed beehive." Sister Augustine reached the dying young man and tried to soothe his last moments as his mother would have done. So he and the dear Sister of Loretto were buried, strangers in every way. Months afterwards, all efforts to find their resting place were unavailable.

Meanwhile, the Indians continued the aggressive fight. The weather was intensely warm, all needed water. The Indians had the advantage. The cholera was doing its work, but no more victims succumbed to death.

It is said that one of the leaders of the party called a few of the men with well balanced minds and gave them his orders: "If the Indians continue the attack for twenty-four hours we are doomed. Make no mistakes in the directions I now give you, but let no man act until I give the order. When I see death is inevitable for us I will give the signal. Then you, Mr. — shoot Sister Louise, you, Mr. — shoot the elder of the Loretto Sisters, and you, Mr. — shoot the younger Sister of Loretto. I will shoot Sister Augustine."

Some people, many hundred miles away, asserted the man could not morally give such an order. This is true, but knowing the treatment of women prisoners in the Kiowa tribe, I would have preferred to have been shot rather than to have been made a prisoner.

The sun was declining. The Kiowas disappeared. The leader of the party asked: "Are any of you men willing to practice strategy by wading the stream and land some boxes of provisions and a barrel of liquor on the other side of the stream? Apparently, it is taking your life in your own hands, although I see no danger. My only regret is to use such means to save ourselves." The freight was safely landed on the other side of the stream. As the sun disappeared, the freighters discontinued their work.

The Indians fell into the trap. They suddenly appeared from nowhere and rushed for the barrel of whiskey. They soon chopped off the top of the barrel with a tomahawk, and each, with scooped hands eagerly drank the liquor.

Word was quietly passed to "Start fires an hour later." By this time the Indians had their fill and were dropping off in a dead sleep. Our travelers, like the Arabs, "Stole silently away." The caravan was safe and on its way to Santa Fe. The men and large boys of Santa Fe and surrounding villages formed a cavalcade and met their beloved Bishop about fifteen miles from Santa Fe and escorted him to his adobe cathedral. Meanwhile the Sisters, priests and seminarians arrived in Santa Fe and all proceeded to the cathedral, the *Te Deum* was sung, with what heartfelt gratitude you may imagine. This was the 15th of August. Since our Sisters left Mt. St. Vincent on May 10th, it is evident it took them three months and five days to reach their destination. The details of the journey on the plains have been omitted. The attack of the Kiowas on the caravan was interpreted in the states as that all males were killed and all females made prisoners. You remember the anguish the news caused our Sisters East, especially Mother Regina.

§ 3

March, 1877.

My dear Sister Justina:

I have been telling you about our Sisters' trials on their journey from Cincinnati to this place. Now I shall write you about our trials here. This is surely a pioneer mission. There is so much to be done and so little with which to do it! The change from school work to miscellaneous, undefined labor needed here, is confusing to me.

Sister Augustine remarked: "You are not interested in the work of this place as you were in Trinidad, are you?"

Sister was right. "I don't know just where to begin or what to do," I answered.

"Well, Sister, I'll tell you. Look around and put your hand to anything you see ought to be done. There is the schoolroom. See how you can improve it."

I went to the schoolroom. There were no blackboards, charts, maps, desks, books — nothing but the teacher and the orphans. I said there were no books, but there were two textbooks, one for the teacher, the other for the pupils! The teacher was doing her best, but what could her best be, under such conditions?

I made my report. "Sister Augustine, we need school supplies. May I order them?"

"My dear Sister, we have no money to pay for them; we have barely enough to purchase what is absolutely necessary for existence."

"Why not ask the School Board to help? If they will give us a teacher's salary we can use it to pay for the supplies," I answered.

"I have applied to them, but as the pupils are residents, the Board cannot allow the salary. It is no use trying," was Sister's discouraging remark.

"If at first you don't succeed,

Try, try again," I quoted. "May I try again?"

"Certainly, Sister, and may our dear Lord give you success!"

Soon after this conversation, the Chairman of the School Board came to see us.

"Sister Blandina, I heard of your splendid school work in Trinidad. What are you going to do here?"

"Teach!" I answered promptly.

"Good! Where?"

"In one of the adobe buildings on our grounds. It occurs to me that we are entitled to a teacher's salary, are we not?"

"If you receive outside pupils, yes," he answered.

"Yes, we shall admit pupils that fit into the grades."

"Then my little daughter will be the first to apply. I shall call a meeting of the School Board and secure your salary."

The check for a teacher's salary was received. No bird ever flew lighter on its wings than I on my feet to tell Sister Augustine and ask if I might order the school supplies, which I did without loss of time.

"You may wait on the orphans in the refectory," said Sister to me one day.

I walked into the refectory. Imagine my surprise at what I saw. Two tables, fifteen feet long, no chairs, knives or forks. Each girl had a spoon, a broken ironstone china cup and plate to match, while some had old pie plates. Each girl is served a piece of bread, and water to drink for dinner, weak coffee for breakfast, and weak tea for supper. The one redeeming feature is that the bread is good home-baked bread. And the children thrive on this diet!

You must remember this is a pioneer mission, poorest of the poor, and working among the poor. I realize that the Sisters do the best they can, that their whole heart is in their work, and that they suffer the privations for the love of God, but I feel we must make strenuous efforts to improve conditions. Saint Theresa says something to the effect that you must make every effort to succeed — then leave the rest to God. I'm going to make the effort, and I'm sure God will do the rest.

A lady, Mrs. Adolph Staab, and her children are here. I have been asked to entertain them after school hours. I am perfectly at home with the children, but I have no attraction for entertaining wealthy ladies. However, since it is given me as a duty, I'll do it. Mrs. Staab really needs attention. She is in a depressed condition, and I must cheer her up.

Albricias! That is what the natives say when they have good news. And that is what I am saying now. Out of a part of the teacher's salary, I managed to purchase tablecloths, knives and forks, cups and saucers, napkins, and some other things. How fine the table looks now! But this is not all. When I was in Trinidad, I had the opportunity to do a favor for a Mr. Thompson. I procured him a wagon to take him to Santa Fe. When he heard I was here, he came to offer his service in his line of business. He has been successful and now has a shop of his own. Maybe I didn't hasten to tell him all the school needed in his line of work: floors to be repaired, pulleys and ropes for windows, blackboards, etc.

"Yes, I'll be glad to supply these things, and anything else you need. I am happy to do so," said the good, honest Mr. Thompson.

"Bread cast on the water coming back on the high waves," thought I.

Just received your letter with the big N. B. "Read the last part of the letter first." It was Mother Josephine's message to you. "Dear Sister Justina, you are missioned to Trinidad to take Sister Blandina's place."

Well, that is a surprise! The Sisters here are as happy as if it were their own sister coming West.

Second week of April, 1877. Mrs. Staab's husband asked me to accompany his wife and children to Europe! I believe he thinks money can do anything, and he expects me to accept the offer. When he was convinced that I could not go to Europe, he said he would be satisfied if I would accompany them to the city of New York. But I am satisfied to remain in Santa Fe.

Fourth week in May, 1877. Sister Augustine tells me that the

Most Rev. Archbishop Lamy wishes me to go with the Staab family to the terminus of the railroad, which is five miles west of Trinidad, Colorado. Mrs. Staab, her two children, Sister Augustine and myself, will occupy one carriage; Mr. Staab and two gentlemen who are going to Chicago will ride in another. Everybody is concerned about our going. Mr. Staab spoke to Sister and myself about the danger of travel (at the present time) on the Santa Fe Trail, owing to Billy the Kid's gang. He told us that the gang is attacking every mail coach and private conveyance.

"We will have many freight wagons well manned, but if you fear to travel, we shall defer the trip." Sister Augustine looked to me to give an answer.

If ever you get this journal, you will see how very little fear I have of Billy's gang. Even if "Billy" has mustered new pals, I'm marked for protection as well as anyone wearing my garb. So I answered Sister's look by saying to, Mr. Staab, "Where could the danger lurk, being in the company of so many freight drivers?" Sister acquiesced; "so it is arranged we will leave Santa Fe the first or second of June. We'll stop off in Trinidad; and, of course, I'll see you."

Las Vegas at the Exchange Hotel.

Rev. Salvatore Personé, S.J., President of Las Vegas College, and two others of the faculty have called to see us. We are to rest several hours before resuming our journey.

I had a very unpleasant experience at this hotel. It was a proposal to me to leave the convent and go out to enjoy some of the pleasures of the world. Do you wonder at my indignation at the insulting proposal? What a wrong idea some people have of the religious life!

Trinidad. — We arrived here June 6, 1877. The greater part of the day was given to making things comfortable for Mrs. Staab and children to travel to New York City. Nothing took place on the plains from Santa Fe to Trinidad to alarm us. But it stood to reason, no gang would attempt to attack a train of freight wagons, knowing that freight drivers are experts at shooting.

June 9. — Dr. Symington wants to know if we would be afraid to return in a hack with himself and Mr. Staab. He says the team is the best in the territory. "But why do you ask if we are afraid?" I questioned.

"The Kid is attacking the coaches or anything of profit that comes in his way," he answered. The "Kid" means Billy the Kid and gang. "I'll consult Sister Augustine and will return to give you an answer." When I told Sister what the Doctor said, she asked me how I felt about venturing. "I have no more fear than if the gang did not exist." "Well, then, in the name of God, we'll go."

It was an understood thing that this return trip was to break the record in time, traveling from Trinidad to Santa Fe. The first day we traveled to Sweetwater, reaching it at about 4 P.M. This is a regular stage station. It did not take us long to see that extraordinary preparations were being made. The stage driver and his passengers were loading or cleaning revolvers and rifles. Ranch men who live in the vicinity showed themselves ready for any emergency. We were told that "Billy's gang was dodging around, and we expect they will attack us tonight." I proposed to Sister that we pray our beads out on the open plain walking up and down some distance from the house. Sister made no objection, but the Doctor did. However, we said our beads and loitered around for some time. When retiring time drew near, both Doctor and Mr. Staab came to say they would remain at our door armed, "So do not be alarmed if you hear firing; we shall protect you."

"Very kind of you, gentlemen, but if you take my advice you will secure a good night's rest and be ready for an early start." The Doctor looked disgusted at my want of perception. All travelers on the plains are early risers, so were we. Breakfast over, the Doctor wanted to know if it would be wise to continue. As wise as to remain, we decided. We started. Our span did credit to its trainer, who was driving. About an hour or so after luncheon, the jockey sent his first message of alarm into the carriage.

"Mas-sah," his voice trembled with suppressed fear, "there am som-un skimming over the plains, coming dis way."

Instantly each man took out his revolver. Mr. Staab told the darkey to keep him informed. A few seconds afterward, Mr. Staab asked, "How now, John?" With undisguised fear, the driver answered, "Coming fas', mas-sah, right fo' us." By this time both gentlemen were feverishly excited. I looked at the men and could not but admire the resolute expression which meant "To conquer or die!" I broke the spell by saying:

"If the comer is a scout from the gang, our chance is in remaining passive. I would suggest putting revolvers out of sight." They looked at me as if to say that a woman is incapable of realizing extreme danger. The darkey in his fright spoke again:

"He am very near."

"Please put your revolvers away," I said in a voice which was neither begging nor aggressive, but was the outward expression of my conviction that we had nothing to fear. Spontaneously the weapons went under cover. The light patter of hoofs could be heard as they drew near the carriage opening. As the rider came from the rear of the vehicle, he first caught sight of the two gentlemen in the front seat, which gave me a chance to look at him before he saw us. I shifted my big bonnet so that when he did look, he could see the Sisters. Our eyes met; he raised his large-brimmed hat with a wave and a bow, looked his recognition, fairly flew a distance of about three rods, and then stopped to give us some of his wonderful antics on broncho maneuvers. The rider was the famous "Billy, the Kid!"

As the carriage distanced itself from the cause of the fright, those two riding opposite us looked their question. I wondered if they could not connect my request of persisting the evening previous in saying our beads on the plains where all knew the members of the gang could see us with field glasses; if the connection could not be made, I had no intention of saying two and two are four, hence I kept silent.

Sister Augustine treated me like a mother who is very fond and proud of her child. Naturally, she cannot understand why I had no fears of "Billy's Gang" — nor does she know who the cowboy is who frightened our party, for she has not asked and she does not as yet know of my meeting "Billy, the Kid" in Trinidad and his promise to protect the Sisters from any attacks of his "gang."

June 12, 1877. Arrived in Santa Fe. The record is broken. We made the fastest trip ever known from Trinidad to Santa Fe.

§ 4

June 12, 1877.

We have on this mission the dearest person you can imagine, Hermana Dolores Chavez de Guiterrez.[15] Some day I will get her whole history and enter it in this journal. Meanwhile, I'm studying her exceptional character. She is a blue blood Spaniard. There are also two native Sisters here, both earnest and interested in community life.

We take our turn in preparing the Sunday dinner for the Sisters. To-day it was my turn, and I gave a series of surprises, though unconscious that they were to be surprises otherwise than intended. I rummaged in the storeroom and brought to light a nice set of dishes which I washed and placed on the Sisters' table. I also discovered table linen, silver knives and forks, and other articles. "I'll make the table look nice, though the food may not harmonize," I said to myself.

I went over the grounds to the place called a hot-house — some wooden frames covered with glazed muslin, and there, to my surprise, I found strawberries! I picked them more quickly than the miners out here dig for gold. But the surprise was on me. When High Mass was over, Sisters Louise and Catherine came to see if they could be of assistance to me. When they saw the table, they turned their amused eyes on me, but when Sister Louise saw the strawberries she laughed aloud and said, "You certainly were brave to pick the strawberries!" Sister Catherine added: "Those dishes are used only when His Grace has company." Sister Louise good-naturedly said, "My blessing on you, Sister Blandina, I'm here much longer than you are, yet I did not know those things were in the house."

But the real surprise came when Sister Augustine saw the strawberries. I realized then I had done something out of the way. Sister asked: "Where did you get the strawberries?"

"In the hot-house," I replied.

"We do not use strawberries for ourselves."

"No?" I questioned.

"No, Sister. The gardener sells them for a dollar a quart; the money helps to support the house." There were several quarts of strawberries on the table! Sister Louise saw I was the one most surprised and managed to turn the tables by asking for talk at dinner.

I wanted my dinner to be a complete surprise, which it was, as far as I am concerned. This turning aside from the usual routine brought facts to my notice which, in some measure, palliate, if not entirely remove impressions already received here. Sister Catherine thinks I am wonderfully courageous to have done what I did. I looked enquiringly at her for an explanation. She looked at me in her very charming way and said: "Sister, not even among ourselves do we speak of the hardships of this mission, but somehow I do not mind telling them to you. If you will be my companion to visit a poor man, whom I think will not survive many days, I shall tell you some of the most frequent hardships we have to endure."

"Do, Sister, it will prepare me for any or all difficulties. Have you kept a record of the first years?"

"Much of the record is not on paper. It is for the All-Seeing Eye of God alone, but the principal events I will give you this afternoon. From what I've heard of you, I know anything I may tell you will not discourage you."

"I shall be glad to hear everything from the first day of your opening in Santa Fe," I assured her.

We started on the road to visit the sick man, but two natives who were going for the same purpose met us, hence I did not get information, because they also returned with us.

June 21, 1877. This day will always remain a memorable one for me. Sister Augustine came to my schoolroom, and in her quiet, formal manner said: "Sister, I wish you to prepare a musical programme for the closing of school."

All our schools here close the latter part of August to give the older boys time to help out at the harvest in September and October.

I replied: "We have no musical instruments unless I use combs."

"Manage as you wish," she replied.

I looked at the pupils who had heard what Sister said. Their eyes fairly danced with pleasure. One of them, Lizzie Krummick, said: "Sister, we have a piano at home. It is a piano and organ in one; no one touches it since papa died. I know mamma will be glad to let you have it."

"After school you and I will visit your mother," I told Lizzie. We went, and so eager was I to make sure the instrument would answer the purpose that while Mrs. Krummick was kissing and hugging Lizzie and saying how pleased she was to see teacher and daughter, I was examining the piano-organ. "Mamma, we are going to have a musical programme, but Sister has no piano."

"If mine will be of service to you, I will have it at the Convent in an hour," said Mrs. Krummick, without waiting to be asked. I tested it, and though it was wretchedly out of tune, I was delighted to get it. How do you think it was brought to us? On six men's shoulders, distance three quarters of a mile!

I gave Lizzie Krummick and Edith McCleary their first music lesson. On these two will depend the accompaniments of the musical programme!

June 29. My old friend, Mr. George Thompson came to say he would make a drop curtain and build a stage. I am testing the voices; one there is that sounds like a frog in a pond, but is brimful of harmony. Her voice must be placed.

I have always maintained that the children of the poor, given an equal chance with the children of the wealthy, will outdo the latter. My theory is now being put to the test. Our orphan girls here are called *Niñas de Caridad* (Charity girls). There are three classes of society here — Blue Bloods, natives and *mistos*. This is as far as I have been able to study class conditions. Those who consider themselves real Spaniards are tenacious of their dignity. None but the rich can send either sons or daughters to accredited academies or colleges outside of the Territory. We have a college for the boys taught by the Brothers, and an academy, Our Lady of Light, for girls, taught by the Sisters of Loretto. The girls of this academy consider themselves the upper ten. As far as money goes, they are, hence the feeling between the Academy pupils and our Charity children. When they attend church the feeling of superiority or inferiority is left outside the church door. This, you know, is about the same as exists in Europe.

July. — The programme for the closing of the school year is written on paper. How I will succeed in carrying it out will depend on the talent I may discover in our protégées. This will be an enlarged study in character-building.

The Vice-President of San Miguel College has come over several times to see what new educational methods we are introducing.

I am told he is an authority on college work. There is nothing for him to learn here, except possibly the growth of character-formation in girls who have felt they possess nothing characteristically their own except the opprobrious name of "Charity Girls." This condition is the natural outcome of social caste.

Because of the enormous initial expense of protecting the students over the plains, which are infested by hostile Indians who spare no one, and seemingly fear nothing except superior numbers and ammunition, students anxious for higher education have to remain in the Territory to complete their studies.

Unfortunate Indians! Yet are there not leading causes for this accumulated barbarity? Carlyle says:

"A lie returns to its starting point though it takes a century to reach it."

The inference is clear. Retribution is one of Nature's laws. What will be the moral standing three generations hence of those educated with no reference to God! Oh! for the singleness of Faith of times past, when the religious body of the civilized looked to things Eternal, and temporal progress was measured by the Everlasting. . . .

I have come back to my musical programme. Here it is:

Programme

Art Gallery .... Tableau
Address of Welcome .... The School
Vienna March .... Piano Duet
Lilliputian Dance .... Sixteen minims
Ten Minutes' Intermission
Girls of Seventeenth Century ....
.... A Dramatic Burlesque (Original)
O Give Me a Home by the Sea .... Vocal Quartet
O Quam Dilecta .... Chorus

July 31, 1877.

"Ignorance is bliss."

To-day a maid who was brought here by a well-to-do family came to see me. She has promised to be the wife of a sergeant at the military post of Santa Fe. She told me also that according to military rule, he may not marry. It took her fully half an hour to say this. Not to waste more time nor hurt her feelings, I invited her to come to the hall where our orphan girls were practicing. When we reached the hall two of the pupils were doing the Vienna March — piano duo — and counting the time aloud.

The wife-to-be of the striped sergeant must have visioned her husband with the epaulets of a general and in thought kept step with him. When the girls came to *finis*, the maid's future greatness could not be repressed. She turned to me and said (imitating fashion): "I've often heard 'One and Two,' but never played so well as this!" Even some of our violets who have been very little, caught the humor of the situation as could be seen by the twinkle of their eyes.

These girls of ours, who have never had an opportunity to know what they could do if the chance presented itself, are surely utilizing every instant of prerehearsal, rehearsal, and post-rehearsal time. They do everything with such enthusiasm that it acts as a stimulus upon me and makes me anxious to study each girl and give to the utmost of myself to evolve the best in her.

The very atmosphere here is impregnated with the spirit of the first missionaries, the Franciscans. Such is not the case in several other parishes, where proper administration was lacking, and morals became loose.

Here is a scene of weekly occurrence. Saturday morning come into Santa Fe the superannuated, the blind, and the lame, who are incapacitated for work. They make their rounds of visits usually in groups of two or three. Each carries a bag or basket into which charitable persons may put whatever they wish. At noon time they all have found their way to our *placita*. They arrange themselves as comfortably as they can in a sitting position where the sun shines, and await the coming of Sister Catherine, who moves among them with an air of benevolence truly charming.

Whatever the convent has been able to put aside for them during the week Sister distributes. Then takes place what in my estimation is the essence of unselfishness. Each recipient looks into his basket or bag. Those who can see do this act for the blind. Then they equalize the edibles. They who have more than càn be consumed for the week give to those who have less, the quality is also changed, giving to those who prefer one thing more than another.

Is not this a beautiful miniature picture of the first Christians?

Our closing exercises will take place August 29. The invitations are limited on account of the smallness of the hall. During the intermission — ten minutes — a cool drink will be served the audience by white aproned gentlemen.

Sept. 1.

The "Charity Girls" had their inning. The closing exercises were a revelation to all present. The first number "Art Gallery" represented a series of masterpieces in painting, the most prominent being Dolce's *Madonna*. The audience was busy studying the paintings in order to name the artists. Meanwhile Bengal Lights were flashed over the gallery to enhance the beauty of the scene. In the audience were several connoisseurs. The study was interrupted by a widow exclaiming in an ecstatic voice, *"Es mi hija! Es mi hija!"* (That is my daughter! That is my daughter!) pointing to the most attractive painting on the stage. Then the talk and laughter began, while the actors remained statuesque. When the curtain dropped the assembly as one became magpies. Every number on the program was greeted with genuine enthusiasm. My theory is fully vindicated. The children of toil given the same opportunity as children of luxury, will excel.

What do you think is strongly agitated? The building of an Industrial School.

§ 5

Jan. 16, 1878.

One year ago I arrived in Santa Fe with the feelings of a shrunken resurrection plant, and a sincere desire to be immersed or remain dry. But lo! I've been plunged into a whirlpool of work.

The Legislature meets in Santa Fe biennially. Members of the present session are arriving from all parts of the Territory. Major Sena made a speech at our closing exercises which gave me thought for a territorial hospital appropriation. The inhabitants here do not seem to have the same diseases as we have in the States. The majority take a daily sun bath — though I do not vouch they take a water bath as frequently. The hospital would be a vacated building, did we depend on native patients. Those who are admitted are men who come from the States seeking health or prospecting for gold; some are under the impulse of wanderlust, and others simply to get away from everybody. These are the ones who are likely to succumb to the climate.

A bill introduced to protect the interests of our native population passed over the Governor's veto. He has the unsavory reputation of being a Mormon, though I believe the odium comes from the fact that he was Governor of Utah before his appointment to the gubernatorial chair here.

A bill has been drafted, the gist of which is to allow the St. Vincent Hospital $100.00 monthly. This will help support the penniless who come for admission.

Jan. 18.

The Territorial Appropriation Bill for the relief of the Hospital passed. *Deo Gratias!*

Our orphans gave a special entertainment for the House and Senate. All members attended. Mr. Jaramillo, a prominent Senator, found out that the piano used was a borrowed one. After the "Little Show" he, in the name of a number of friends, placed money enough in my hands to order a new piano. The order goes in the next mail.

April, 1878.

The question of building is assuming large proportions. I smile, knowing the financial condition of the convent treasury. . . .

Sister Augustine called me to her office and very suavely broached the subject of building. In part she said, "Most Rev. Archbishop Lamy thinks one great need in the Territory is a Trade School for girls. Now, Sister, will you undertake to build it?"

"How much money have we with which to begin building?"

"Nothing, Sister. Do as you did in Trinidad. I was told you had not a cent when you started to build your adobe schoolhouse, and you finished it without debts."

"Ah! Sister, that was only an insignificant matter compared to what a Trade School should be."

"Well, Sister, keep the size of the building within the boundary of your judgment."

"And the money within the same boundary?"

She smiled and continued, "Use your originality as you did elsewhere, and with God's blessing you will get through."

I immediately thought of the young artist, Mr. Projectus Mouly, son of Antoine, whose feelings made him shrink from meeting his friends.

Mr. Mouly has come to the Convent. I saw at once he was strangely touched that I should send for him. I told him my plans for building an Industrial School. The plans are out of all proportions to any building here, and far away from the imagination of the present population of Santa Fe. Keep in mind the fact that the inhabitants of the territory are still on terms of enmity with the Apaches and Navajos, and any railroad is yet three hundred and some miles from here.

Was it the extreme pressure of mental distress being experienced by this young genius, or his determination to get away from what he believes would be his ultimate downfall, or my enthusiasm in plunging into a great undertaking requiring large sums of money and not a cent on hand, that made him say: "I'm with you, Sister, when do you wish to begin?"

"As soon as I consult with His Grace and the Rector of the Cathedral."

I must confess, I have a strong repugnance to building; not on account of the hardships the work will entail, but because some things are not clear to me. At an interview with His Grace, he said: "One great need of the territory is a Trade School. Go at it with my full blessing." Here is the interview with the Rector of the Cathedral, Rev. Augustine Truchard. He thinks the object of the training school is most laudable and greatly needed.

"How much money have you to begin with, Sister?"

"Not a cent, Father."

"And you want to build a three-story house in a country where there is not a planingmill, not a brickyard, nor a quarry of your own, nor limekilns, and, worst of all, not a cent on hand! Yet you want to begin to dig the foundation Monday morning. Do you know what some of us will say of you?"

"I can surmise, but if you will do what I ask of you I'm not afraid to begin work Monday morning."

"Let me hear, Sister, what you wish me to do."

"Simply to announce at the next Sunday Masses that the Sisters of Charity wish to build a house where girls in need can be trained in industries by which they can make a livelihood. Please say that our present wish is that a number of peons be paid by those disposed to do so, and sent to our front grounds to work on Monday and continue daily until the foundations are laid, each man to bring pick and shovel."

"Well, Sister, I will make the announcement, but I do not believe the men will come."

Monday, June 3, 1878.

Seven o'clock. Twelve men with picks and shovels came to work. I registered the names and became timekeeper.

June 17, 1878.

Two weeks ago we started work on the foundations for an Industrial School. Part of the land excavated makes a natural foundation, so we are ready for masonry work.

I had another interview with the Rector of the Cathedral. When he saw me he said: "Now, Sister, what do you want?" The answer was, "Wagons, mules, drivers."

"And how do you propose getting them?"

"If you please, in the same way we got men, picks, and shovels."

"Well, Sister, I shall announce your second plea at all the Masses to-morrow."

Meanwhile, a quarry had been opened and the men who were not needed to work on foundations were quarrying stone. After the second announcement in the church so many men and wagons were sent to us that they were in one another's way. A Mr. Antonio Ortiz y Salazar,[16] who has taken an active interest in our plan of building without money, said to me:

"Sister, when you dismiss these men and wagons, I shall send you a regular team on one condition that when the mules need shoeing and the wagon needs repairs you send them to Mr. Paul's blacksmith shop and charge to me."

"Thank you, Sir!" I said gratefully. You will note, Sister Justina, that by this arrangement we will have a steady team to depend on.

Dr. Longwell said to me this morning, "Sister, there is an American who has a splendid pair of horses which he will let you have on ninety days' time."

"And the price?"

"One hundred and fifty dollars."

"Please tell the American that I shall take the span on his own terms."

Some time before this I had seen a jolt ranch wagon warping in the sun and ascertained that the owners had no further use for it. As the family who owned the wagon was poor, I asked them to let me have it for some time, which they cheerfully did. You know, Sister Justina, that there are here no planingmills, no brickyards, nor regular limekilns.

We have given a contract to a native who will employ his own men to cut the trees and handsaw the lumber to the dimensions required. The nearest place trees are available for lumber is twenty-three miles from Santa Fe.

We have started our own brickyard. 250,000 bricks will be burnt at the first firing. We have eight gentlemen pledged to send workingmen to wait on the bricklayers.

The intersecting interior walls are to be of adobe laid in mortar. This will make the school cool in summer, and warm in winter. The work is to settle for months before the bricks and adobe walls are interlocked.

We have neither gas nor water-works here, but we are going to install pipes for both commodities in case we ever "wake up." This place is not a "Sleepy Hollow" only "Sunshine Asleep."

July 26, 1878.

The bricks are all piled ready to use.

I sold the span of horses and the wagon for $200, paid the owner of the horses $150, and gave $40 to the poor family who had no use for the wagon, and thereby gained $10. This will help pay for lime.

We have made no financial appeal to the people of Santa Fe, yet they have shown themselves most liberal. Seldom do I go to the plaza to order supplies, but I return with much more money than I started out with. God provides when one does his best.

August 14.

We detected white bulging spots in the bricks. Mr. Mouly sprinkled them. Vapor smoke arose, which means there is limestone in the clay and the bricks are useless! A sample of the clay had been sent to France and pronounced good brick clay.

Poor Mr. Mouly! He sat on a stone, placed his face in the palms of his hands, and remained immovable for a long time. I broke the silence.

"Mr. Mouly, what is required to make that clay available?" I asked him.

"A crushing cylinder, Sister, but I put every cent I had into the brickyard."

"What do you think the cylinder will cost?"

"Six hundred dollars, and I would have to go to Denver to buy it."

"Very well, Mr. Mouly, when do you want to start for Denver?"

"I have a mule, but no credit there."

"The credit will arrive in Denver sooner than you will on mule back. A check will be sent you by mail, so go when you are ready."

"May I suggest that I remain until after the open air exercises, for which you are preparing the orphan girls, are over?"

"I am more than pleased at your suggestion, because I know I could not carry out the drafted programme without your help."

About two months ago I was measuring lumber which had been hauled in when I heard someone say, "Ma, I wager that is the Sister we want to see."

I turned to face a tall woman, who introduced herself.

"I am Mrs. Dana, the General Quartermaster's wife. This is my daughter, Mary."

"You are speaking to Sister Blandina," I said.

"Mary thought so. My daughter would like to read *Promessi Sposi* with you and review some of her music."

"My work is such that I cannot assure you a lesson without interruption. If you are willing to come with that understanding, I accept you as a pupil."

Mary came. Miss Dana is much interested in our orphan girls. She has every lady at the military post anxious to assist us in any way she can. For quite a while I was annoyed at her calling our girls "brats," so I asked her what meaning she attached to the word "brat." She laughed. "By 'brat,' I mean every girl in your school is a love of mine."

Miss Dana is a unique character. She comes frequently to assist us. When she leaves she goes straight to the Cathedral — the side chapel opens into our placita (yard) and there remains half an hour in His presence. The Danas are not Catholics.

A messenger from the General Quartermaster says that he will send an orderly and a squad of soldiers to put up awnings for the open air exercises. The rainy season begins about the middle of August.

If the programme we have on paper can be carried out in reality, no one in the audience will regret the dollar entrance fee. I was coerced in charging for entrance.

The stage is topped by two large acacia trees. The stage proper is divided into three stages, each with its curtain. Carolina's voice has been placed. One year's training has accomplished much. Her voice is a rich mezzo-soprano, and can easily support twenty-five voices without effort.

Carolina's mother had been a traveling opera singer and harpist. Years ago she left this child with the Sisters and forgot to call for her.

Sept., 1878

The Open Air Exercises surpassed all I had hoped. I am going to explain two scenes.

First stage. The curtain rose on a tableau of our Blessed Mother, angels clustered about her, ascending into heaven. Slowly she disappeared, the angels accompanying her. The illusion was perfect. No one suspected a second stage.

The second curtain rose. Carolina, a captive knight, dressed in the full armor of knighthood, sang, "The Captive Knight." Above the dungeon scattered in two acacia trees were many brilliantly dressed fairies, with bows and arrows, awaiting to defend the Knight, in case of treachery. A third curtain rose, showing a garden. The fairies had carried the Captive Knight to the fountain, which was throwing intermittent sprays of sparkling water, and the Knight was made to drink. This turned him into the leading fairy just as the court officers came to recapture him. During all this scene, dreamy music was heard from the distance. The would-be captors fell asleep. The fairies disappeared. The perspective from the first stage to the end of the garden was enchanting. The play was part of an original one, written to meet the capacity of the orphans.

As nothing of this kind had ever been produced here, the circulating gossip had it that the trainer of the orphan children must have been an actress!

Without the aid of Mr. Mouly and the General Quartermaster, I could not have succeeded. I must acknowledge, it is stimulating to meet emergencies.

The people have renewed interest in the building of the Industrial School.

Mr. Mouly has gone on muleback to Denver to purchase a crushing cylinder.

§ 6

Oct. 1, 1878.

Our new Governor is General Lewis Wallace.[17] It is difficult to predict anything about him, except that he has a difficult task before him. Not the least of which will be to check the depredations being committed by Billy and his gang.

The work of the "Gang" is arousing the anger of good men. Mr. Turnstall, a rancher, was brutally murdered by "Cattle King" Major L. G. Murphy's men.

"Billy," cowboy for Turnstall, witnessed the deed and swore to shoot down like a dog every man he could find who had part in the murder of his friend.

Here was a man with qualities to make him great, smothering his best instincts, to become a murderer and an outlaw.

Mr. Lucas, one of our cultured Americans, came to say, "I will bring Bob Ingersoll to introduce him to you. Is it agreeable?"

"Not at all, Sir."

"Why not, may I ask?"

"On account of the soul destruction he is causing among his audiences in the United States, especially among young men. The premises upon which he bases his agnostic teaching are false. His oratory is so fascinating that the majority of his hearers drink and relish his flowery speeches without searching into their correctness. I understand our estimable Governor (General Lew Wallace) has received him at the Palace several times."

"Yes, Sister, he has. May I bring Mr. Ingersoll?"

"No, thank you, I forfeit the honor."

Governor Lew Wallace and Mr. Bob Ingersoll were on the train from Santa Fe to Las Vegas.

Mr. Ingersoll, looking at the mountains of white clouds and their background of perfect blue, addressed Mr. Wallace in this form:

"Wallace, what is beyond those clouds? . . . ether? What beyond that . . . space? And then . . . I don't know. Do you?"

Mr. Wallace made no reply.

When his book, Ben Hur, came from the publisher, one copy was forwarded to Mr. Ingersoll with this statement: "This is the answer to your questions to me on the train from Santa Fe to Las Vegas."

1878.

The new architect whom the Most Rev. Archbishop Lamy has engaged to continue the building of the cathedral came to see us this morning. He does not impress me favorably.

Our work on the Industrial School is at a standstill, owing to the fact that we are waiting for a clay crushing cylinder. To-day I made a point of having a talk with Mr. Mouly. Mr. Mouly is the young artist whose nature was so wounded by a person in authority who constantly nagged at him to "work like the other men" that, having warned the inspector, "If your nagging continues, I drop the work" — he did. The work meant the completion of the cathedral and the chapel of the Sisters of Loretto.

The unfinished chapel of the Loretto Sisters has been a thorn to me since I came to Santa Fe. So to-day, after discussing the work yet to be done on the Industrial School, I said to Mr. Mouly:

"I'm going to ask you a personal favor."

He answered: "Is it possible I can do you a favor?"

"Yes. Please resume work and continue until you complete the chapel of the Sisters of Loretto!"

The expression that revealed his eagerness to show appreciation for what had been done for his artistic life suddenly vanished, and a look of anguish, revealing a fierce struggle within, took its place. I quietly waited while he was fighting his battle — I, too, was pleading with his and my guardian angel. Presently he drew a long breath and said:

"Yes, Sister, I'll do as you ask."

Half an hour after this conversation I went to visit Mother Magdalen. The first words Mother Magdalen said to me were: "Sister, I've been wishing to see you. Will you try to induce Mr. Mouly to complete our chapel?"

With enthusiasm I told her I had anticipated her desire and that within the last half hour Mr. Mouly said he would resume the chapel work. Then I added: "You know his talent — his artistic conscientiousness; you will make no mistake by leaving the work to him without anyone's interference."

"I think the same, Sister, and I thank you very much for doing what you did. Rest assured the prayers of the Community will be offered for you before and after the completion of the chapel."

Sister Mary Stanislaus (Chavez) of the Loretto Sisters came into a portion of her family inheritance and sent us a nice slice to help with our Industrial School. For some time, Miss Manderfield and her sister Eugenia, have been insisting on my visiting their garden. I went, taking a few of our orphan children with me. Every step we took in the garden caused an exclamation of surprise.

The strawberries, with no exaggeration, are three times as large as the largest strawberries in Ohio, but the taste falls far below. Miss Manderfield thinks they may have used extreme cultivation methods.

§ 7

August, 1878. We had a long walk to-day in the "Archbishop's Garden." This and the old Cathedral are the two objectives of all tourists who come to Santa Fe. The dear old Archbishop showed us a pear tree trained to grow like a grape vine and pears were on the branches of the tree entwined in the grape vine which also had grapes hanging.

His Grace asked me, "Have you seen the Jesuits' garden in Albuquerque?"

"Yes, Archbishop."

"What do you think of it and Brother Pandolfo?"

"I easily compared it to what we might suppose Eden was, and as for Brother Pandolfo — his personality and conversation gave me food for many meditations. There is an agriculturist that could the unborn speak, they would clamor for his assistance. His generosity is on a par with his knowledge. He makes choice of natives to work with him who can assimilate what he imparts, and who, in turn, will make use of his teaching to instruct others. With a dozen of trained men — such as Brother Pandolfo will turn out — the Rio Grande Valley has a chance of becoming a miniature Eden."

Then His Grace said: "Well, my children, shall we visit the fountain and the fish?"

The group answered: "Please, Archbishop."

His Grace led. At each line of trees bearing fruit he stopped to explain — such as — "these peach trees were transplanted five years ago — this is their first bearing year. You must notice how few and large the peaches are: that is because Louis pinched off many of the blossoms." Coming to a row of apple trees he remarked: "Six trees of fall and six trees of winter apples," then turning to me he said: "Did you visit the jail this week?"

"Yes, Archbishop. Juana is there, and the great pity is that any periodically insane person should have to be placed in jail. So, as soon as she is over this attack, we are going to take her to the hospital."

We reached the fountain and fish pond, and His Grace explained the careful attention required to preserve the lives of the goldfish.

You can realize, Sister Justina, what a pleasure it was to have the Archbishop show us through the garden. He asked (during our walk) if any of us had been told how Sister Vincent spoke Spanish. No one had. Then he said: "I was her teacher and one day a number of army officers, among them General Carleton (who brought an Indian Navajo baby here which was found on the battlefield) wanted to get acquainted with the Sisters of Charity. I brought the gentleman to the Sisters' Community Room, the door of which was partly glass. Sister Vincent saw us coming, so when I rapped she said: *"Entran, caballos!"* (Come in, horses). General Carleton remarked: "Is this a specimen of your teaching?"

§ 8

Spring, 1879.

Our Spring begins in February. In the course of this journal, dear Sister Justina, I have mentioned what a charming character we have in the person of Hermana Dolores Chavez de Guiterrez, and also promised myself to ascertain her history before she entered our community.

Sister Dolores is so markedly unpretentious that I had to be tactful to have her speak of her youth. Unquestionably she belongs to the blue bloods. The Chavez family from which she descends is noted for its sagacity, but particularly for having made great financial sacrifices to educate the male members of the family. The females are taught the refinement of a Christian home, and how to keep themselves aloof from the contamination of the unchristian worldly fashion. Fashion in this sentence means everything not ethical in the Catholic sense.

Sister Dolores cards and spins wool in the Community room. This carding and spinning is considered one of the accomplishments of our Lady Doñas. Whenever I can manage to spare half an hour from my duties, I take my mending and sit patching, while Sister tells me incidents in the life of her people and the Indians as far back as she can remember. Of course, I try to get her to speak of herself. In this way, I have learned a great deal about her life. It took many sittings to gather what is here condensed:

"When I was a little girl I was quite timid. We always had

Mexican and Indian servants. The Indians were prisoners of war, or children picked up from the battlefield and reared by my parents. Many families obtained their Indian servants in this way. My mother told me the older Indian captives worked in the fields, but seldom could they be trusted to remain.

"We had an Indian — a Navajo — who was nice. Mother had reared him from the time he was a papoose. He had been taught to read. One day mother sent me to the jars to get a handful of gold money. The coins were in five dollar gold pieces. I got the handful, but told her I had to put my hand way down in the jar to reach the money. While I was telling this to my mother, our Indian came into the room. When he raised his red handkerchief to wipe his face, a number of five dollar gold pieces fell to the floor. My mother asked José where he got the gold money. He hung his head.

" 'How many times did you go to the jar?' mother asked.

" 'I don't know how many times,' he answered. 'I gave one piece to every Indian I saw, and to every Mexican family who has many children. I saw you give to the Mexicans, so I gave to the Indians, too. You always look happy when you give. I was happy too, until I remembered you did not send me for the money to give it away.'

"The Indian had access to the jars the same as I had, but this was the first time he had used the gold for any purpose except the one intended.

"My mother was studying how to tell my father when he would return from Albuquerque. We were then living in Pajarito, the other side of the Rio Grande from Albuquerque. A short time after this event my father and some of the ranchmen came in. My father gave quick orders. '*Alma mia*' (my soul) to my mother, 'get the children quickly. We must hasten to Albuquerque where we can protect ourselves against the Apaches who are heading for Pajarito and Atrisco. The Apaches were told the men are out of these villages. José, put all the gold money in as few jars as possible, each of you men carry a jar to the raft. Children, help your mother to choose the clothes you most need, and all be on the portico in less time than you can count one hundred.'

"In a very short time my father returned, and mother and the children were led by my father to a raft made of hand-sawed lumber. We got on it and all covered our eyes. We were afraid of falling into the water. The men did not get on with us. They first pushed the raft, then they used long poles to drive it forward. José was on the raft with us. We heard the yells of the Indians when they found out the people had gone. We were very much afraid. My father was speaking to us and telling us not to be afraid, because we were out of reach of the Indians. José turned quickly and said: 'I will give my life to save you.' When he turned, he took his hand off one of the jars and it fell into the Rio Grande. My father said: 'Keep on, men, never mind the money.' We got to Albuquerque. My sister Juanita lived there, and we went to her house. My sister's husband was brave. The Indians did not come to Albuquerque, but we did not go back to Pajarito. We went to Los Algodones.

"At this time I began to think how much I should like to be a nun. The thought was in my mind all the time. All my sisters got married, but I said I loved my parents too much to leave them.

"One day I asked my father to take me to Durango. He asked me:

" 'To see your brother Tomás?'

" 'No, to enter the convent.'

"He looked at me, and I could see he did not know whether to laugh or be serious. But as he saw I was in earnest, he said: 'It will cost ten thousand pesos (dollars) to get up a caravan to travel to Mexico. Many tribes of Indians are disturbed at the change of government here. They do not know whether to side with the natives, or with the Americans. Everything is uncertain. Wait a while until matters are settled, and by that time you may have changed your mind.'

"I waited one more year, then asked father to take me to

Durango to the Convent. Meanwhile, the family had arranged for me to enter another state of life, but I insisted I wanted to be a nun. Then my father got up a big caravan to take me to Durango. There were many wagons and many men in the caravan. There were also a number of Mexican scouts who followed all new and old trails, to discover if any of the Indian tribes were in ambush to attack us. We had reached Franklin[18] (El Paso) three hundred miles from where we started, when two of the best scouts reported that Indians were warring among themselves and attacking indiscriminately. So my father ordered a return trip. I still waited another year in hopes some way might be proposed that I could go to Durango. The bad feelings between the Mexicans, Navajos and Apaches continued, which made it impossible to travel. My parents asked me if I had not better choose another state of life. I married Mr. Guiterrez. The first thing I did was to inform the Indians and servants belonging to our ranch that I would give them catechetical instructions every day.

"My nephew, Francisco J. Chavez, I took under my special care. He was so bright, but so mischievous, that he was in constant trouble. Since those far-off days Francisco was a delegate to Congress, and as you know he is now President of the Senate here. When he comes to see me he always speaks of the time I taught him how to pray and keep out of trouble."

"Where did you make application to enter our Community?" I asked.

"From Puertecito. My husband went annually to oversee the shearing of the sheep. He was always accompanied by ten or fifteen men. There were expert shearers. At the last trip he made he left his escort so as to reach home sooner. When the sheep shearers came within twenty-three miles of Las Vegas they found my husband's body, murdered and scalped, by some unknown Indians. This happened in 1859.

"My children were all settled in life. I had no ties to hold me back and my mind constantly ran on the idea of being a nun. I was told that Mother Seton's Community admitted widows. I determined to seek admission to the Daughters of Charity in Santa Fe.

"When speaking to my confessor he remarked. 'The Sisters of Charity are practical women; they fear no work.' At once I thought the only work I can do is card and spin, but I can learn. The day after I had spoken to my confessor I went into the kitchen and told the head cook I wanted to learn to cook. She and her assistants humored me, thinking, as I plainly saw, that my husband's tragic death had affected my mind. I studied cooking till I satisfied myself that I could cook an ordinary meal. Then I went to the laundry, and from that to the chicken yard. It took me nearly one year to learn to do what I might be called on to do if I could be received into the Community of the Sisters of Charity. I was then sixty years old.

"Broaching the subject again to my confessor, and telling him I had learned to do domestic work, he said: 'You have my full consent to enter the novitiate of the Daughters of Charity. I, myself, will go to Santa Fe and represent your case for admission.'

"I was received. The only complaint I have is that I expected to be put to hard work and I've only been given carding and spinning with the addition of darning stockings. I have seen my family to the fifth generation, and am sometimes annoyed for fear I'm only in the way."

I must note here that Sister Dolores, up to the time she fitted herself to enter the Community, had never crossed the threshold of the kitchen, laundry, or chicken yard. Orders were given from the open door of each department, and that completed her work.

Sister Dolores has two sisters, both married, but who have never been known to leave their homes on any pretext except to flee from Indians, so Sister Augustine has planned to make a visit to her sisters and relatives, going down on one side of the Rio Grande and coming up on the other side.

§ 9

A hasty message came saying Big Jim has been mortally wounded and is being brought to the hospital on a stretcher. Big Jim is the tallest man in Santa Fe, our beds are only six feet in length, so we hastily made an addition to the length of the bed in one of the rooms facing the street. The under sheet had been stretched when six men walked in with the patient. To inexperienced eyes he was a corpse. He was placed on the improvised bed and the men who carried him had just got outside the door when a policeman appeared and said, "I want to examine Jim's pockets." Rumor had it that some of the policemen were in the habit of examining the pockets of those arrested, but if the contents were of value, no return was ever made to the owner. So I said "Mr. Jim's pockets will be examined." The policeman threw aside the lapel of his coat to show me the star. I remarked: "We know you are a policeman, but we will attend to the contents of Mr. Jim's pockets."

I called one of the convalescent patients and asked him to bring pen, paper and ink and another witness. When the two men came, one was asked to search the apparently dead man's pockets. Some trinkets and a roll of bills were placed on the table. The money was counted; it amounted to three hundred and fifty-seven dollars. The policeman said, "I'll take charge of the money." The reply was, "You two have witnessed the amount of money found in Big Jim's pockets. You, Mr. Mahoney, please go to the bank and ask that a messenger be sent here to take this money to the bank and deposit it to the patient's credit."

The policeman walked off.

Turning to see if any change had taken place in the condition of the man who caused the above scene, Big Jim said in a subdued voice: "You're a brick" — a new expression to me. Instantly I thought of our first kiln of bricks which were porous and worthless, but how to apply the term to me was a conundrum, so I let it go by, as I do many other things beyond my comprehension.

Big Jim had received many flesh wounds inflicted by a pal of many years. All that annoyed Big Jim was that his pal might send one or more of his friends to finish the job, because, said Big Jim, "I bit off my pal's ear. Do not let any of that gang come near me." At every visit I made, the patient invariably asked if any of his enemies had asked about him or had come to see him. In a week's time he was ready to leave the hospital. He cautioned me to say he was not here. That such a giant as this man is to be so afraid is another conundrum for me.

My parting words to the giant were, "Find your pal, make up and be good friends again."

Three days after this, a man with bound up head applied to be taken in. The weather was quite chilly and the man looked sick and ill-at-ease. "I have need of hospital care, but before registering I would like to know if Big Jim is here?" He was assured Big Jim had been discharged.

This was the man who had had his ear bit off by Big Jim. Each was afraid of the other, having been good friends, they were now bitter enemies, yet loving each other unknown to themselves.

Erysipelas had set in. He was placed in a room to which his supposed enemy could not have access.

About three weeks from this time Big Jim came to see me. "Sister, I'm sure my pal is here. I want to see him."

Five-feet-three looked up at six-feet-four and answered, "He is here, but you may not see him unless he wishes to see you." Big Jim's facial expression was: "With my little finger I can brush you aside and go to my pal," but quickly changed into a blank stare which I interpreted, "but I don't know where he is." Jim spoke. "Sister, I want to make up; we have been good pals. Tell him that, and tell him, too, I'm on the police force."

I went to the sick man's room and casually mentioned that Big Jim would like to see him to make up. The patient trembled and shook the bed with fear.

"Sister, please do not let him come; I am helpless and he will finish me."

"If I tell you what I think will you believe me?"

"Yes, Sister, but I'm very much afraid of him."

"I am convinced he is sincere in wanting to become friends again. If you say so, I'll bring him in and remain during the interview."

"Just as you say, Sister."

I showed Jim up to the room. Two loving brothers could not have shown more genuine pleasure at meeting each other after an estrangement. So that feud was ended.

§ 10

April 4, 1879.

Most Rev. Archbishop Lamy is much pleased that Sister Dolores will get to see her relatives.

Our first stop will be at Pena Blanca — to Bernalillo — to Albuquerque, cross the Rio Grande at this point — down the Rio seventy-five miles.

Work on the Industrial School is at a standstill. Mr. Mouly has not returned from Denver, nor have we heard from him. The check sent him to purchase a crushing cylinder has not been cashed. Many persons, among them his partner, have urged me to continue the building in stone work instead of brick. All interested have given up hopes of his return. I contend that, unless he has met with foul play, he will have a satisfactory explanation.

Next Monday, the third week in April, Sisters Augustine, Dolores and myself, start on our trip. The greater part will be following the banks of the Rio Grande[19] (Big River).

What do you think is the greatest pleasure I anticipate?

Crossing the river in a ferry boat![20]

I've been told the river is crossed at Albuquerque on a ferry boat. Even to see a boat's smokestack will give me a thrill. Many things of everyday use in the East are never heard of here.

Pena Blanca. So far is our first day's travel — about twenty-eight miles. Doña Maria Los Angeles, Sister Dolores' sister, has sent her family coach to take us to her ranch.

From now on, we shall have two search scouts to guide and protect us. Doña Maria Los Angeles is the wife of Don Antonio Baca. We are now at the ranch. Goodness is depicted on the countenance of every member of the family. A nice chapel speaks their Catholicity.

The scouts and Don Antonio are discussing the shortest and surest route for us to Bernalillo. Unless we take the La Bajada route, we shall have to retrace and travel, all told, about sixty miles to reach San Felipe Indian Pueblo, which is some eighteen miles from Bernalillo. The conclusion is, we take the La Bajada road — La Bajada means "The Descent." When we reach the base, we see San Felipe. This route saves one day's travel. All decided on the short route.

"We have to cross the river again at Albuquerque, do we not? And there is a ferry boat there?"

"Yes, ah! yes, a boat!"

You can not realize, Sister Justina, the joy the thought of seeing a boat gives me, I care not how black the smoke or thick the soot; they will resemble some items in Cincinnati.

We are now in Bernalillo. Sister Dolores has many relatives here. Don Alejandro Perea has built a private chapel for his family, but his living family extends back to five generations. This gentleman is called the Patriarch of Bernalillo. Every Sunday from all directions of Bernalillo County, and from the town itself, arrive all kinds of private conveyances and line up on both sides of the Perea residence. These conveyances bring sons, daughters, and their children to the weekly visit. He receives each family with equal courtesy. The deference and love shown "The Patriarch" is within the memory of the oldest inhabitant of Bernalillo. What about his wife? She is an unassuming, charitable, prayerful creature, who keeps in the background when public honors are distributed, but who can be found ready to help in any public distress. The family chapel was built to please her, and was named "Dolores," after her.

Saturday, first week of May, 1879.

At 1 P.M., we leave for Albuquerque. 2:30 P.M. we are delayed. The scouts have gone to a ranch to procure planks. From this point I saw a very high smokestack and asked the driver if it is the ferry stack.

When we reached the descent we saw the Rio Grande. From the summit to the base only scientists could tell approximately when the volcanic upheaval occurred. The prospect of driving between rocks where every turn had to be eye-measured, and where if either of the mules made the slightest slip the conveyance would come in contact with large rocks, was not reassuring to Sister Augustine. I asked the scouts if any wagon had ever attempted the descent.

"Yes, yes, but we never heard of ladies attempting the La Bajada in any vehicle."

Sister Augustine at once said, "I shall walk down." Sister Dolores is well past sixty years, and has never been known to walk a mile on a smooth road, so I asked again. "Is it safe to drive on this zigzag road in this conveyance?"

"Sí, Hermana, sí, sí." (Yes, Sister, yes, yes.)

"Then, Sister Dolores and myself will ride." We did ride, but at a snail's pace. When we came to the bank of the Rio Grande the scouts looked at the ripples of the water, then said in Spanish, "This was a fording place last week, but not today."

We drove about a mile along the bank, when again the scouts studied the ripples, and in a few minutes started to cross, telling the drivers to follow. One of the scouts was communicative:

"Only Indians and Mexicans understand the treachery of the Rio Grande sands; many Americans have been deceived and lost their lives by attempting to cross where, with guides, they had crossed before, not understanding that the sand in the Rio Grande is always on the move. If you get on the accumulated sand the suction is so strong nothing can save you."

"No, Señora, no ferry has a smokestack, only the mill of the American has it."

"Well, then, how do they ferry across the Rio?"

"Oh! The Mexican, he smart; you see by and by."

We are now on the old bed of the Rio Grande, six miles from Albuquerque. The river has changed its bed twice within the memory of the inhabitants.

Four miles from Albuquerque! We are the guests of Doña Juanita Chavez de Armijo, one of Sister Dolores' sisters.

This is too good not to jot down. Sister Dolores and her sister had not met for many years, so I managed to walk away (the grounds are ample) to let them enjoy their meeting. But Doña Juanita followed me and said, "You are so young to take such long rides. I want you to take a good rest." Showing me into a room, she remarked: "We do not even allow the servants to enter this room, for reasons I will explain later on. Now I insist you take a siesta in that comfortable bed!"

Doña Juanita left me and I went to the resting place. It looked hilly to me. Feeling the spots made itself plain there could be no rest, so I took a chair and read. About an hour after, in came Doña Juanita and seeing me reading, said:

"You are young, but you have used more sense than some others I know. Now, because you were so good, I am going to let you see where I wanted you to rest."

She turned up the coverings and there I saw a large quantity of family plate. Heavy solid silver. One spoon would make six solid silver spoons of ours. The plates are possibly one and one-half pounds each. The cups ditto. Some of this table silver is marked "Chavez." This came from her family. The Chavez family has a solid gold table set as well. Then Doña Juanita said, "I desire you to accept a quantity of this family plate in remembrance of your visit and that of my sister's." We took it and will send it to the Cabinet at Mt. St. Vincent, Cincinnati. We have been told that the Communion rail in the Cathedral of Mexico City is solid silver. Their revolutions and counter-revolutions are so numerous that one is never surprised when news reaches us of the spoliation of any of the churches.

Undisciplined minds must be fed. Their action is like to ungovernable children wounding their mother — who is ever ready to forgive.

The scouts and conveyance are ready. So now for Albuquerque and the great pleasure I anticipate in crossing the Rio Grande on a ferry boat!

Albuquerque! The only things restful to the eye are the Church and plaza in front of it.

Atrisco. — We crossed the Rio. I remember the blank looks of a child of six when he discovered that Santa Claus was not Santa Claus. Picture me with that look when the driver pointed to some heavy planks nailed together in an oblong form and other less heavy planks put on these to make a solid floor, and you have what the driver was sure would be a big surprise when he said to me:

"Oh! The Mexican, he smart, you see by and by."

I came, I saw, but I did not conquer the feeling that I wanted to see a little bit of the things that once were. It seems we crossed the river in the same place that Sister Dolores and family did over fifty years ago when they were pursued by the Apaches. The ferry boat is the same model. Yet this demonstrates the sagacity of the natives. The river is not navigable; the sand is constantly moving. Man power is used to propel the raft from the river bank as far as it is safe for the men to wade. They then got on the raft and with long poles worked the "ferry boat" until we were near the opposite bank of the river, when they jumped into the water again and used their physical engines to land us. During this performance, the engineers wore what at one time was white muslin made into the shape of a bag, head, arms and legs free.

After we landed on the Atrisco bank the driver said, "I no say you the Mexican he smart?"

We are now a few miles from Pajarito where Sister Dolores spent her childhood.

Gallup. — This spot makes me feel that God takes delight in

giving it sunshine. I have not seen its equal anywhere else. We remained here one day. This morning the Doña brought us breakfast before breakfast time to our rooms. Sister explained this delicate attention is given by the old Spanish families when they want to show *Cariño* (love).

We rested two hours at Mrs. Connelly's of the Chavez family. Doctor Connelly, her husband, was governor from 1861 to 1866 under the Organic Act. Mrs. Connelly is one of the old school saintly matrons. We stayed long enough to have the two friends recall their youth. J. Francisco Chavez belongs to this branch of the Chavezes. He is a figure in the territory.

La Constancia. — We expected to rest for an hour or so, then go to Tomé. But Doña Carlota Otero de Chavez, Sister Dolores' niece, ordered her coachman to unhitch our vehicle in the stable. Scouts, drivers and horses were lodged, and we were informed that we were to remain until the morrow, when she would accompany us to our next stopping place. I counted fifteen servants here. They are in one another's way. Father, son and daughter are lords of the mansion.

Los Lunas. — We made short stops at Peralta and Tomé. We are guests of the Los Lunas family. Don Tranquelino Luna is one of the most popular men in the territory. He is called "The Handsome." His sister is positively the most beautiful girl I have ever seen. She carries the atmosphere of a convent education, and is entirely unspoiled by adulation. Mrs. Luna is a saintly woman. We are going direct to Las Vegas, the "Meadow City."

Las Vegas. — It surely must give Sister Dolores many sensations to review the places where her husband and children lived part of their lives and transacted business from Puertecito to this place. Her visit is like a jubilee to her relatives and friends. We passed San Miguel, Glorieta, and are now at Santa Fe. Our trip is accomplished. Dear Hermana Dolores looks and feels many years younger than when we started.

§ 11

June, 1879.

Dear Sister Justina:

"Not ours to know the reason why unanswered is our prayer,
But ours to wait for God's own time to lift the cross we bear."

This Mr. Mouly I speak of is the young artist who so interested me while still in Trinidad.

All I knew of him was that he was a highly-talented artist and that he had given up the unprecedented honor — for one of his age, not more than seventeen years, the building of the Cathedral and the Chapel of the Sisters of Loretto, because his sensitive artistic nature could not brook criticism from one who was not capable of drawing a circle on a square, and yet had the power to "Lord it over him." He withdrew into solitude — that is, from all except one man. Providence gave me the opportunity to discover him.

Before leaving Santa Fe for Denver, he had received a pathetic letter from his father telling him that he had been informed that he was doing common masonry work. "You, who are capable of doing the highest work of art — you are degrading your profession. I beg of you, my son, give up that work." This letter stung the sensitive artist to the heart. His father's informant was no other than the person who had so unintelligently criticized him at his work.

Mr. Mouly had no intention of bringing the unjust critic to the notice of his father, but this letter was the culmination of his suppressed indignation.

"No one, my dear father, questions your capabilities in art, and when God deprived you of your sight and you were asked to find a substitute you presented me, and your honesty could not be impeached. I was accepted as your choice to continue the work for which you had been brought to America.

"I made no change in your prints, nor in the treatment of the workmen, keeping you ever as my master-model. Your informant visited the work at least once a day. When he found me inspecting instead of working — according to his idea — he invariably asked: 'Why are you not working like the other men?'

"For a number of times I answered courteously, but the same question was so often repeated that at last I said: 'Sir, I believe I understand the work and its supervision, I cannot endure your repetition, work like the other men. Please understand, if you repeat that, I drop the work.'

"The next time he visited the work and found me inspecting, he repeated his taunt. I only said 'Good-bye, you may now look for an architect, superintendent and workman.'

"I went to room with . . . You know his failing. I found myself sliding down the scale of proper living, and could not rise above it. Steel was working toward my heart and wanted to pierce it.

"Constantly did I think of you and the members of our family. Nothing could arouse me from the depression I was in, and the degradation I was facing. At this juncture, a Sister of Charity sent for me. She did not moralize, but said, 'I have heard of your artistic talents and that you have no engagement at present. Are you willing to take work that will only gain merit in God's sight?'

"While Sister spoke I read her sincerity and felt like kneeling to thank her for the opportunity to get away from my hiding place, and shall I say it — from ways that point to destruction.

"I asked, 'What are your plans, Sister?'

" 'To build an Industrial School wherein our native girls can be taught trades to help maintain fathers and mothers.'

" 'And funds to build?' I asked.

" 'Not a cent, Mr. Mouly,' Sister answered.

"Sister told me that she hoped the Rector of the Cathedral would co-operate with her plans; if he did so, the work on the foundations would be begun at once. Once under way, in her opinion, it meant success. An Industrial School is one of the Most Rev. J. B. Lamy's long-standing desires. For this object he asked the influence of Most Rev. Archbishop Purcell — ec-

clesiastical Superior of the Sisters of Charity of Cincinnati —
to have certain Sisters sent to Santa Fe, which request was
granted. I give the above information because I know I have
wounded the family pride, but, my dear father, you might
have heard things of me which would have grieved you beyond
my reparation if I had not been found and literally snatched
from my downward course."

The answer came in decisive words.

"My Son:

"Every member of our family joins me in thanking the Sister
of Charity who took that big interest in you, and I want you
to feel that I am doubly proud of the victory you have gained
over yourself. You have raised the plane of masonry work. We
honor you as a true artist. We shall write a grateful letter to
your friend, the Sister of Charity.

"We all subscribe ourselves,

"Yours, honored by your action,

"Your Father and Family."

Dear Sister Justina:

From this correspondence you can notice that father and son
let each other see their inmost thoughts. Mr. Mouly told me
that I would never have known the strained feeling between
his father and himself were it not that he feared some inter-
loper would consider it his duty to inform, or rather misinform,
me.

The work on the Industrial School has been resumed. A new
kiln of bricks is being fired.

June 15. A Mr. Shelby came to-day to say that he and some
friends desired me to accept this trap — pointing to a rig and
finely groomed horse. "You have so much walking to do. This
will save your energy."

"Thank you, Mr. Shelby. Our native people are so willing
to assist with their labor to help build the Industrial School,
and you know the sacrifice that most of the laborers are making,
that, were I to ride while the laborers helped me, I would

feel wretched. I thank you and your friends, but I prefer to walk."

The next time I went to the plaza a carriage drove up to the curb and the driver said: "Sister, we have orders to pick you up wherever we see you, and drive you to where you wish to go."

Understanding this to be the sequel of not accepting the fine rig, my companion and myself stepped into the carriage. From this last incident I took the precaution not to walk where carriages could be driven. Remember, Santa Fe is built on the squatted plan, but the inhabitants are more alive than an unobservant person would give them credit.

§ 12

July 16. — Intensely warm.

One belonging to the "Santa Fe Ring" — political, of course — came to ask me to visit "Big Jim" who is in jail for the murder of a policeman. Unfortunate Jim! He has not even the shadow of a loophole to defend the homicide.

To-morrow we take our orphan children to an outing.

My intention is to remain home to visit the jail. The Governor has given orders to the warden that I be permitted to see any prisoner.

Picnic day! Such a day is not noticed in the States, but here it is causing a lively commotion. Our orphans are overjoyed. Citizens came here in number to see their happy faces. When all were seated and signal given to start, a clamor arose from the citizens who had got up this pleasure. "Sister, you must take off to-day. We have sent an extra carriage for you."

I hesitated. Too well I know the retributary, unwritten law of the Southwest. Our nested town is all alive with protests against the murderer of an innocent man. Mr. Shelby said: "I know your work will accumulate. I will instruct the driver to leave the picnic grounds at 2 P.M. and return you and your companion home."

2 P.M. came — so did one of our torrential rains. Seated in the carriage when the pouring began, my companion and

myself were drenched when we arrived at the Hospital. Immediately I began to make preparations for visiting the jail.

Sister Louise said: "Sister Blandina, you shall not go out again to-day. You are not over the effects of the drenching you have just received. To start out again means you might be caught in another downpour. Two such dampings could easily result in pneumonia."

"But Sister," I said, " 'Big Jim' is in jail."

"One day more or less will not hurt 'Big Jim,' " answered Sister. With untold uneasiness I submitted. Next morning the *New Mexican* in large letters had "Retribution!" Before "Big Jim's" case could have a hearing, justice was meted out to him.

I did not read the account in the *New Mexican*, but I write what those who read it told me. As for myself, I feel too wretched to have lost the opportunity in some way to prepare him to appear before the final Judge. Yet that Judge who knows the clay that moulded "Jim" will pronounce sentence in accordance.

Here is what was told me partly by those who read it in the *New Mexican*, and mostly by one who had the act narrated to him by a participant.

"We went to the jail, twelve of us. We blindfolded the jailer and gagged him. Two of us held him. 'Big Jim' was in bed; he was ordered up. Each man had a revolver and aiming singly at arms and legs, they fired at Jim. By the fourth shot he fell, but not dead. He was then told: 'This is what you brought on yourself for taking the life of a good man, and you did it for money. We will now finish you.' Then all discharged another shot.

"The corpse was carried to the first adobe house that had a portal and hanged to a crossbeam, head downward."

It is not the tragic end that affects me so much, but to realize that he had no time to ask God's mercy outwardly. What he did in thought, God alone knows.

§ 13

August 1, 1879.

Grave problems are ahead of us. The A. T. and Santa Fe road is working its way toward Santa Fe.

What of the great number of men employed on the work?

Some will succumb to the climate, others to accidents, and only one hospital within a radius of five hundred miles. The sick or injured will have to be taken either to Phoenix, Denver, or Santa Fe. Our hospital is the central point. Figure this out for us who are trying to do the most good with the least amount of money. Has God ever forsaken those who put their trust in Him?

Progress is in sight — so is disaster to a certain portion of our native population.

The labor of our pioneer missionaries on our natives will be destroyed by money-making schemes. Deceit and dishonesty will rob the poor natives of everything.

I saw this process take place in Trinidad, Colorado. Nothing too bad for the natives — nothing too good for the land-grabbers.

Understand, dear Sister Justina, those I designate as land-grabbers are not representative Americans, but restless characters who wish to get away from law and order and make their own rulings.

Among my forebodings I foresee the disastrous effects on the spiritual life of our people.

Here is a fact: Sister Rose, of the Cornette Community, St. Louis Hospital, wrote me to visit a young invalid who is traveling with his mother. Sister knows the young man cannot live long and she is anxious to have him receive the last Sacraments of the Church.

Taking the address given me, and an orphan for companion, I went to the residence named. To my surprise, the lady harboring the invalid and his mother is the wife of a prominent business man of this place.

She welcomed me most cordially. After hearing the reason for my visit, she went to see if the patient were awake.

"In ten minutes' time he will be happy to receive you," said she on her return.

During our conversation she said to me: "Sister, I marvel at your tolerance of the 'Greasers.' I would not let one come within a forty-foot pole of me."

"On the contrary, I admire most of their characteristics. The majority are guileless," I answered.

I saw the patient and made sure the last Sacraments would be administered to him.

On my return, Rev. M. M. Meara, of Columbus, Ohio, who was sent here for his health by Rt. Rev. Bishop Rosecrans, met me. Our Most Reverend Archbishop had invited Bishop Rosecrans to come to Santa Fe and rest after the arduous work of building his Cathedral. His reply was: "Father Meara has broken down under the work and needs a complete rest. Please receive him as you would have received me, and oblige your old friend." This was the last of many kind acts of Bishop Rosecrans. He died immediately after the dedication of the Cathedral.

When Father Meara met me he handed me a St. Louis paper, saying: "Read that article. Is there such a person as Mrs. —— in Santa Fe?"

I replied that I had just come from her residence.

"Is she not a bigot?"

"I cannot say she is, though she has little sympathy for our native population."

I read the article the Reverend gentleman had marked. It is too lengthy to reproduce in this journal, but it produced in me a profound contempt for all shams.

Here is a quotation from the article:

"My dear Co-laborers: — Could you see me surrounded by these benighted Mexicans and realize how anxious they are to know something of Jesus and the Bible, you would not hesitate to draw from your pocketbooks and send me what would help me continue to enlighten their dense ignorance of things holy and the Bible."

And she had just told me that she would not let one of these Mexicans come within a forty-foot pole of her!

Here is a scene on the same subject:

A Mr. P—— and Mr. G—— were shown into my office. Mr. G—— introduced his companion as "Bishop P——." "I am minister G—— from Tiptonville, New Mexico. We are missionaries and we have been told that you like the Mexican people. Now, if you will join us we can do very much to bring the light of the gospel to them. You are not allowed to read the Bible and your Church does no charity. If you join us, we will teach our poor people to read the Bible and to love Jesus. We expect to preach on the Santa Fe Plaza to-day, and if you are with us, we are sure the Mexicans will take to the Bible."

The Bishop, whom I have been told is of low mentality, said not a word.

As for myself, the humor of the whole scene was so great that all I could do was to listen. Mr. G—— exhausted his poll-parrot speech, and I recovered from my astonishment. I said: "Mr. G——, you realize that being a Sister of Charity makes me a part of the Catholic Church!"

He answered: "Yes, Sister." Then I said:

"Since the tragic death of your father (you and your mother know what caused his death), your two sisters have been fed, clothed, and educated free by the Sisters of Charity. Is there no charity in that? As for our being forbidden to read the Bible, where did your sect get the Bible, if not from the Catholic Church? The Catholic Church takes wise precautions to prevent first grade pupils from interpreting the Bible to their own destruction, as you interpret the charity of the Catholic Church. One thing more I wish to say to you. This town is well named 'Holy Faith.' If you and your companion go to preach on the Plaza to falsify the faith of our native population, I shall be there to listen."

Dear Sister Justina, I never allow myself to be drawn into any religious controversy, but the provocation of this mendacious person made me lose sight of the spirit of tolerance. The two zealots left Santa Fe without preaching on the Plaza.

These incidents give me to understand what we may expect in the future.

August 16.

For many months we have had at the hospital a Mr. O'Leary, who sits in his chair, eats when the tray is set before him, but shows no interest in life, nor anything around him. The doctors are puzzled. So far as we know, he has no one belonging to him, nor do we know how he drifted here.

August 19. — Mr. O'Leary died.

As this case baffled the physicians, Dr. Longwill proposed a post-mortem. Sister Augustine asked me to remain at a little distance from the mortuary room in case anything would be wanting. Dr. Bartlett from the military post attended the post mortem also. Like a statue I placed myself where I could be seen in case my services were needed, facing the opposite direction from where the doctors were to do the dissecting. I stood waiting and hoping I would not be called. I began the standing at nine o'clock A.M. and I only realized how long I had been standing when the Cathedral bells rang the Angelus. As I turned I noticed that the dissecting room door was ajar. I went toward it and rapped lightly. No answer. I looked in and saw the corpse and where the cuttings around the heart had been made and court-plastered. I took in the whole scene at a glance and instantly I began to tremble with an indefinable fear and an ungovernable impulse to run away, which I did, and only stopped when I reached the Community Room, a distance of at least three hundred feet. When I got there the Sisters had all gone to the dining room and I had gained normalcy. I said to myself: "Sister Blandina, walk back and look at the corpse until you have conquered yourself."

Slowly walking where a few moments before I had run, I reached the mortuary room door and cast my eyes toward the corpse. The same impulse to run again urged me. I commanded myself and said: "Walk in and stand near the corpse until fear leaves you." I went and stood and looked, but the impulse to run was strong.

"Are you afraid now, Sister Blandina?"

"Yes, I am."

"Well, stand until you have conquered."

"Now, will you walk out slowly?"

"Yes."

After this soliloquy I walked to the door and that irresistible impulse to run came again.

"Well, Sister Blandina, you will stand still, look at the corpse, then leisurely walk away," I said to myself, which I did. I had conquered at last!

Going to the dining room I made an apology for my tardiness and looked to see if any Sister smiled; but all was solemnity. The secret of the battle fought was my own.

The next thing I did at 1 P.M. was to tell Joseph Quintella to come to the carpenter shop. "I will help to make the coffin," I told him.

No undertaker here. The usual mode of burying has been a winding sheet for the poor. The rich can import their needs.

This Joseph Quintella we found on the plains near Glorieta, and we invited him to our hospital. The man's left hand had been caught in some machinery, he said, and two of his fingers cut off. The arm was much inflamed. This patient's gratitude has been continual. He is determined to do the fancy carpenter work on the Industrial School and stipulated his charges "75 cents per day when I ask for it." He is a compound of genius and childishness. His cabinet work is done with the precision of a tradesman.

A few days ago I heard the "Anvil Chorus" played with good technique and followed by "Ah, I Have Sighed to Rest Me" in excellent tenor tones. I hastened to see who was in the music room. Whom did I find at the piano but Joseph, who blushed as if he had been caught doing something wrong.

I am sure this man is not out here to land-grab, but — and one's judgment is suspended — why find him on the plains near Glorieta, with no money and with an inflamed arm caused by two missing fingers on the left hand? Time will tell.

The men working on the railroad and unable to cope with our high altitude are being sent to the hospital.

To date, no serious accident has occurred on the works this side of Las Vegas. Heavy blasting is expected near Glorieta.

The only woman patient entered in our register since the opening of our hospital ten years ago is a Mrs. Herbert. Neither native man or woman takes to going to a hospital to be cured of any physical ailment, but of course, with the influx of strangers everything will change.

To-day Dr. Longwell, head of our staff, said to me: "Sister, let everything go to Hades, but you go and supervise the care of your Archbishop who is in a critical condition. Those attending him have too much reverence for him to compel him to follow my orders, which, if not carried out, means death."

We all love and revere Archbishop Lamy. In a few moments' time my work was transferred to other hands and I was on my way to his residence.

The attendants were reluctant to leave, though they fully realized the necessity of doing so.

Ten minutes after my arrival it was necessary to follow instructions. I said: "Now it is time to carry out the first prescription."

"But, my little Sister, I prefer to remain quiet."

"Yes, I realize how you feel, but I also realize your time for rest is not yet, so we shall follow orders."

This is the great man whose eagle eye can read one through and through, but I believe his reading of me to-day was not correct.

While carrying out the doctor's instructions, this heart of mine was transposing in different keys; it played to high C more than once, but perfectly determined to do or die.

When Dr. Longwell made his next visit he said: "Saved, Sister, he is saved!"

§ 14

Sept., 1879.

Dear Sister Justina:

Looking over the scribble I wrote on scraps since January, I notice they were not entered in this journal, which I trust some day you will enjoy. I have condensed the scraps and here is the result:

The Legislature was in session the early part of the year.

Many tramps came from the East and Northeast.

Need I say that, as usual, everywhere attempts were made to get rid of them?

Yet these same poor tramps are human beings with immortal souls. Repeatedly we were told that many of these trail-pilgrims were succumbing to fatigue, climate, and want of nourishment. Those who reached Santa Fe found their way to our hospital and often gave us the information that quite a number of fortune-hunters were perishing on the Santa Fe Trail. At the time I scribbled this on waste paper every bed in the hospital was occupied. Like King Richard who offered his Kingdom for a horse, I would offer mine for a mattress. But there were no mattresses to be had. I took the mattress from my bed and had it placed on the porch for a patient. Then came two more patients. By the time their brief history was recorded, another mattress was placed by the side of the other. Without a word, every Sister deprived herself of her mattress for the poor patients.

Then came the question of nourishment. Sisters denied themselves milk and sugar to give their portion to the convalescents.

Please remember I am treasurer with an empty purse. Some of the patients admitted can pay their way. This gave me the new idea to place those who have money in some private house and let them pay for their keep. We can send the doctors to visit them. I said to Sister Augustine: "Sister, I propose that patients applying for admission and having money be sent to some private family and that we retain those who have no money; this will give the latter a chance to live!"

Sister looked at me compassionately, then said: "Child, how will you meet the bills?"

I answered: "The day I cannot meet our bills, I will say: 'We can admit no patient who cannot pay' !"

Again Sister looked at me searchingly, then said: "Child, in God's name, do as you propose."

I hastened to Sister Catherine and told her that we have permission to take in patients and disregard the pocketbook. "Now, we must redouble our prayers and our activities. You know God helps those who help themselves.'" In Sister Catherine's gentle manner, she replied:

"Well, Sister Blandina, the idea throws much responsibility on Divine Providence; but I have seen you get through situations equally as difficult as this. You can always rely on my assistance."

"The first thing we must do is drive about four miles until we come to an L-shaped adobe; there are four men there, stranded and sick."

I want to tell you, dear Sister Justina, the genuine charity of this mission makes me forget the hardships attached to it.

Since I arrived, January, 1877, I have not heard a murmur or complaint. Our urgent needs are many, but we are all cheerful and happy.

During the legislative session which took place the early part of the year, a thought came to me: "Why not invite the law makers to visit the hospital?"

Knowing the Speaker of the House made it easy to address a note of invitation, which I did. Not being acquainted with the President of the Senate, I addressed my note of invitation "To the Senate." Punctually at the time appointed, every member of the House and Senate, except the President of the Senate, was here to be shown the work being done.

The Hon. Santiago Baca, of Albuquerque, unobtrusively whispered to me: "Sister, Colonel Chavez, President of the Senate, did not accompany us because you addressed your invitation 'to the Senate' instead of 'to the President.'" At once I rushed an invitation to him asking for half an hour of his busy time. Meanwhile, the visitors had noticed how few were the facilities we have to care for the sick. A gentleman representing the sympathy of all asked: "Sister, what can we do to assist in ameliorating the present condition of your hospital?"

"Before I answer the question, please read our daily record."

When the record had been examined, he said: "Gentlemen, the records show that not a patient admitted during the last three months has paid anything."

"Now, Sister, what can we do?" was repeated by one of the members.

"Pass a Relief Bill allowing the hospital $400.00 per month," I answered. One member remarked: "That is not enough."

I rejoined: "It would be $400.00 more monthly than we are getting at present."

One gentleman remarked: "The credit of assisting in the progress of our territory ought to be more evenly divided."

The visitors took their departure and I waited for the President of the Senate. In ten minutes the doorbell rang. I was there to answer it. In a glance I saw a well-groomed gentleman, with an angel sleeve coat and waxed moustache *à la Victorio Manuel*.

"I am Colonel Chavez," he said.

I replied: "I am Sister Blandina, who asked you for half an hour of your valuable time. Please follow me."

When we arrived at the surgical ward and he glanced at the patients, he exclaimed: "Sister, please excuse me from the rest of the tour through the hospital."

"These are our daily scenes. You promised one-half hour of your time."

He courteously followed. When every object of interest had been seen, he remarked: "We must all join to promote the progress in sight for our territory. I stand for whatever the members of this session will propose for the welfare of the people following the trend of your work."

The "Relief Bill" was passed, but it will be some months before we receive any benefit from it.

Some weeks after we had permission to take in patients who had no money, the head of the culinary department said to me: "Sister, we have not a handful of vegetables to prepare for dinner, and seventy-two patients, thirty-five orphans, and sixteen Sisters to feed. Please figure it out, you, who, I have been told, are never daunted!"

Smiling, I replied, "That problem will be solved in ten minutes."

I went to the rear of our empty vegetable garden and looked over the adobe wall into the Archbishop's garden. There I saw an abundance of cabbage, turnips, carrots, and what not. Most of the vegetables were buried heads down in the ground, roots showing above ground. I made one athletic spring (old habits die slowly) and landed near the cabbage patch. Throwing over into our vacant garden at least two dozen cabbage heads, I did the same with each of the other vegetables, only in greater number, as the sizes were smaller. Then I went to His Grace's door and rapped.

"Come in."

I opened the door and stood, saying: "I have come to make a confession out of the confessional." He looked at me with that benevolent expression which once seen can never be forgotten. In that look he also saw that I was covered with dust, and he said, "My little Sister, what have you been doing?"

"Stealing, Your Grace. With never a thought of restitution, I dug up enough vegetables from your garden to last us three days."

"And then?"

"Whatever you say."

"Tell Louis to give you all there are."

"Thank you very much," is all I could say.

Shortly after this, Mr. Frank Manzanares, of the firm of Browne and Manzanares,[21] sent sacks of coffee and sugar. I think His Grace is guilty.

The contractors working on the A. T. and Santa Fe advertised for me. "Free transportation. Big pay." Men were shipped by carloads. The contractors, having chosen the able bodied, the unsuitable were left to shift for themselves.

Picture the condition of affairs!

To the credit of the officials of the A. T. and Santa Fe, I shall say that Mr. Conant, the station agent, informed us that when we needed transportation for the men all we had to do was to give them a card on which should be written: "Pass this man or these men," and signed by the Sister's name.

Mr. A. A. Robinson, General Manager of the A. T. and Santa Fe, came to see us and inquired if he could do anything for us in transportation or freight. It was after his visit that Mr. Conant sent the above notice to us.

Jan., 1880.

My old acquaintance, "Billy the Kid" is using his gun freely. The people of the territory are aroused and demand his capture, dead or alive. Rewards have been offered for his capture.

Our Governor, Lewis Wallace, has shown heroic bravery by going to Lincoln County to try to pacify the storm. He had a number of interviews with "Billy," but to no effect. New rewards have been offered both by the Governor and the people to capture "Billy."

The work on the Industrial School continues, so does the hospital expense, but see what God does when other things fail.

The Reverend Antonio Fourchegu came this morning and said: "Sister, I want to help you a little. I am going to turn over to the credit of the Sisters of Charity 600 ewes, bringing 25 per cent interest yearly, and a two thousand dollar note, bearing 10 per cent interest, which you can claim very shortly, as you will notice by the date on the note. For these gifts I make the condition that I am to have a private room at St. Vincent Hospital, beginning in 1880. If I am not ill, I shall not come, but should I take sick, I want to secure a place to recover or go to God." So you see, Sister Justina, when one door is closed, another is opened.

I am going to write an incident of this good Father's missionary life. Galloping on the plains near Pecos, he saw a very strange looking animal — a quadruped. He determined to capture it. The animal ran swiftly away. Father Fourchegu followed till it was exhausted, when it backed against a tree, faced its pursuer, and with glaring eyes and sharp teeth, defended itself against its enemy, fighting and scratching furiously.

The Reverend Father captured the savage animal wrapping his coat around it. It was a little girl!

Father Fourchegu brought the child to us. With great difficulty we subdued her, cut her long, tangled hair, her long nails, and dressed her like the other girls. She retained that frightened look and propensity to scratch and to dig into the ground. At first she could not speak, only grunt, but in time she learned to speak also.

Some years before, a little girl had disappeared. The parents thought she was dead.

When the girl was brought to us she was the talk of the day. People came from far and near to see the wild girl. The newspapers had broadcasted the fact. Then came a man and his wife to see the child. They recognized her as their little daughter, Carmela, who had disappeared several years before.

Father Fourchegu's health continued good, and he did not claim the private room he had secured at the hospital.

Every time we — Sister Catherine and I — are seen going out in a borrowed jolt wagon, the message is broadcasted, "The Sisters have gone to pick up sick men on the plains. We must prepare for emergencies." When this was brought to my notice,

I could only smile. Everything available for the sick had already been placed at their service, but somehow or other our hospital became a regular omnibus; we did not refuse one penniless patient. We may be imposed upon, because we never question a man when he is too ill to answer.

A certain new physician brought in a patient one day, who was running a temperature of 105. The physician insisted on his fee before leaving. The patient mumbled with great difficulty, "My pocketbook is somewhere." I motioned the doctor to follow me, handed him the $10 fee, which he was trying to get from the patient and said, "Do not bring any more patients until your credentials are presented to the hospital authorities. Our hospital staff will attend to your patient." Dr. Longwell, chief physician, is nobly seconding our efforts to save the lives of the indigent sick strangers in a strange land, and, at the same time, he is trying to ease the physical work of the Sisters economically by discharging patients three days after they leave their beds.

To avoid a relapse of men that I fear are not strong enough to battle for work or something to eat, I have ordered wood by the cord and keep the weak men out of sight by having them sit in the rear yard and have them chop wood occasionally for five minutes. This will give them an added chance for life.

So far every man has understood my motive, but to-day an Irishman from the North of Ireland made this speech in one of the convalescent wards, "Men, when that little boss comes in again and tells any of us to go to the wood pile to chop wood flatly say, 'No, I am a patient. You receive plenty of money, or else you would not go on the plains and grading camps to hunt for the sick!'"

This speech was told me by a young Protestant who had also been discharged, but whose weakness made me fear for his life; so I concluded to have him dust my desk three times a day! I went directly to the ward where the man from the North of Ireland was trying to raise a mutiny and said:

"I understand that someone here has advised the men not to

chop wood when I ask them to do so?" A great big burly fellow took the floor.

"I am the man who told the men not to chop wood, and that you are well paid for what you do, or else you would not go hunting for the sick."

"Suppose you put this question to every man in this ward, beginning with yourself, 'How much have you paid since you were received into the hospital?'"

"I did not pay anything — you did not ask me to."

"No, sir, you were too ill when we found you on the Santa Fe trail. You may put the same question to any patient in the hospital. The reason I have been asking the discharged patients to go to the wood pile for five minutes is to let them gain strength gradually and avoid the danger of a relapse, fearing they may not soon get work and in all probability, have nothing to eat."

"I'll be hanged, Sister! I thought you were making money on us. I am a brute and could not understand why not a man here agreed with me. I will take my bundle and start on the road."

"Very well, some other poor fellow can have a chance for his life. Good-bye, and God speed you."

This afternoon twelve injured men were brought in from Apache Canyon. The men were working in a cut; the fuse went off prematurely, and twelve men were caught in the blast. How we did have to work to find place for them!

Six o'clock. As we were praying our beads in the Community room, I saw a big blaze from the hospital chimney above the rooms where were the last patients brought in. I made a spring, saying at the same time, "Mother of Mercy, help us!" I went to the convalescent ward and told all who were able to form in line to carry water to me to the second story. I sent one man for a bucket of salt, with instructions to bring the salt to me before the men handed me the water. I marvel how composedly I acted, because the thought uppermost in my mind was that the last patients will be cremated if the fire is not extinguished quickly.

I went to the roof of the first story. From here I looked to the roof of the second story. There a blaze was issuing from the chimney. There was nothing in sight to help me get to the hospital roof. I touched the three-inch drainer tin spout and soliloquized, "I cannot ascend on that." My next act from the hospital roof was to say: "You two men stand and let the third man get on your shoulders to hand me the bucket of salt." I threw the salt down the chimney. The sparks rushed out, but the blaze subsided. Water was handed me in the same manner. I poured one bucket down the chimney and nothing came out but black smoke; the fire was extinguished!

Suddenly I heard Dr. Symington ask the men: "Where is the ladder that Sister used to get on the roof? How did you reach salt and water to her?"

"We two men stood and Mike got on our shoulders and handed Sister what she wanted."

"That's all right, but how did Sister get up there? I saw the fire from my residence about a hundred feet from the hospital, and came immediately. Now that the fire is out, I want to know how Sister got on the roof?"

This question made me think, and, meanwhile, I began trembling, so much so that I had to sit on the roof. The reaction made me weak.

Diving quickly into psychic phenomena I knew I had been the subject of mind over matter. Dr. Symington belongs to the volunteer Bucket Brigade. After looking around a few seconds he did not refer to the subject again. I doubt not the men think I'm either a saint or a witch.

The whole scene could not have taken more than ten minutes.

While I was resting on the roof, the Sisters had gone to the different rooms to carry the blast-injured men to safety in case the fire could not be controlled.

Dear Sister Justina, so many unexpected events occur that I am at a loss which to jot down and which to omit. . . .

Please remember, I never speak of politics or the acts of politicians, but I consider this incident worth while. There are two political parties here, Republicans and Democrats. The first party goes by the name of the "Santa Fe Ring." This party has been doing things to suit themselves, so the Democrats say. This is how we came on the tapis. One of the "Santa Fe Ring" said to me, "Sister, Mr. —— will take my place on the Board of County Commission by one vote. I feel certain he will come to see you before the election and make many promises to help you!"

I had my own thoughts on the subject, but nothing annoys us except the want of means to care for the sick, to bury the dead, and to save the lives of strangers among strangers.

As was predicted, "The one to take my place by one vote," came to see me. Sure enough he intends to do much for the public through us. "The Republicans have carried things their way long enough. We, the Democrats, will do some bossing now," he announced. "The Democrats expect their whole ticket to be elected. I'm going to be a true friend to you, Sister."

"Thank you, sir, whatever you do for me will be for the benefit of those whom we serve."

The County had been allowing us $8 for every indigent patient who dies and whom we bury . . . that is, we prepare the deceased for burial, procure the grave and have it dug, make the coffin and transport the body to its resting place. To this I add a wreath of flowers, and when I return from the graveyard I invariably write to those connected with the deceased, mentioning the fact that, in lieu of his having passed to God among strangers, we endeavored to supply the place of those who loved him by giving full attention to his needs, after which we placed a wreath of flowers on his coffin and accompanied him to his place of rest.

Among the powers that be, there is graft. County warrants are issued for debts assumed by County Commissioners. These warrants are depreciated to fifty per cent of their face value. The graft comes in when those who have the power to depreciate, purchase, and turn in at face value. This graft has not affected the $8 county warrant allowed us for the burials of the penniless.

Yet we have come to the end of our resources on the amount allowed, though I help to make the coffins.

At present we have a patient who cannot survive the day, so while attending to some business on the plaza, I stepped into the store of our new County Commissioner. He expressed himself pleased to see me, and asked that I look at the new equipment of his office. "You see, Sister, I want to do honor to our party." (Political, of course.)

"I noticed by this morning's paper that you buried unfortunate John."

"Yes, he was buried."

"Presumably it entails some expense to bury a man."

"I used the prisoners to do the work, still it cost the county $30."

"It does not require any stretch of imagination to see that it would cost $30," I answered. "While we are on the subject of burials, I wish to mention that we have a patient who will scarcely pass the day. We have been receiving $8 for the burial of every poor man. Of course, you know we have not been receiving patients who can pay, in order to save the lives of those who are sick and penniless. We can manage to bury a corpse for $15.00, which, of course, you will allow."

"Just because I am chairman of the County Commissioners I must economize. Now, Sister, do as you have been doing — charge the county $8.00."

"It cannot be done, Mr. ——." With this I took my leave. On arriving at the hospital I was informed that the moribund patient had passed away.

I returned to the Commissioner who intended to do so much for me and said, "The person of whom I spoke to you a while since was called to eternity. Will you allow $15.00 for his burial?"

"Now, Sister, you must help me to economize. Bury him for what you have been receiving, $8.00."

I made answer, "In fifteen minutes the corpse will be brought to your office. You can economize as you wish. Good-bye."

I had walked about forty steps when the Commissioner's voice said, "Sister!" I stood. "We will allow you $15.00 for the burial of each poor patient."

"Thank you, sir."

The Vicar-General has given us a long strip of land in the burying ground in the rear of San Miguel College.

I may as well mention that often I scribble on waste paper, slip it in my desk drawer, and it or the slips remain there until such time as I am able to clear it, hence some have no date.

This day — no date — a convalescent and myself lowered somebody's darling into a coffin. I borrowed a wagon and made a round of the hospital to find patients available to accompany the corpse with me to the graveyard. My companion is always an orphan girl. The only available help I could get was a weak patient to drive, a one-legged man who carried a crutch, and a one-armed man. The funeral cortege started. All went well until we had to carry the coffin. The mules were skittish, so the old man stayed with the wagon while the one-legged man and one-armed man were asked to carry the light part of the coffin. I took the heavy weight. No vehicle is allowed in the graveyard. The grave that had been dug was four rods from where we had to carry the dead weight. All went well with me for a few minutes when I felt the weight too much for me. I exercised my will to the limit so as not to let the coffin drop. But suddenly my sight left me. I asked, "How far to the grave?" From a tired voice the answer came: "Not very far, Sister." At last we got to the grave. I heard one man say, "Here we are. Lower!" after which I stood. I was on the point of telling the two men that I had lost my sight, when I saw as quickly as I had been deprived of sight. Of course, weakness was the cause. The men rode to the hospital. My companion and myself, to save time, took a short route. When we were near the entrance of the hospital, an agent of the A. T. and Santa Fe, who apparently had seen us from some distance, said, "Sister, will you please step in my office a minute?" Which my companion and myself did. The agent introduced me to four officials of the A. T. and Santa Fe. Mr. Goddard said, "May I ask what you have been doing?"

"Burying a dead man."

"Could not others have done it?"

"Possibly."

Mr. A. Robinson, general manager, repeated his desire to be of service to us. I remarked: "We may soon have to freight from Chicago."

"Just let me know, Sister, when I can do anything for you."

The stone and brick work on the Industrial School is nearing completion. A messenger came to say that Mr. Mouly has typhoid fever. We had him brought to the hospital. Both doctors and Sisters gave him every attention, but God took him — a talented young artist. He goes to his Judge with a good record.

§ 16

Jan., 1880.

We are drawing on amateur talent in Santa Fe for a concert we intend to give at the opening of the Industrial School. Mr. Wedles will preside at the piano. Mrs. Symington will give one number, a vocal solo. Our orphan girls will fill in the greater part of the programme. It is a well known fact that Mrs. Symington and the doctor were the actors in the largest romance ever enacted since the Spanish invasion.

Mrs. Symington's parents and the parents of a distinguished, rich and powerful family in Old Mexico, arranged an alliance between the two families. Neither of the betrothed had ever met. The day for the wedding was set and elaborate preparations were being made by both families. The groom gathered his retinue in marching order, cavalry style, a coach drawn by a span of the best bred horses decked in green and gold and all mountings solid silver — on horses and coach. The cavalcade approached the splendor of old time princes going from one kingdom to another to claim a bride.

A musical band rejoiced the travelers. When the groom and

his followers arrived in Old Albuquerque (as the Spaniards express it) "All the world turned out." The servants were told to prepare the bride-to-be to meet her affianced – the bride was nowhere to be seen. A note stated that she and Dr. Symington had gone to Santa Fe to be married.

Dr. Symington had followed the Santa Fe Trail as a teamster and landed in Old Albuquerque, where he met Miss Armijo. Miss Armijo had been educated in St. Louis at the Visitation Convent and had imbibed the idea of choosing her own mate for life.

The Doctor had his M.D. degree, but came out as a teamster for frolic and ended in marriage.

Jan. 25, 1880.

To-day one of our patients asked: "Do you know that Joe dances to the moon?"

"I do not know that he dances at all," I replied.

The patient added: "At about 10 o'clock P.M., Joe will go to the convalescents' adobe roof and dance as queer a death dance as any Apache can do."

Last night after we had retired, the inside doorbell rang. Intermingled with the sounds of the bell were groans, and occasionally the word "Sister" could be distinguished.

Five of us were dovetailed in a room 15 by 15 feet. I noticed all had heard the bell and groans. I prepared to meet the trouble. Meanwhile, Sister Catherine's gentle voice whispered, "Sister Blandina, that is our Joe. I am going out to see what is the matter."

Sister stood near me, but made no effort to go toward Joe. I went where Joseph stood ringing the bell and groaning and asked: "What is it, Joseph? Are you sick?"

"Yes, Sister, yes, Sister. I am afraid."

"Sister Catherine and I will go with you to your room. You go in and go to bed, then we will come and pray a third part of the Rosary with you."

He went to his room and to bed. We followed and began

the Rosary. The prayers calmed the worried mind. When we were ready to leave he said: "Sister, I must make a confession."

"Shall we go for the priest?" I asked.

"No, let me make it to you in Italian while I have the courage. What I did is so much on my mind that if I do not get it off I will go crazy."

"Joseph, my friend, we will remain on our knees until morning, then call the padre to hear your confession."

"No, no, Sister! I must get rid of this horrid oppression now, or I will die or go crazy." With the last sentence he began a tale of grievance against himself.

Ah! Guardian of his soul, soothe his anguish and offer these spasms of pain to the compassionate Heart which rejects no one who is repentant.

Joseph, the scientist, the musician, the home embellisher, the gentle, voluntarily exiling himself! All saints are not buried.

My dear Sister Justina, mountain high are our problems piling.

Consumptives, men with money looking to become millionaires, land-grabbers, experienced and inexperienced miners, quacks, professional deceivers, publicity men lauding gold mines that do not exist. I could use a half a dozen more adjectives and yet not touch on all the methods of deception carried on. They are all here in advance of the railroad.

This morning Mr. Seligman — one of our merchants here — sent me a paper with news from the mining camps. The headlines gave me a nightmare surprise. In a semi-circle with capital letters was printed:

"Sister Blandina's mine is being worked. Gold found in abundance."

I had heard that some persons in St. Louis were in danger of being financially ruined by bogus advertisements; so when I read this, I took a Sister companion and rode to Los Cerrillos where the supposed mine was located. From some men we had befriended I ascertained who had the untruthful heading printed. I was also told that arrangements had been made to sell stocks of this bogus mine to a certain lady in St. Louis. So I faced the originator of the scheme.

"Mr. ——, I understand you are prepared to sell shares on Sister Blandina's mine, which, according to your statement is yielding lode that produces more gold than any mine discovered to date. In a friendly way I advise you to drop your method of getting-rich-quick and resort to hard work instead. You remember when you and your so-called company came to me at our hospital in Santa Fe, showing me a specimen of yellow clay claimed by you to have been dug from the southwest corner of our land and which you said had been assayed and showed proximity to a vein of gold and your company corroborated your statement and you asked permission to put your men to work to verify your words? You may also remember my answer: 'More to us is the life of the men perishing for want of proper care. If there is gold on our land it can wait a little longer to be discovered.' Instinctively I knew you were scheming to deceive, but my intuition did not cover your present line of action. So change your mode of trying to get rich, because it will not work to your benefit either here or hereafter."

"Do you intend to expose me?" he asked.

"You have exposed yourself. A large number of the men whom we have been instrumental in saving have left us with grateful feelings and more serious thoughts than they had when they started on their hunt for riches. Many of those will not forget that all for them would have ended in an unmarked grave had not willing hands stretched toward them. Their serious thoughts will prevent your carrying out your nefarious designs, because the consciences of those befriended are your exposure."

"All right, Sister. You win."

Our mountains are literally choked with rich metals, but it requires capital and experience and patience to reach success. Here and there some hard-working miner does strike a rich lode. The discoverer, not having capital, usually sells out to the man who can purchase his claim.

We expect the railroad to reach Santa Fe some time in February, 1880.

Ordering merchandise from a distance has not been satisfactory with regard to our roof material for the Industrial School. I wrote to a firm in Chicago which had sent us a catalogue of roofs and material, and asked if their corrugated iron could be worked on a mansard roof. The answer was positive:

"Yes, our corrugated iron can be used advantageously on your mansard roof." So the roofing recommended was ordered and landed in El Moro, Colorado, from where it was freighted to Santa Fe on ox teams. This was over a year ago. You see we have to look ahead when depending on mule or ox teams. At the time of our freighting the conditions on the Santa Fe Trail were not secure from attacks from either white desperadoes or savage Indians, although the United States Government had dotted forts here and there on the Trail to protect travelers and freight caravans. The corrugated iron cannot be used on our building, so there remains nothing to do but go on to St. Louis for our roofing.

The A. T. and Santa Fe Railroad reached here February 9, 1880. The Governor, Lew Wallace, and people were overjoyed when the last spike was driven in. Now Sister Augustine and myself will go on to St. Louis to purchase roof material and return with an expert man to put it on.

I must tell you, dear Sister Justina, that the erection of this building has brought out many ludicrous opinions. Some asked: "How can a building sixty feet high, and a cupola on top of that, stand? The first big wind will blow it down." Others said that if the inside adobes were not laid with mud, the first rainy weather would melt the building. These critics thought the roof would be mud-covered. So many were the criticisms on the building that the Vicar-General said to me one day:

"Sister, you remind me of the crocodile, which looks to neither right nor left, but makes straight for its prey." I confess my ignorance, I do not see the analogy.

The natives who have been educated abroad are our standbys; the others, who are afraid something disastrous will happen to the building which was erected under the most peculiar circumstances, are those who have not seen anything but one-story adobe buildings and mud roofs.

We started our own brickyard, opened our own quarry, had our lime burnt to order, and had our lumber hand-sawed by our natives. After this had been done, a sawmill was started at Glorieta and a planing-mill was opened in Las Vegas. There was a sawmill sixty miles this side of Trinidad, but having to rely on teams to haul the lumber, it was better economy to do as we did. Can you picture what work this entailed?

We have a very witty Sister here. Spanish is her mother-tongue. During the process of building she would come one time with: "Sister, there is a gentleman who wants to see 'La Hermana Mayor' (the most elderly Sister)," then place herself at a distance to see the gentleman look over my shoulders to watch for the coming of the elderly Sister. Again she would come and say: "There are some rancheros who want to speak to the 'Sister of The Sheep.'" Possibly the next day she would come to me and say: "The lumber men are here and want to see the 'Sister of the Lumber.'" I have had as many adjective names as are the names of the material we have used, though we did not use sheep in the building — but we did use sheep to pay off some of the workmen. To add to this I found a laughable rhyme (written by the witty Sister and placed on my desk) referring to every name that has been applied to me. No one quite understands what my particular work is, as they see me everywhere.

I am sorry I mislaid Sister's effusion. The most amusing incidents brace me up, but too much time cannot be given to any one thing. There is certainly no monotony in our work.

Feb. 12, 1880.

Here is the latest criticism on the Industrial School Building.

Some ladies who are not troubled for want of money took this view: "If those Sisters who had no cash to build succeeded in putting up the finest building in the Territory, why cannot we, who have money, build our own homes?" It would take pages to note all that has been said about the structure.

The San Miguel College is also building. The President, Brother Rudolph, came to see me under the impression that we intend to make an appeal to our people in Santa Fe, in order to furnish the Industrial School. Here is our interview:

"Sister, do you intend to collect in Santa Fe to help you?"

"I have not given the subject a thought."

"Because if you expect to make a collection I will temporarily have to stop work on the new college. Brother Baldwin (vice-president) expects to raise $3,000 here to meet our next payment, which will be due in April."

"I am happy to tell you that none of us thought of soliciting in Santa Fe, perhaps the reason is that our people have been so wonderfully good to us."

"Well, Sister, I was misinformed."

"Please tell Brother Baldwin I wish him all the success his endeavor deserves."

§ 17

April 10, 1880.

Dear Sister Justina:

We have just returned from St. Louis with a workman who is an expert and will lay the slate on the Industrial School. Mr. Burke comes with the intention of doing prospecting work. This will exempt us from paying his expenses to return to St. Louis. Our roof will be the first slate roof in the territory.

April 12. — This morning I made a survey of the premises and missed the ten boxes of corrugated iron. Sister Louise was in charge of affairs while we were in St. Louis. I asked Sister Louise what she had done with the corrugated iron.

"Did you not order it to be sold and taken away?"

"Who took it?" I asked.

"Really, Sister, I did not ask his name. He said you told him to sell it, which he succeeded in doing."

I saw we had been over-reached.

The point was to find out who took the iron.

Before we left for St. Louis some gentleman spoke of forming a gas company. With this in mind I went to the only hardware store in town and asked if anything came of the proposed gas company.

"No, Sister, not yet."

I went to the station agent who asked many questions about our trip. This gave me a chance to ask questions and this was the first:

"Have you had any heavy freighting lately?"

"The heaviest from Santa Fe," he replied, "was your corrugated iron consigned to Colonel Carpenter at Los Cerrillos. I hope Mr. —— paid you a good price for it, because it was just what the Colonel wanted for his smelter."

So now I know who shipped the iron.

This party has a planingmill and is soliciting orders. I gave him one for some doors and sashes. The order was delivered quickly and in good condition. I gave a second order which likewise was filled promptly and satisfactorily. For the first order I mailed a check by return mail. After the second order was filled, this notice was mailed him:

"Mr. ——, there are forty dollars due you; this being the difference between your bill and the price of the corrugated iron, which you sold. Shall we mail you a check for the amount, or will you be in town soon?"

The next train brought Mr. —— to Santa Fe.

"Sister, what am I to understand by your letter to me stating you owe me $40.00?"

"Forty dollars is the difference between the last order we gave you, and the price of the corrugated iron which you sold."

He asked: "What has corrugated iron to do with your order to my mill?"

I told him: "Only this. When you pay for the iron which belonged to us, we shall pay your bill."

He answered: "I see, Sister, you compel me to resort to law to have you pay me what you owe me."

I said: "Suit yourself, Mr. ——."

Thirty-six hours after this interview his wife came to see me.

"Are you Sister Blandina?"

"I am."

"I'm Mrs. ——. Is it possible you are trying to ruin my husband and family by claiming money not owed you?"

"I trust not, Mrs. ——."

"My husband tells me you claim money for a sale of which he knows nothing. Sister, I cannot imagine a Sister of Charity trying financially to ruin a family. My husband put forth every effort to establish a mill for the benefit of this Territory. Now, that he is established, you claim money not owed you."

I replied: "Mrs. ——, suppose you let your husband and myself settle this business. I would suggest that you do not make this public — unless your husband tells you to."

"I will make it public. I will not see my husband and family ruined because you claim money not due you. I am going now to your own lawyer and expose you."

"Let me beg of you to permit this affair to be settled between us without any publicity," I entreated, "this I ask for the sake of yourself and family."

Impetuously she answered: "Your plausibility has no effect on me. I go straight to Mr. Catron." With this last answer, she turned toward the door.

I spoke again. "Mrs. ——."

She turned and gave me an indignant look.

I continued: "I will speak more clearly if you will calm yourself."

She retorted: "I am as calm as a wife can be when she sees her husband and children on the brink of ruin and that by a Sister of Charity."

Then I added: "Will you return to your home and deliver to your husband a message from me which I believe will settle our differences?"

Mrs. — cheerfully responded, "I will be glad to deliver your message."

This was the message I wrote him:

"Mr. — I had hoped this affair would be settled without anyone's intervention.

"You are the consignee of our corrugated iron to Colonel Carpenter at Los Cerrillos. Mr. Conant, the freight agent, has your signature. I did my best to save your reputation and have you retain the love and respect of your wife and children; which to hold or lose is in your hands.

"Yours to rehabilitate and not to destroy.

"Sister Blandina."

April 23, 1880.

Three days later, Mr. — sent a lawyer to receive $40.00 from us, and who gave us a receipt in full for the second order delivered to us.

April 30, 1880.

My Dear Sister Justina:

I am beginning to learn that human nature, since Adam was too pliant, and Eve too curious — is a strong mixture of good and evil.

The thing that puzzles me most is that they for whom we make the most sacrifices become the shrewdest in over-reaching us.

The latest that causes my wonder is this: A hasty message was brought me at 9:30 P.M. "Mr. — is on his way to the hospital. He is bringing his wife, who is in a dying condition. The high altitude has affected her heart."

We managed to make place for her. She was carried in at 10:30 P.M., and passed away at 11:00 P.M. The husband was inconsolable. He has a sawmill near Glorieta and she did the cooking for the hands at work, which helped him to carry on the sawmill. He gave me a pathetic story of his troubles and wanted to know if we could not accept a note on thirty days' time for lumber which we still need for different purposes.

"Whether you want the lumber or not, I'll be at the bank to pay the face value of the note. By doing me this favor, I can pay my men and save my mill."

After consultation, we thought no greater act of charity could be performed.

He told us he was a church-going man, but none of his denomination lived in this part of the country. Being a church-going man had no effect on me, but having seen his wife die and buried, and knowing that every man who drifted this way and had no capital to rely on, would claim his money for work done, and would surely endanger his mill if hands were not paid, we treated him as we would wish to be treated ourselves.

We got notice from the bank that the note was due, and we paid it. No sight of the mill man, nor have we heard from him. I repeat what I wrote of "Our Joseph" — time will tell.

Of the many patients brought to the hospital, only one remains of whose cure we are in doubt. This patient was caught in a blast; one eye is entirely gone. Dr. Longwill thinks there is a possibility of retaining the sight of his other eye, but the patient would have to be under the care of an eye specialist.

I wrote to Sister Gabriella in charge of the Good Samaritan, at Cincinnati, asking if she would admit Tom Gleason in hopes that he might retain the sight of one eye.

The answer was prompt from her kind heart: "Send him on, Sister Blandina. I understand you are doing your share. I must do mine."

The contractor for whom Mr. Gleason worked sent word along the line of workers saying, "Tom is going to be sent to Cincinnati in hopes his one eye can be saved. Let us make a collection for him." The collection was made, and we sewed the money in a bag and helped Mr. Gleason to store it away on his person.

We put him on the train *via* St. Louis to Cincinnati — Good Samaritan Hospital.

To-day, May 2, 1880, Dr. Symington was angry with me for attending to a patient without my gloves.

He remarked, "Do you realize the danger you run?"

I answer, "Yes, Doctor, but I am not afraid."

He countered, "And the disease is not afraid of you."

This patient literally fell to pieces.

"Our Joseph" and myself made his coffin, but when we were ready to place him in, piece by piece, every convalescent patient disappeared, including "Our Joseph." So piece by piece I placed the corrupted body in the coffin. The stench made me think of the descriptions of the lower regions given by Dante in his *Inferno*. I was just putting the lid on the coffin when "Our Joseph" came to the mortuary room door.

The expression on his face showed his fear of infection and shame at having left me alone. Though Dr. Symington professes no religion, I believe he was much disturbed because I gave so much time to this Lutheran patient. "A man is a man for all that."

§ 18

June, 1880.

How embracing and encouraging the atmosphere when you see a woman of distinction give her earthly possessions and herself entirely to God's service. Such a person is Doña Ana María Ortiz. She is the sister of the late Vicar-General Ortiz, who had been appointed Vicar-General by the Right Reverend Bishop Zubiria, Bishop of Durango, Old Mexico.

When our present Most Rev. J. B. Lamy was appointed to the bishopric of Santa Fe, Padre Ortiz was Vicar-General depending on the Bishop of Durango, Old Mexico. Hence, when Rt. Rev. J. B. Lamy came to Santa Fe to claim his See by appointment from Rome, Vicar-General Ortiz calmly said: "You will have to get your credentials from the Bishop of Durango." It was then that Rt. Rev. J. B. Lamy performed an act, the heroism of which was never known before, nor can it ever under the same conditions be repeated — to travel from Santa Fe to Durango on horseback to ask for the necessary documents to have himself accepted as the lawful Bishop of the newly established See of historic Santa Fe — a vast expanse of over 400,000 square miles.

The wealthiest inhabitants of these regions would consider a journey from New Mexico to Durango, Old Mexico, a hazardous undertaking even when accompanied by a caravan of one hundred wagons and twice as many men, not counting the advance scouts and rear watch. Yet our intrepid French missionary waived aside all human considerations, though at least six Indian tribes were constantly on the alert to attack any being that would give exercise to their war propensities to kill and appropriate anything that came their way.

Picture the work of this brave heart on his return. He showed his right to the See to Vicar-General Ortiz who acquiesced and remained in his position. But what of those who had gradually put aside the discipline of the Church and whose conscience pricked hard? When the capable historian will review the life of the Most Rev. J. B. Lamy, beautiful revelations will surely come to light.

My Dear Sister Justina:

That corrugated iron took so much of my time and thought that I neglected to mention an incident of our stay in St. Louis. While there we were guests of the Sisters of Loretto. Mother Magdalen, Superior of the Loretto Sisters in Santa Fe and vicinity, made us promise we would be her Sisters' guests in St. Louis. This Mother Magdalen is the essence of Charity. I must tell this about her. Her Community does not make use of mirrors. Three days ago I was traveling from Albuquerque to Lamy Junction. The conductor came to speak to me.

"Sister, is it possible for a person to forget what he looks like?"

I replied, "Well — yes. Would a person recognize himself after a solitary confinement of three years?"

He continued: "Last week on my morning trip from Socorro, I noticed a Sister in one of the cars. When I got to her she told me please to ask that Sister at some distance in front of her to come and sit with her. I replied: 'You are the only Sister on the train.'"

"'Pardon me, conductor — please look again.'"

"I looked again and saw only the Sister's image in the mirror opposite her! I then asked, 'How long since you saw a looking-glass?' 'Forty-three years,' she said."

While in St. Louis, Mr. Martin, manufacturer of men's clothes, had us under his special care. He took us to High Mass at the Cathedral. At the Offertory *Madre Del Som' Amore* was sung as a quartette and in excellent Italian. Mr. Martin informed us that the Offertory and Mass (Mozart's 12th) was selected to please us. After Mass he drove to Mrs. Slevins (formerly of Cincinnati) and there a very pleasant surprise had been prepared. Just as the signal for Grace was given, the folding doors were thrown open and Rt. Rev. Bishop P. J. Ryan entered and said Grace. Bishop Ryan is considered one of the best orators of the day. Though our trip to St. Louis was merely a business one, our friends added much pleasure to it. My only regret was that Sister Augustine could not see her way clear to give time enough to visit our Motherhouse, being so near Cincinnati. No pleasure without its corresponding pain.

§ 19

July, 1880.

Sisters Augustine and Pauline have gone to some near springs in hopes of being relieved of rheumatism. The only worth while act I have done since Sister Augustine's departure is to dismiss a postulant who underhandedly sent for her relatives to come for her, but repented the act after they arrived. With her people is her place. It is difficult for me to understand anyone putting his hand to the plow and then looking back. But in this case there was no vocation to the religious life.

Several others have applied, but we are careful whom to admit. Personally, I would prefer the time of probation to take place at Mt. St. Vincent. Why should the subject in question have recourse to a dishonorable way of leaving? She came of her own free will, and all she had to do was to say she desired to return to her home.

July 5. Monday. — We celebrated the Fourth of July to-day. While explaining to our orphan girls the full importance of this day, a messenger came to speak to me privately. The knowledge he imparted aged me ten years in a few minutes. The interview ended by the person (one of the highest theologians here) saying, "I had no idea the subject of my visit would so affect you." The import of the interview was to form a separate community from our Motherhouse. My answer was such a firm "NO" that my allegiance to the rules and constitutions of the Sisters of Charity of Cincinnati, Ohio, cannot be called in question. I have the key now to things that have puzzled me for the past few years. The proposition will come up again.

The reasons given for a new community are, "You are so far from the Motherhouse, and the local Superior is restricted by rule in many ways; waiting answers to permissions asked is a slow process. Moreover, few understand the needs of our southwestern missions. Only those who are actively engaged in the work are fit judges."

I reasoned with the theologian, "The Jesuits are here and (in my estimation) they are one of the best organized and one of the best governed Orders in the Church. Their General resides in Rome; it is somewhat farther than Cincinnati." The theologian left me saying, "I will not take this as your final answer."

July 23. — "Billy the Kid" is playing high pranks. The Governor and the people of the Territory have offered big rewards for his capture, dead or alive.

Aug. 30. — Many events have taken place since July 23rd. We expect Mother Regina. The subject of establishing a new community has been threshed out with a number of our best theologians. The pivot upon which the new community relies is immovable in her loyalty to Mother Seton's Daughters; hence I predict there will be no new community. The Motherhouse archives will receive the proceedings of conferences on the subject.

October. — Mother Regina and companion, Sister Baptist, have come and gone. Five new Sisters are added to our working force. Sister Augustine has been recalled to the Motherhouse. Sister Louise missioned to Trinidad. While Mother Regina was here, the present Superior of the Jesuits in the Southwest, Rev. Father Gentile, S.J., and the ex-Superior, Rev. Father Gasparri, S.J., came to apply to have our Sisters open a school in Old Albuquerque. Mother sent me in to make such arrangements as would be agreeable to both parties. It was agreed that the Jesuits would build a house for the Sisters, furnish it, and give them the deed in fee simple.

The Sisters were to support themselves.

All spiritual needs were to be rendered by the Jesuits. We at once began to put aside articles which will be of service for the new mission.

Feb., 1881.

Rev. Donato M. Gasparri, S.J., wrote to say that Doña Nieves Armijo wants to see me in Albuquerque in order to make us a donation. Sister Augusta and myself went down. We were met and escorted to Doña Nieves' residence and ushered into a room where Lawyer Werner was seated surrounded by a stack of papers. After a few words of greetings, the lawyer told us the reason for wishing our presence. He said: "Doña Nieves desires to donate to you this residence and all that surrounds it, garden and vineyard, etc." The offer did not elate me one iota. I thought of the daughter, her husband and their children. Meanwhile the daughter passed the door, and one glance showed me she was much disturbed. A few seconds after, her husband rushed by, and I drew my conclusions. The mother,

Doña Nieves, is doing some sort of retaliation, so when the lawyer said, "Sister, will you accept the deeds in fee simple?" I replied, "No, sir." He looked at me sharply and said:

"Do you know what you are rejecting?"

We spoke Spanish so that Doña Nieves might understand. She withdrew while the lawyer was trying to convince me to accept the gift. Presently she returned and announced she had gone to see Father Gasparri, S.J., to beg him to advise me to accept the property. His answer to her was:

"Sister understands her business."

As you may judge, dear Sister Justina, I did constructive work on this trip. Sister Augusta is puzzled at my closing the subject as I did, especially as both location and building are ideal for a convent.

March, 1881.

The contractors on the A. T. and Santa Fe road have been insisting on our going to make a collection for the hospital, so Sister Catherine and I went to San Marcial where workers from Kansas were employed. To save time, Sister went to one group of workers, I to the other. The first workman I spoke to was a tall black-bearded, sharp-eyed man who impressed me as one who had read plenty against nuns; he was between two minds — whether to ignore me, or insult me. He stared at me while I said, "We are making a collection for the Santa Fe Hospital. Will you subscribe?" In surly tones he answered, "No, ma'am, I never get sick."

"In case you should need our services, do not hesitate to come. The surest admittance card is sick and moneyless," was my response to his surly answer.

From San Marcial we went to Socorro, and returned in four days to San Marcial. We make it a point to look up the sick, because the climate plays havoc with newcomers who are not properly nourished.

The proprietress of the only private hotel heard we were in town and sent a messenger to us to invite us to be her guests.

We accepted the courtesy. The neighborhood wanted to give us a pleasant evening, so it was one stream of visitors. While we were taken up with one group of visitors the doorbell rang. The person who answered the call came to say that it was a railroad man with his arm in a sling asking shelter for the night.

The landlady said there was no place for him. The message was delivered, but the man began pleading to be taken in. He said, "I have a large splinter in my hand and it is beginning to fester. If I remain out all night and catch cold, I know I will lose my arm. Please let me in, if only to sit near a fire." The answer was given again, "We have no vacant place." I said to the proprietress, "If you will permit, we shall give up one of our rooms and attend to the man's arm." The lady of the house said, "Here is what we will do, Sister, put a cot in the kitchen for him." I was highly pleased over the arrangement and asked if I might attend to his arm at once.

In the last group of men who had come to see us were four young Jews, as kind-hearted as they were alert, on business matters. The four put themselves at our service. In half an hour's time we had the patient as comfortable as could be. The instant I saw the sufferer I recognized him as the man who told me, "I never get sick." I gave no sign of recognition, but said:

"Tomorrow morning I shall put you on the train for Santa Fe. Go at once to St. Vincent Hospital. There you will receive the attention you need."

§ 20

March, 1881.

Dearest Sister Justina:

Here is a wee bit of news for you. I am to be in Cincinnati at the Motherhouse to make the July retreat!

When I was sent to the Southwestern missions in 1872, owing to the difficulty of traveling, we did not expect the pleasure of meeting at the Motherhouse for the annual retreat. The advance of the railroad has brought great progress particularly in facilities for traveling. Unquestionably there will be many climatic changes.

Dr. M. Beshoar, of Trinidad, Colorado, who is a scientist as well as a physician, claims that at one time tropical fruits grew in this latitude. Another student of climatic changes calls attention to small mounds that grow weeds which must have been produced by water-covered earth, hence he asserts that at some age, far removed from us, these dry regions of sea-growing weeds were a vast volume of water.

None of us would murmur if the clouds opened their gates oftener than once a year. Our rainy season is during the middle of August, September and October. I have seldom seen umbrellas or overshoes, because when it rains it generally pours. Immigration and the cultivation of the soil will, of course, make for more rain. . . .

This morning Mr. La Casagne came to say that a friend of his had put a revolver to his temple and fired, but missed his intent by a small margin. The man spoken of has cancer of the mouth.

Up to yesterday he could room by himself and order what he wished. His money having given out made him attempt suicide. He is very sensitive. Mr. La Casagne persuaded him to apply to the hospital for admittance, which he did through his friend, but on consideration that only one Sister should ever see him "and Sister, I promised him no one would wait on him but yourself," added Mr. La Casagne.

As I am going to Cincinnati, I had to refer the case to Sister Cephas, who is in charge. The dear soul was much perplexed when I mentioned cancer. Sister asked if it is usual to admit cancer patients. I told her it was the only application from a cancer patient we ever had.

"Well, Sister, if you think he should be admitted I suggest he be placed in an outside room by himself."

I told her that we had no vacant room either inside or facing the street, but that we could have one built before sundown.

Sister smilingly said, "Well, have it built."

I went to one of the convalescent patients and said, "Mr. Atkins, we are obliged to put up a one-room house before sundown. We have seasoned lumber, two window frames and sashes and one door. The rainy season will not be here for some months. This will give time to waterproof the roof."

"Yes, Sister, but what about the foundation?"

"This is an emergency room. We shall build it on props of which you will find enough in the carpenter shop. By the way, Mr. Atkins, the person who is to occupy the room is a carpenter who studied in a trade school. Put Joseph and Tom to dig the prop holes, while I go order more nails and screws." When I returned, willing hands from the convalescent wards were in each other's way trying to have the room built before sundown. By 5 P.M. the house on props was ready for occupancy; by six, the patient was in it. I was as happy as when the last spike of the A. T. and Santa Fe road was driven in.

Unfortunate "Billy the Kid!" His marauding has drawn the attention of the whole Territory, and the "Kid" is as confident of safety as though he had a battalion at his command. It has been bruited about that he intends undoing Governor Wallace. Friends of law and order are on the *qui vive* that no harm come to the author of *Ben Hur*.

April 24. We have a patient who is a real tenderfoot, and who came to prospect. He tells me he is going to Los Cerrillos. He is splendidly groomed and wears valuable jewelry. I advised him to leave all valuables at the bank for safe-keeping and wear miner's clothes while in camp. He did not take the precaution necessary. Two weeks later his corpse was consigned to St. Louis, his home city. Sunday he dressed in fine clothes. The miners take off Sunday, not to honor God, but to debauch. When one of the miners saw our patient so well groomed, he said to him, "You have no right among us," and with his words went the shot which killed him. The murderer was intoxicated and is now in jail with "Billy the Kid," who attempted to carry out his threat against Governor Wallace, but the latter was well guarded by every honest man in the Territory — hence Billy's capture. My first free hours will be given to visit the prisoners.

May 16 — I have just returned from the jail. The two prisoners were chained hands and feet, but the "Kid" besides being cuffed hands and feet, was also fastened to the floor. You can imagine the extreme discomfort of the position. When I got into the prison-cell and "Billy" saw me, he said — as though we had met yesterday instead of four years ago — "I wish I could place a chair for you, Sister."

At a glance I saw the contents of the prison. Two empty nail kegs, one empty soap box, one backless chair, upon which sat the man who had shot our patient. After a few minutes' talk, the "Kid" said to me:

"Do what you can for Kelly," pointing to the chair, "this is his first offense, and he was not himself when he did it. I'll get out of this; you will see, Sister."

Think, dear Sister Justina, how many crimes might have been prevented, had someone had influence over "Billy" after his first murder. The plains are broad. His ascendancy was instantaneous over the minds of our free-lance cowboys, who are spurred on by a freedom that is not freedom. Finding himself captain and dictator, with no religious principles to check him, he became what he is — the greatest murderer of the Southwest.

I marvel at the assurance of the chained youth. No one can surmise how he can escape punishment this time. Mr. Kelly, his companion prisoner, is much dejected — fully realizing the enormity of his crime. Were not the doings of these two captives publicly known, I would not mention them — for what a prisoner says to me remains my property.

June 12 — Picture me with a dozen odd jobs attending to the needs of the would-be-suicide cancer patient; but for his soul's sake it is worth while. His attitude toward God has changed — still here is my dilemma. I dare not leave him when I go to Cincinnati, and how presume to bring him to the Good Samaritan? To-day I will send a letter to my dear large-hearted Sister Gabriella and ask her to admit him into the Good Samaritan. Well I realize he is nearing eternity, but his peace with God is not complete.

June 20 — On the fifteenth of last month, Mr. Lionel Sheldon[22] took his place at the Palace as Governor. A committee of two lawyers have asked me to make an appeal to the new Governor in behalf of Mr. Kelly, the murderer of one of our patients. Mr. Kelly makes no pretense. He is weighted down by the act he did while intoxicated.

This 2 P.M. a wire from our dear, dear Sister Gabriella says: "Bring your patient." What do you think of that for charity without gloss?

We — myself, Sister Pauline and a postulant, Doña Carlotta, and our patient, of course, started for the East on the 22nd. I must tell you some traits of this new aspirant who wishes to serve God. The first time I met her at her home she was surrounded by a bevy of servants. I thought at the time that she was training them to acts of benevolence, despite the fact that they were employed to wait on her, her father and brother.

A few months after this, the Rev. D. M. Gasparri, S.J., wrote, "Doña Carlotta is on her way to you — care for her — soul and body."

She came and made arrangements for a private room, "but allow me to make one condition — I wish to be served the exact kind of food the Sisters have at their table."

I hesitated — then she added — "I must test myself, for I hope to enter your community. So please admonish me when you see me do anything that is not in keeping with what I wish to become." Seldom could I give her more than a few minutes' visit, but on one particular day she insisted I should remain "just ten minutes." Among the furnishings in her room there was a library table on which lay two unsealed letters about an arm's length removed from her. She called her maid to hand her the unsealed letters, sealed them and told the maid to mail them. As soon as we were alone I said, "You will make a fine Sister of Charity, but I would advise you to employ more maids to prevent your moving at all."

"Oh, Sister, Sister, I did not think. I will pay this maid an advanced wage and send her to her home. I should have had common sense to see that the Sisters do not have maids to wait on them." The next thing the lady did was to bring me her jewel case. I looked at the contents — diamonds mounted in many shapes, and a crescent was especially beautiful — gold watches in numbers. As I looked at the "baubles," she said to me: "Do what you please with them." I asked, "Have you no relatives?" She answered, "A number of them, and particularly one who did my family a great injustice."

"Then give that relative a portion of these jewels," which she did, and the breach between the two families was closed.

Meanwhile I can tell you about our cancer patient. Before the wire from Sister Gabriella reached us I mentioned that as I was going East some other nurse would wait on him. He became very much dejected — he is so sensitive about anyone seeing him. As soon as Sister Gabriella wired, "Bring your patient," I told him. He revived wonderfully. The accommodating conductor gave us the double rear seats for our sick man. At each stopping place I will jot down any incident of interest.

La Junta, Colorado. Our Trinidad friends must have been annoyed when they saw the train move off and Sister Pauline, my companion, still on the platform.

After she got on the train, still panting, she told me she had said to the group, "Sister will have the train stopped, you will see."

Naturally I had to play guide to Doña Carlotta who had never traveled on her own responsibility — not suspecting that Sister Pauline needed my attention. The conductor happened to pass at the same instant I missed Sister. He asked, "Did you enjoy your friends?"

"Yes, but one Sister is still on the platform." He at once pulled the rope and signalled to back, remarking at the same time, "We are not running on schedule time."

St. Louis station. One hour to await our train for Cincinnati.

Two incidents occurred from Trinidad to St. Louis, which I think are of interest. The first is we were slated for dinner at one of the Harvey's restaurants. The Pullman car was stopped on a rather high place. The conductor placed a stool to assist the passengers off the train. All went well until it was Sister Pauline's turn to be helped. She quite positively said, "I can get off by myself, thank you." I prepared to pick her up. I knew she would fall. While leaning on me for support she said, "I did not want him to touch me." Trying to keep from laughing, I remarked — "Less noticeable had you allowed yourself to be assisted than to draw the attention of our fellow passengers on a sprained ankle."

The second incident. Three times a day I left the Pullman to attend to our patient. I noticed I was closely watched by some of the occupants of our car. On the second day of our traveling, just as I got through with his dinner and had covered his sores, I turned to face at least ten surprised mortals. Their looks were so puzzling that for a few seconds I stood still, when spontaneously a fine collection was handed me, which made me happy to give to the forlorn man. After I resumed my seat I was told the group who followed me were determined to find out what I did away from my traveling companions.

§ 21

Cincinnati. Motherhouse. July 10.

Sister Gabriella has come to make the retreat which begins this evening. She tells me our cancer patient received the last Sacraments and died in peace. His soul was worth the effort made. R. I. P.

Dear Sister Justina:

I shall continue this journal at the Motherhouse. I began the journal in 1872 while traveling to my allotted station in the Southwest, and to add new sensations in the East to those I had in the West, gives me thrills that none save those who have experienced the like can conceive.

From what Mother Regina has asked me, I surmise I have been slated for Fayetteville, Brown County, where a building for a boys' boarding school has been started.

Doña Carlotta makes herself quite at home sweeping, washing dishes, and emptying garbage buckets. I have often noticed that those who give up most are also the most generous in God's service.

Is this the consequence of the first renunciation or pursuing one's ideal of Christian perfection? You ought to be able to answer the question.

July 26. Mother Regina is undecided whether to send me to Fayetteville or to Albuquerque, the school mission that is to be opened in September. Letters have been coming and going between Rev. D. M. Gasparri, S.J., and Mother Regina, so she told me. I received my share too. The plain facts are that every temperament cannot be moulded to fit requirements for duty in the Southwest.

I stand as Patience on a monument, receiving the winds from the east or the west with equanimity. At last, August 21, the question of my returning to New Mexico or remaining in the East is decided. I am going to Albuquerque as music teacher and remain one year. Those appointed to open the Albuquerque mission are: Sisters Mary Josephine, S.S., Pauline, Gertrude, Agnes Cecilia, M. Alacoque and myself. With the thoughtfulness gained by experience, Rev. D. M. Gasparri, S.J., asked to have the Sisters stop at Trinidad and Santa Fe before going to Albuquerque, in order gradually to acclimate the new recruits. . . .

The first band of Jesuits lost one of their most exemplary and promising members shortly after they began their work. It was winter and Rev. Father Bianchi was giving a mission. He remained in the confessional many hours. There was no heat in the church. When he left the confessional he had the germ of pneumonia. In three days he went to God — the first missionary Jesuit victim of the Southwest. Those who knew him spoke of him as an "Angel in human form." Such men as those are the Jesuits on the missionary field of the Southwest. To my knowledge, three of them are from noble families, educated at the Collegio dei Nobili, Rome, from which they entered the Jesuit novitiate. Do you think they ever mention their ancestry? Not they. Most of the Jesuits in the Southwestern missionary field have been given names by the inhabitants of the Territory of New Mexico, which portray personal characteristics:

Rev. D. M. Gasparri, S.J. — The Walking Encyclopedia
Rev. Salvatore Personé, S.J. — The Vanisher of Sadness
Rev. M. Marra, S.J. — The Writer Who Scalps
Rev. A. Gentile, S.J. — The Man of God

It has been frequently remarked that whenever Father Personé walks the streets, groups of children follow him, non-Catholics as well as Catholics. Another charming trait is — and many have tested the fact — he can make you cheerful by simply looking at you; yet he is dignified and blessed with such benevolence as charms all who meet him.

Rev. Donato M. Gasparri is the man of the hour under any conditions. This is told of him by one of his companions:

He did not enter College until he was thirteen years old. He had devoted much time to music. To enter College at thirteen in the United States is considered marvelous — not so where the best tutors are secured and live in the mansions of the wealthy with full power over the students' studies.

The hazing among the college youth at his time of entering was disdain and hissing.

"Look at Donato! Bravo! When we get homesick, Donato will

MUSEUM OF NEW MEXICO PHOTO

Print depicting arrival of stage coach in old Santa Fe

Northwest corner of the Old Palace which served as Santa Fe Post Office in the 1890's

MUSEUM OF NEW MEXICO PHOTO

MUSEUM OF NEW MEXICO PHOTO

Ox trains arriving in Santa Fé, near the Plaza, 1870

Print of Seligman Bros. store and Exchange Hotel, about 1860–1870
Present site of La Fonda Hotel, Santa Fe

MUSEUM OF NEW MEXICO PHOTO

give us Trovatore for dessert — only do not cry if we are already surfeited, etc., etc."

All this because he was considered backward in his studies. Donato looked at the students in silence and formed a resolution:

"Lord, I promise to give up music, but let me lead this student body in three years from now."

The first campus day Donato requested the infirmarian to let him remain in the infirmary.

"*Poverello!* Do as you wish," answered the infirmarian.

Donato had his books with him, went to the infirmary, allowed himself to be comfortably waited on, after which he got out his books and began to study.

At night in his room he managed to have candle light, stuffed the keyhole and the doorsill to prevent the light from being seen on the outside, then studied until midnight. He kept this up, and as he was perfectly docile, his dislike for campus day was attributed to the fact that he was a home boy. No one suspected his night vigils. In three years' time he was the leader at college. That day he said: "Where is Donato now?"

After his ordination his first sermon was delivered in Naples. A number of men in the audience waited outside of the church and when he appeared raised him on an improvised arm-seat and carried him through the principal streets of Naples. This demonstration was to show appreciation of his first extraordinary sermon. A few weeks after he received a letter from the Provincial telling him he was named for the New Mexico mission.

It was in 1867 that Rt. Rev. J. B. Lamy went to Europe to obtain recruits and Rev. D. M. Gasparri was one of the first five Jesuits sent to the Southwest.

It was he also who cheered and encouraged the Loretto Sisters and our Sisters Augustine and Louise on their journey to Santa Fe. When the cholera broke out in the caravan on the plains, Father Gasparri recognized all the symptoms in himself. He withdrew and under one of the wagons made a soliloquy with Saint Ignatius.

"This is your Feast Day (July 31) dear Saint Ignatius, but you might have treated me better and procured for me a chance to do some work in these arid regions. A fine thing to do for one who desired to do all for Almighty God!"

When hours passed and he did not die, he resumed his helpfulness wherever needed.

These events of his life have been told me by his confreres. I will mention two more:

When Father Gasparri was a novice it was the custom to send novices to certain places with a wallet and beg alms. This was done to test the novice's humility. He was sent to his home where the servants told him they did not feed beggars and idle men. This speech had been arranged by his own father who wanted his son to be a true religious. Poor Donato lowered his eyes and walked away from the paternal roof, not knowing the cause of such treatment.

On the occasion of pronouncing his first vows, his father dedicated to him a lengthy poem on the religious life which Donato often read to stimulate himself to religious fervor.

Speaking of him as a writer, the *Denver Inter-Ocean* said of Father Marra: "When he goes after a man's scalp he leaves not a hair." Father Marra is at present Editor of the *Revista Católica* — yet he is one of the most silent and most humble of men.

Endurance and self-sacrifice are expected of "The Woman" but when I study the lives of these Jesuits I conclude they reach the heights, while those like myself are on the first degree of perfection.

Let me tell you something about Father Leone, S.J., a scholar —as all the Jesuits are — at one time assistant to Right Rev. Bishop J. B. Lamy, and a preacher who thrills his audience. On a certain occasion he returned home sooner than expected. He had been out several weeks on branch missions, many miles apart. His daily meals had consisted of *frijoles* (beans) and tortillas — flour and water, kneaded into dough pressed between the hands and baked. He was tired and hungry, but the cook was out.

Father Leone went into the kitchen, prepared some *chili con carne* and dined as contentedly as if at a sumptuous feast. This is not an isolated case. The life of missionaries out here and everywhere for that matter, requires self-sacrifice, but the love of God sweetens it all and they are the happiest of mortals.

This is one side of missionary life. There is another with which we have nothing to do. It is the missionary in a comfortable home with his wife and family, going around misinforming the natives, calumniating the Church and alienating her unfortunate children from her.

I wonder if they really believe they are doing God's work and drawing souls nearer to God?

So, Sister Justina, I return to what I love — to be of some service to the native population of New Mexico, to Albuquerque, to the parish of San Felipe, Father Gallegos' parish, who allowed himself to go into politics and gave up his priestly character to become a delegate to Congress.

Of course, the normal train of disorders followed his defection from the priesthood. I was stationed in Santa Fe when he was brought to our hospital. Shortly after, he had a paralytic stroke, lost his speech, but retained his senses. He made all sorts of signs for something he wanted. Many things were named to which his countenance said "No." A priest was mentioned. He brightened and said "yes," but by the time the Vicar-General, Rev. Equillon, arrived, the repentant soul had gone to the Great Judge. One thing is certain. Those connected with his life as a delegate are doing sincere penance.

All who live in the Territory know of the scandal given by Father Gallegos; hence I do not hesitate to write about it. Should you ever be sent to the places mentioned in my journal, you will hear of the heroic lives of so many of our secular clergy that will astonish those who are censorious in their remarks on the lives of those consecrated to His service.

Draw a picture of a college man — and some are university men — following trails and more often no trails to reach the abode of some lone soul who was baptized and practiced his religion whenever the priest could reach the far-off place, and now pleading for a priest to absolve him before he makes his last accounting. The priest may have to travel forty miles or more on horseback to answer the call.

August, 1881. At the Station, Kansas City.
Dear Sister Justina:

Nine years ago I was traveling this same route alone. On this trip I am one of a group — Sister Antonia, of the Emmitsburg Sisters, and our artist, Sister Stella, are among the travelers. These two are to return. Both are on the *qui vive* and somewhat nervous. "Kansas City, three miles from Central Station," said the porter. Quicker than I can write the incident, Sister Antonia grasped her satchel. Sister Stella did likewise, the other three followed. 'I recognized the mistake, but as I had the pocketbook I, too, followed. No sooner had I reached the platform than the train moved off. We were in darkness save for the station light. Sister Antonia asked: "Is this Kansas City?" I answered: "No, Sister, we are three miles from the Central Station." There were a number of hacks around, engaging one, I said: "We must lose no time to reach the Central Station before the train for Trinidad leaves."

So here we are.

Santa Fe, New Mexico.

The Sisters who have to be acclimated were left in Trinidad, Colorado. They will follow as soon as they experience no difficulty in breathing. Being a veteran, I came on to Santa Fe to help prepare pillows and mattresses for our new mission.

I doubt if I will ever enjoy anything more than to see Sister Mary Josephine at work washing wool. She is brimful of good humor. Her many beautiful traits of character are condensed in these two: "The religious and the lady."

Sister Pauline and myself are going down to Albuquerque[23] to look at our future residence before the Sisters take possession.

PART
III

Albuquerque

A NEW public school to open. A new mission to begin. The valiant Sister was pioneering again. San Francisco de Albuquerque (later changed to San Felipe de Albuquerque), was founded by Governor Cuervo y Valdés in 1706 and consisted at the time of its establishment of thirty families. The first recorded marriage was a mass celebration of fifty-six couples at Zia by Father Michael Munez in 1701. The Villa was a military base from the time of its founding and was taken over by the Texas Confederate Army at the time of the Civil War when the Confederates invaded New Mexico.

Old Albuquerque, to which Sister Blandina was sent, had been visited by the Spanish Conquistadores under a lieutenant commander of Coronado's, Hernando Alvarado, who established a military camp for the winter of 1541 at a point not far north.

Simultaneous with the Villa's founding, was the building of the Church of San Francisco by the Franciscan Friars. The name of the church, as well as the town, was changed from San Francisco to San Felipe. Later the church was renamed San Felipe de Neri. It was in this stately, two-towered adobe church that Sister Blandina directed the choir in the presentation of Mozart's Mass, Christmas, 1881. During her first year in Albuquerque the public library was established. December 3, 1882, the first paper was printed in the town by steam. It was *The Daily Journal* consisting of eight pages, $10.00 a year, in advance; and the Albuquerque Bridge opened December 12. Each person on foot paid five cents to cross it. During this same period, the *El Paso Lone Star* announced: "For the first time in the history of New Mexico all the members of the legislature can sign their names." The population of the state at this time was approximately 150,000.

Our Lady of the Angels, the name of the Old Town Public School, opened September 21, 1881, with the Sisters of Charity in charge. The school offered elementary and grammar subjects with the adjoining convent offering lessons in music, art, languages, and other subjects requested. Each teaching Sister received a salary of $12.00 monthly from the town. In the *Albuquerque Morning Journal* for September 3, 1882, there appeared the following advertisement:

"School
of
Our Lady of Angels
Under the direction of the
Sisters of Charity
will re-open
Monday, September 4, 1882

All useful and ornamental branches taught: Painting, drawing, and wax work, Spanish classes and private lessons. For particulars apply at the convent."

The convent mentioned was a log-raftered, mud-floored adobe built next to San Felipe Church in Old Town. It served simultaneously as school, hospital, and convent. Sister Blandina always referred to it as "Wayfarers House."

Despite the flourishing appearance of Old Town, Sister Blandina predicted shortly after her arrival there, that Old Town would not long remain the metropolis and that people would begin to build adjacent to the railroad station which was fully one mile from adobe Albuquerque. Sister was given charge of building the New Town Academy in the Armijo addition. The first wing of the new school of Our Lady of the Angels at New Town was completed January 9, 1884, and was known as Public School, Precinct Number Twelve. The subjects taught in both schools were those required by law: writing, spelling, arithmetic, English, Spanish, geography, and United States history. The private schools, in conjunction, offered religion, higher arithmetic, philosophy, botany, physiology, Latin, music, and drawing.

Sister Blandina never slackened in her struggle for perfection. She tried without ceasing to bring people so close to God that they would not even wish to offend Him by sinning. "To teach and meet emergencies as I see them," was her motto.

§ 1

Albuquerque, Sept. 8, 1881.

We are disappointed. The house that Father Gasparri intended for use for the Sisters has a lease on it, and though Don Nicolas Armijo, the lessee, and family are willing to vacate, it has been impossible for them to do so. The house has eighteen large rooms, plaza and corral. Everyone can see Mr. Armijo will have to build a home for his family. As soon as Father Gasparri realized that the residence was not available, he began building the Sisters' residence next to San Felipe Church on land that had been used for a cemetery. Meanwhile, the rainy season set in and crumbled down one of the corners of the house. The design of the residence is for two stories and the workmen here have never been known to build anything higher than a one story adobe. The first time the corner collapsed the workmen were jubilant — it confirmed their previous verdict that nothing but a one story adobe would stand the climate.

The Jesuits asked us to remain a few days to look over the necessary preparations for the coming of the Sisters.

Doña Nieves came to escort us to her home. Showing us to a well-furnished room she said: "This room is named Saint Blandina, and no one but Sister Blandina and her companion may ever use it."

After supper we withdrew to say night prayers and retire.

It was about eleven o'clock when I heard some one trying the shutters. Then the window was raised and a man was in half way. I sat up and said: *"Qué quiere?*￼ (What do you want?) He sprang out and let the window drop. The noise awoke Don Santiago Baca (Doña Nieves' son-in-law) who ran out with two six-shooters. This was told us the next morning. You may be sure poor, timid Sister Pauline was trembling and saying her prayers fervently.

In the morning when we went to the dining room everyone was brimful of mirth. Don Santiago said: "Sister, your friend, Judge Romero from Peralta, came to hold court. He is not with us at breakfast, fearing you will have lodged a complaint against him for housebreaking. The Judge was to be our guest, but he was delayed for some hours by friends. When he came and saw a light burning in the front room, he concluded that was the place he was to occupy and not wanting to disturb the household, he attempted to get in without calling anyone. He was half in through the window when he heard someone ask him what he wanted. He was so frightened that he dropped the sash and ran away, not knowing but that a shot would follow him. The fact is the Judge is too chagrined at his mistake to bear the laugh that he knows would greet his appearance here."

We remained in Albuquerque till we were convinced that school opening will be unavoidably delayed.

We returned to Santa Fe to learn that Rev. Doctor Sebastian Byrne will accompany Mother Josephine and Sister Mary Agnes[1] to the Southwest.

Poor, poor "Billy the Kid,"[2] was shot by Sheriff Patrick F. Garrett of Lincoln County. That ends the career of one who began his downward course at the age of twelve years by taking revenge for the insult that had been offered to his mother.

Only now have I learned his proper name — William H. Bonney.

The Rev. S. T. Byrne, D.D., Mother Josephine, and Sister Mary Agnes have arrived. Everything is arranged that we will open the school in Old Town Albuquerque.

September 20, 1881. I am enjoying several byplays. Big men

and women like to have their say on subjects they have not tried out practically. This reminds me of what was done during the time the General Manager of the A. T. and Santa Fe was taking opinions on the dangers caused by the rainy season. The most trying place was Galesto. The General Manager, A. A. Robinson, had several experts with him who all agreed that the Galesto danger of washouts could easily be overcome by heavy and deeply driven piles. Among those whose advice was asked was an old Mexican, who did not agree with the *Americanos*. He gave explicit reasons for his opinion. Yet the opinion of the engineer carried. So were several millions carried from banks to meet the destruction caused by washouts — much of which expense could have been avoided, had the ideas of the old Mexican been carried out — not that he had the faintest idea of engineering, but he knew by practical experience what velocity water assumed when rain comes down the depressions of the mountains resembling a continual water spout.

So to return to my first idea of big men and big women wanting their say on subjects on which they have not practically worked, but the power is there both "on the throne and behind the throne," and those who have worked their hands and mental faculties to accomplish, to the present hour, keep silence until the non-workers will have discovered their glaring mistakes. Even then the workers will not say, "I told you so," but only resume where the non-workers' mistakes began.

Rev. Father Fayet is determined to have our Sisters in San Miguel. He asked me to plead for him. I said: "Better apply to someone else to plead for you to have our Sisters open a school in San Miguel. The mission will be all one can desire while you are there — but eliminate yourself — what then?"

So he applied to Mother Josephine to plead for him. The Sisters are to go to San Miguel.[3]

§ 2

Sept. 21, 1881.

We open school to-day. To shelter ourselves from the sandstorms, which are of daily occurrence, we, or rather the Mexican workers, have put up a sort of windshield at the corner of our residence — the corner has collapsed three different times. Father Gasparri has said to me, "For God's sake, Sister, please take it in hand." Mother Josephine thinks I am self-conceited to agree to attend to the constant collapsing adobe wall.

I went to Santa Fe, engaged an Italian stonecutter, had him lay a stone foundation and carry the stonework half way above the first story. Naturally, there was no more collapsing. The visitors, Rev. Father Sebastian Byrne, Mother Josephine and Sister Mary Agnes, are desirous to visit the Isleta Indian Pueblo. We are to go there to-morrow.

I predict this Old Town Albuquerque will not long remain the metropolis. Two years ago when Sister Augustine, Sister Dolores and myself came in a private conveyance to Albuquerque there was not a house where the railroad station is now, but the houses are springing up like mushrooms. I foresee that both the Mexicans and Americans here will combine to remove the capital from Santa Fe and have this the capital city. I will continue predicting. The capital will never be removed from Santa Fe while Mr. Thomas B. Catron lives. By the time Mr. Catron disappears, other interests will have taken hold of the minds of the inhabitants outside of Santa Fe, and many will realize that the capital cities in the United States are not usually located in the largest populated towns.

I am going to make a further prediction. The "land-grabbers" will do tremendous havoc among our native population, both spiritually and financially. When you read this, dear Sister Justina, you may be inclined to think I am suffering from indigestion. I wish it were that, and not the clearness of vision which makes me apprehensive for our natives.

Progress will come, I do not doubt, but spiritual death will also come. And "what doth it profit a man if he gain the whole world and lose his own soul?"

You may not know that the Sisters of Loretto had a school in

Albuquerque, but withdrew some years ago. The house on the site they occupied is in ruins.

We have taken over the day school taught by the Jesuits. The natives have fallen in line as though we had been here since the place was founded and named after the Duke of Albuquerque. There is quite a history connected with Albuquerque, but more particularly with the Territory. For the past fifty years no geographer could map the territory with any certainty, because by the time the map was completed, names and boundaries had been changed. The situation would strongly remind one of some of Europe's wars for certain possessions — Alsace-Lorraine, for instance. The Civil War played havoc with Albuquerque property — not so much by legal confiscation as by illegal contrivance. The territory was a "play ball" for many years. The Navajo and Apache tribes of Indians kept the natives in constant turmoil. So in the end, the "Gringo" was a welcome intruder. This is the information I gathered from the oldest inhabitants, many of whom belong to the old school of Spanish aristocracy. No one can deny the refinement of the Spanish race.

Excerpts from a speech made in the House of Representatives, Washington, D. C., taken from records in Santa Fe:

Mr. Richard H. Weightman, Representative of the Territory of New Mexico, 1852–1853, has this to say:

"Should I close my remaks without speaking in their behalf (the natives of New Mexico), I would be unmindful of the courtesies and kindness and hospitality I have invariably received in every part of New Mexico, and be unworthy to represent people who, with frankness and confidence, have trusted me to represent their true condition and promote their interests and happiness. . . . I have never met in any part of the United States people more hospitable, more law-abiding, more kind, more generous, more desirous of improvement, more desirous that a general system of education should be established among them — more desirous that the many and not the few, should govern, more apprehensive of the tendency of power to steal from the many for the few, more desirous of seeing in their own idiom the Declaration of Independence, the Constitution of the United States, the history and words of the Father of his Country, the messages of presidents and state papers illustrative of the spirit and genius of our government. Among them I have met men of incorruptible integrity, of honor, refinement, intelligence and information."

Some biologists stress the idea that the most refined can become the most cruel. My contact with the Spaniards, natives and mistos, has been most pleasing since my residence in New Mexico. I find a natural culture among the native inhabitants. So much has this impressed me that I lose myself studying the different castes and in each discover an innate refinement never noticed elsewhere. When this village (town now) was founded in 1706, it consisted of thirty families. It requires only an ordinary foresight to picture this sand-stormed place of fifty years hence.

The advent of the A. T. and Santa Fe road marks the first stage of progress. Already the rumor has got abroad that a connecting link between the Atlantic and Pacific oceans will be made by a new road whose terminus will be Albuquerque. We are told by the natives that there are gold and turquoise mines not far distant. There is no doubt of coal fields between Lamy Junction and Albuquerque. Granite can be had for the quarrying. Good stone abounds throughout the Territory. With "Yankee Pluck" — "Land-Grabbers" and "Get-rich-quick" people, what is now sand banks and adobe houses will have been transformed into green fields and stone buildings. The transition period will cause many to forget the end of man's creation. When the sane period comes, there will be a clearing up of madhouse activities. The conscientious and level-headed will emerge serene. The dishonest will fear exposure, the unsophisticated will be submerged, and the Catholic missionary apprehensive and on the alert to prevent wolves in sheep's clothing from entering the flock.

Many former pages back of this journal will have told you I

went through this mill-grinding experience. It might more correctly be called an imbecile period. Trinidad did adjust itself, so will Albuquerque. The want of any moral standards is much to be feared. There is an influx of undesirables mixed with those who have thrown their lot with sincere intent to make good lawfully. No hospital, no place to care for abandoned children, no committees to care for the needy. So imagine my work after my teaching period.

Our first attention will be given to the inmates of the jail. As soon as we can get possession of the first house we were to occupy, we will use it for emergency cases. The house has eighteen rooms and a large plaza. I need not mention the want of time to practice on any musical instrument, so will rest on my oars until headquarters sends us reinforcements.

I enjoy many silent laughs at the daintiness of some of our Sisters. Coming home yesterday, we met a Mexican sitting in the public high road. From exhaustion he waited for Providence to assist him. One foot had been cut off some months ago. The stump was festering and bleeding. I became his second crutch until we reached the Convent, where the stump was disinfected and dressed. Our dear Sister Mary Alacoque suffered torture, only to hand the dressing bands. I acknowledge the sight was not a bed of white lilies. The man's hair had not felt the teeth of a comb for months. No one could surmise the last time he had dropped into the river for a bath. His clothes shone with ground-in grease. But what of that? You ought to see how Sister Mary Josephine meets every incident with charming serenity!

December 10, 1881. We are preparing for a Christmas Tree. None of our native children have any knowledge of Santa Claus.

Our academic department is attended by American young ladies of all denominations.

We are already securing land where eventually New Albuquerque will be. The railroad station is fully one mile from adobe Albuquerque. Ere long, progress will build adjacent to the railroad station. The Jesuits are planning to put up a Church in the same direction. While fortune-hunters are making mad rushes to find Aladdin's Lamp, the servants of God work strenuously to land subjects into His court. . . .

Most Rev. J. B. Lamy has been in the Territory since 1851. The Sisters of Loretto came in 1852; the Christian Brothers in 1859; and the Sisters of Charity in 1865. From these dates you can see His Grace lost no time in supplying the needs of our native population.

I looked up some old records while in Santa Fe. The facts they contain throw Don Quixote's imaginary occurrences into the shade.

May, 1882. Preparing a programme for the closing of our schools. Besides our academic departments we teach in the district public school. I am going to tell you my latest on some of our "Want-to-get-rich-quick" people.

A middle-aged lady came to see me. She began by saying: "My sons do not know I came to see you! I want to give them a surprise. I heard them say to each other that if they could interest Sister Blandina in their scheme it would be a· success. My sons are working to get the right of a ranch, and all they need is a sign like this — X — on paper, and the ranch will be theirs."

I asked: "Is anyone living on the ranch?"

"Only some kangaroos," she answered.

"Kangaroos?" I questioned.

"My sons tell me those who live there are like kangaroos or like coyotes."

I began to understand.

She continued: "My sons thought of shooting them, but my Jim said the road is not clear enough."

I saw the mother was being deceived, and asked:

"Do you realize what your sons mean by a kangaroo, or a coyote?"

She replied, "Animals that cannot talk, I take it."

This conversation took place in our front music room facing the street. I led her to the window, hoping that some of the natives would be passing. To my great satisfaction, Don Perfecto Armijo, with a group of his friends, was standing in earnest conversation. I drew her attention to the gentlemen and asked: "Do they look like dumb animals?"

"Bless my soul, lady, those are nice people!"

"And these people your sons call 'kangaroos or coyotes.' My dear friend, I am going to give you the true facts. Your sons are trying to steal land and call it lawful. You may tell them for me that there is a Vigilant Committee which would be highly pleased to meet them. The committee always carries a rope for just such emergencies as your sons are trying to create."

The dear innocent woman looked at me in surprise, not understanding my meaning. I only repeated, "Tell your sons the Vigilant Committee is active. They will understand."

§ 3

Feb. 28, 1883.

Dear Sister Justina:

I want to tell you something about our Jesuits. There is Rev. D. M. Gasparri, the essence of kindness and generosity. "Brother," he said to the gardener, "take the first ripe fruit of our garden over to the Sisters. Mark the best row of grapevines, and let the Sisters have the pleasure of picking the grapes themselves."

This morning on returning from Mass, we found at our kitchen door a gunny sack which moved about and squeaked — no wonder! On opening it, we found a cute little white pig! As we have resident pupils, there will be enough left over from their meals to feed the little creature.

These thoughtful acts of kindness in small matters are indications of what Father Gasparri does in matters of importance. Many a noble deed have I known him to do. Here are some examples:

Information reached him of a wedding that was to take place ninety miles away. Father Gasparri knew that the man had a wife and family in the old country. The girl he was going to marry belonged to a good Catholic family. The banns had been published three times. As is the custom, an altar had been erected in a large assembly hall, the invited guests filled the hall when Father Gasparri arrived on the scene. He spoke to the girl's mother and the marriage was called off.

To prevent this marriage, Father Gasparri traveled twenty hours in the inclement winter weather, in an open buggy. No one except those who have traveled on the plains in winter can realize the suffering he endured to save that girl.

On another occasion, Father Gasparri was notified that one of the girls in his parish had just been enticed into a house of questionable virtue. The moment he heard it, keeping on his soutane and biretta, he walked quickly to the house. The mistress answered the doorbell. She was alarmed when she saw the priest at the door, and she was frightened when he said: "I demand Miss ——, who has just been brought here!"

A man stepped out to answer his demand. "I am the one who brought the girl here, because she wanted to come. If you make any more fuss about it, I'll shoot you."

"You may shoot, but while I have breath I demand that innocent girl."

Quickly the man drew out his revolver. Just as quickly the girl sprang between the priest and the man.

"Black Gown, you win!" snarled the villain.

By deception, the girl had been enticed to that house.

The priest took the girl by the hand, and without saying a word left the place with her. At a short distance away he said, "Walk on as fast as you can to relieve your mother's anxiety."

When the men from the States came out West to dispossess the poor natives of their lands, they used many subterfuges. One was to offer the owner of the land a handful of silver coins for the small service of making a mark on a paper. The mark was a cross, which was accepted as a signature, and by which the unsuspecting natives deeded away their lands. By this means, many a poor family was robbed of all its possessions.

As soon as Father Gasparri discovered the fraud, he, with a number of men, went from house to house to warn the natives not to make any mark or sign any paper that might be presented to them, "because," he told them, "you will be giving away your home and land." By this means, he saved many a family from utter destitution.

The case of Doña —— will illustrate the tricks practiced by those land-grabbers.

Doña —— was one of the victims of these unscrupulous men. She was a benevolent old lady. When two handfuls of silver coins were offered her for merely making a cross on a paper, she did it gladly, because it would enable her to help her poorer neighbors. A few months later she was notified to leave her home — she had signed away her property! The poor, unsuspecting woman had nothing left but a few of the coins which she had not yet given away.

Father Gasparri gave her the use of an adobe cottage on the mission grounds, and the promise of work as long as she lived.

This is only a sample of his acts of benevolence, and he is only a sample of all the Jesuits out on these western missions. It is wonderful how these priests — some of them belong to the nobility and are college men — can accommodate themselves to the hardships of this pioneer life, but they do it, and do it joyfully for the love of God and their neighbor.

May, 1883. My attention has been called to the actions of some of the Indian agents. They are depriving the poor helpless Indian tribes of the supplies sent by the government to make up partly for what was arbitrarily wrested from them.

The "survival of the fittest" must not deprive those judged "unfit" of the means of living. The Indian has the vices of barbarism, but he also possesses a nobleness of character, by which, with just treatment, religion and civilization, he can attain to the ideal man.

I am taking a deep interest in the Indians. An Indian school is located here. Complaints have been sent to Washington in regard to the immorality of the school. What else could be expected — no God, no morals.

The superintendent and teachers at the Indian school have been dismissed. The new superintendent offered us a monthly salary to teach Christian Doctrine to the pupils at the school. We proposed that the Indian pupils come to us on Sunday and we would open Sunday School for them, grade them into classes, supply all teachers needed, and after instructions, conduct them to church. We would do all this without any salary. The offer was accepted, and now we are glad of the opportunity to teach the poor Indians about God, and take them to Mass.

May 16, 1883. Rev. Father Fede, S.J., came to-day to tell me that the chief of the Apaches wants me to go teach the squaws and papooses of his tribe.

"You tell the chief to write that request to my chief, and if my chief says 'yes' I'll gladly go to teach the squaws and papooses of the Apache tribe and remain with them till the Great Chief of us all calls me to His Home."

Rev. Father Stephan, of the Indian Bureau, offered me $12,000 to go to the Apaches. "Get me the permission from my superiors, and companions to go with me, and I'll go without any salary. You can use the money for other charitable purposes," I told Father Stephan. To go to the Apaches would be the height of my earthly happiness.

This tribe has been giving a great deal of trouble, because their grievances are many. Our ancestors have left us a saying, "The mills of the gods grind slowly," which is quite applicable to our times. . . .

My dear Sister, I am going to tell you about the greatest disappointment of my life. Two years ago, discussing in the presence of His Grace, the Most Reverend Archbishop Lamy, the most urgent need of the people of the territory, we came to the conclusion that a central Industrial School to teach trades to our young people would render more practical service than any other improvement that could be devised. His Grace emphasized the needs of such an institution by saying: "Put this project through and you accomplish the greatest good that has ever been done for our Territory."

We obtained all needed permissions, then planned our work. Lawyer Catron told me that he had a large grant of land. "Select a thousand acres and they are yours in fee simple, for your Industrial School," he said to me. Father Hayes offered us his whole grant — 42,000 acres, in Socorro county. We consulted Colonel Chavez in drafting the bill to present to the legislature. The Colonel is President of the Senate and an authority in these matters. Governor Sheldon approved of the Industrial School as an admirable transition from the old shiftless methods to the new methods of alertness. It will give the coming generation means of support.

After receiving information from the states of New York, Illinois and Louisiana, that the wording of our prospective bill would in no way conflict with law or constitutions, C. B. No. 51 was introduced, read, the first and second time, and by suspension of rules, a third time, and passed unanimously — a gentleman not in favor of the bill absenting himself to avoid voting. The members of the Board were representative men of the Territory. At the first meeting of the Board, a blunder was made in assigning the appropriation to ten different towns — one thousand dollars to each, thus nullifying the object of the central Industrial School.

Governor Sheldon and Colonel Chavez wanted to call a second meeting to clear the misinterpretation of the bill, but our superiors judged that if the Board divided the appropriation at the first meeting, it would find means to do the same at the second. "Keep out of it," advised our superiors.

Putting on a smiling face to hide the cruel disappointment, I told the Governor and Colonel Chavez who still insisted on rectifying the blunder that "the action of the Board was final."

I could not say as someone said of Charles Carroll of Carroll-ton, "There go millions," but I did say, "There lies buried five years of serious thought and hard work, and the central Industrial

School which would have been such a great blessing to the people of the Territory.

I wonder if you will read between the lines what will be written in full for the archives of our Community!

I cannot help regretting the blunder which an influential member of the Board made though I feel he did it with a good intention. God has permitted it, His Holy Will be done! . . .

The closing exercises of our school gave great pleasure to all concerned, to the pupils themselves, to the teachers, and above all, to their parents and friends.

§ 4

Vacation, 1883.

The Elpasoans have asked us to open a hospital in El Paso. With the request they offered us generous inducements.

Rev. Carlos Personé, S.J., of the same place, has twelve aspirants to the religious life and wants to know how soon he may send them to our novitiate. The Council has decided to transfer the novitiate from Santa Fe to Albuquerque. I was told to see the postulants.

Whilst in El Paso, I obtained all information possible in regard to the opening of the hospital there. A hospital and sanitarium in El Paso would complete a chain of prospective hospitals, including Albuquerque, Santa Fe, Trinidad, Pueblo, Colorado Springs, and Denver. The altitude would be beneficial to invalids, particularly to tuberculosis patients.

Patients in the first stage of tuberculosis could be cured at Colorado Springs by the climate without the aid of medicine, by their doing only light work, forgetting their ailments and their worries, eating nourishing food, and living as much as possible in the open air, and being contented and happy.

Second stage tuberculosis patients would require lower altitude. Patients with heart trouble could not stand Santa Fe altitude, but in a chain of hospitals, under the same management, every patient could be allotted to the best suitable to his condition.

Sister Pauline and myself are going, at the request of a number of contractors, to make a collection on the railroad works. At our Santa Fe hospital, while I was treasurer, I proposed the receiving of patients who had no money, and placing those who could pay into homes where our hospital staff could attend them at call. This was done and many lives were saved. Possibly this is the reason why the contractors are so insistent to have us collect among their workmen.

August, 1883. When I wrote you last it was just before Sister Pauline and I started to make a collection for the hospital. We returned the last of July. Seldom do I make any money provision for traveling, having railroad transportation. When we arrived at El Paso the first friend we met was ex-Governor Anthony of Kansas, who is General Passenger Agent of the Mexican Central in course of construction. "You will want passes to the end of the construction line, which is just forty-two miles this side of Chihuahua, and, of course, you will go to Chihuahua before returning," said he kindly.

"We did not think of going to Chihuahua," I told him.

"I will send Mr. Parker to Chihuahua tomorrow to protect you," said Mr. Anthony. This collection trip took on importance when there was need of being protected, though it caused no apprehension in me.

Those highest in authority in New Mexico literally forced letters of recommendation on us, and though I knew from a number of persons of Old Mexico that the religious habit was not tolerated, it made no impression on me — possibly because my object was the end of the construction line, and not Chihuahua.

We boarded the train at Juárez and arrived at the end of the line on Saturday, 4 P.M. A crowd of workmen saw us and at once came to speak to us. Most of the men were Irish.

Sister Pauline called my attention to the fact that it was Saturday; if we did not go to Chihuahua we would lose the Sunday Mass. I told Sister that we were forty-two miles away from any church, and that we were justified in not attending Mass.

"I'll tell you what we shall do. Here are many good Catholic Irishmen. We shall let them know we are going to read the prayers for Mass for those who are unavoidably absent. They will all come, and we shall have the opportunity to say a few words about God to them."

Sister said to me in Spanish: "You know you can go to Chihuahua if you want to." Meanwhile, a good-hearted Irishman said: "Sister, if you go to Chihuahua there is one of us in jail there, and you know he will be kept there until he will be nearly eaten up. Do what you can for him."

"Now," said Sister Pauline, "you have two reasons for going where we can hear Mass."

The coach was waiting for passengers. We went toward it. Eight dollars is the amount someone handed me as we arrived. I asked the coach driver the cost for each to Chihuahua. He said, "*Ocho pesos cada una*" — (Eight dollars each).

"Will you trust me until we return?"

"Are you little nuns?" (*Monjitas.*)

"Yes, sir."

"Yes, yes, I will trust you. Come in the coach."

We got in to find one seat occupied by a distinguished looking Spanish lady with a child. She cordially welcomed us and introduced herself as Doña Garlotta's half-sister (our Sister Mary Teresa Otero de Chavez). This lady has a romantic history into which I shall not enter.

At the first change of mules, both Sister Pauline and myself wished to view the heavens. There was just enough moonlight to make the surroundings visible. Above were the pure white floating clouds — some slowly following, others piling on one another in terrace form with a background of inexpressible blue, a scene which makes one raise his mind to heaven and bow his head to think of the time when shadows will be no more and reality begins. Yet more than this impulse toward God was the fact that both faith and prayer were intensely stirred in our hearts. I wondered how Sister Pauline was affected and asked:

"How do you feel, Sister?" She answered: "Everything speaks to me of God." I concluded the atmosphere was impregnated with faith, yet I knew the Constitution of Old Mexico leaned toward irreligion.

When we were nearing Chihuahua I asked the driver to let us off at any Church where we could hear Mass. He left us at the Cathedral, and we knelt halfway up the side aisle. Presently all the bells in the tower and many silver bells rang joyously. The sound was enchanting. The main altar was a blaze of light and at the music of the bells the Blessed Sacrament circled to a position on the Tabernacle. Then Mass began. The sermon was on the gospel of the day. After the sermon I became quite uncomfortable. I felt something touching me repeatedly. Looking to see if we were kneeling in the proper place, I saw we were with the women to the left of the church, the men were at the right. I noticed Sister was uneasy too. After a few moments I decided to go on with my prayers and leave the cause of uneasiness to be discovered later.

Mass concluded, and we arose to leave the church. When we turned, behold! A number of women were kissing the hems of our habits and others waiting to do so. As quietly as possible we reached one of the doors. One asked us in the name of the others in what way they could serve us. I said we would like to be shown Doña Corrina's residence. *"Ah, la hermana de Caridad!"* (Ah, the Sister of Charity!) Doña Corrina had been given this title on account of her charity.

A large number volunteered to escort us to the lady's home. How the inhabitants learned of our being in Chihuahua we did not know, but here is what happened: All along the road doors and windows were thrown open, and the most frequent exclamation was *"Las Monjitas, las Monjitas — Gracias a Dios!"* (The little nuns, the little nuns! Thanks be to God!) The reception given us by Doña Corrina was truly sisterly. We had been there about an hour when a messenger from the acting governor, Don Luis Terrazas (the governor being abroad), was received. "The

Governor returns the eight dollars you paid the coach driver and wishes to say that his carriage is at your disposal. We would also wish to know how long we shall have the pleasure of having you in Chihuahua."

Not having calculated on anything except to hear Mass, I ventured the answer "Three days." Several hours after, the same messenger returned. "I bring you the highest regards and compliments of the Governor, who desires to know if you will find any inconvenience in attending a *junta* (meeting) of the aristocrats of this city who wish to welcome the Sisters."

"Please tell the Governor the obligation is all ours. We shall be pleased to meet those he designates."

"His carriage will call for you," he added. Meanwhile, we were feasted with ripe figs, and we had the pleasure of seeing them picked off the tree. Sister Pauline said and repeated: "I feel more Catholic than I ever felt before. I have wondered if Catholicity is in the atmosphere."

On Tuesday the State carriage came to take us to the meeting of those persons who wished to be introduced to the Sisters. The appointments in the salon were exquisite, the company in evening dress. The introduction was given by the Major-domo, a title equivalent to the Mayor in our cities. After the introduction he remarked: "According to our Constitution, you are our prisoners." I glanced at the rich draperies and paintings and answered: "Rather a gilded prison." After some half hour's conversation, we were presented with a beaded purse filled with money. A request had been previously made to have us driven to the palace. The Governor received us with Spanish courtesy and introduced us to the assembly as "*Monjitas* that we want to keep here," and continuing, he said, "To induce you to remain, we shall give you the Franciscan Monastery and Church, and the House of Benevolence."

I asked, "How did you acquire the property?"

"By confiscation."

"Ah, I see, you wish to make restitution. Then it belongs to the Franciscans. We would not touch it."

A distinguished looking gentleman said: "I have my *quinta* (summer home), which is valued at $500,000. I will present this to you in fee simple — retaining a suite of rooms for myself until I die. This is personal property; no confiscation. Will you remain?"

I answered: "Gentlemen, our coming to Chihuahua from the terminus of the railroad line was to hear Mass on Sunday. We know the mind of our American Sisters. None would volunteer to come unless under the protection of the Stars and Stripes. Why not amend your Constitution?"

"It cannot be done."

"If the minority passes objectionable laws, why cannot the majority demand laws to annul them?"

The Governor repeated, "We would so much like to have you Sisters here. Your costume is so nearly like that of many of our ladies that it would pass unnoticed by those pledged to maintain the law."

"Ah, that would make us hypocrites!" I answered, then added:

"Ladies and gentlemen, in the name of the Sisters of Charity of the United States and of my congregation in particular, I thank you sincerely for the generous propositions made us, though we cannot accept them. But this unpremeditated visit of ours has deepened my conviction in the loyalty of the majority to the Catholic Church. Why the minority should lord it over the majority, I cannot comprehend. Let us say adiós to the subject until, in God's own time, the Constitution of this glorious country will represent the desires of your best inhabitants."

With this the Governor asked what places we would like to visit. He remarked that "visitors like to see the place where we have our bull fights."

"We would like to visit the jail," I answered, remembering the poor Irishman recommended to us. Our leave-taking was a repetition of deep regret expressed by the assembly. We found ourselves in the Governor's equipage — driven by a driver in livery. Presently my attention was drawn to a crowd of soldiers in motion. I recalled that in Mexico, jails were guarded by soldiers. So that problem was solved. I looked at Sister Pauline — she was reciting her beads. The driver stopped about ten feet from a double line of soldiers. The orderly came to the carriage door, looked in and did not see the Governor or his suite — saw only two black-gowned nuns. The look of astonishment! Spanish politeness quickly aided him.

"A *su servicio de Uds.*" (At your service.)

I answered: "We wish to visit the prisoners." The orderly accompanied us to the double file of soldiers between whom we had to pass while they presented arms. In that instant I recognized the saying in the United States "Keys of the City."

When we reached the prisoner's iron cage, a voice vibrated, "Thanks be to God!"

I answered, "You are the man we are looking for."

"Now, Sister, what can you do for me?"

"We ought to be able to do something for you. Did you not see the presentation of arms as we came in?" I hoped he had not seen my kerchief covering my face to prevent my laughing aloud. Sister Pauline noticed nothing but her prayers. After speaking to all the prisoners and distributing medals and scapulars our last words of cheer were given to the Irishman for whom his co-laborers had pleaded.

We returned to the palace where the Governor met us and wanted to know if there was any favor he could bestow.

"The release of the Irishman in jail, if you please."

"*Ya está.*" (It is done), meaning your wish is granted.

From the palace we were driven to Doña Corrina's where a young gentleman, Angelo Carnero, asked a favor of us. Every step had been a thrill since our arrival, so nothing could surprise us. This was the young man's request: "To walk with me through the principal streets of Chihuahua in order to make reparation to the memory of my father who was instrumental in having the religious expelled from our city." After complying with his request, he asked us to visit his family who desired a favor of us. We went to his residence. After all the Spanish preliminaries we were told the family begged us to accept the residence they occupied which had been a convent and given to the head of the house by the government. Saying some words in commendation of their desires, and assuring them that some day, in God's own time, Mexico would come into its own, we returned to our hostess. On the way we met Mr. Parker who had been requested by ex-Governor Anthony to protect us in case we went to Chihuahua. He simply asked, "Everything all right?" "Yes, sir," we answered.

On the third day of our stay the same coach driver who had driven us into the city came to take us to the terminus of the railroad line. Coming, we had traveled at night, now we were traveling in daytime. When we arrived at the first eating station, which was also the relay change for the mules, a large crowd of natives welcomed us. Naturally we were nonplussed. Matters were soon made clear. The Governor had sent word, "The nuns are my guests." The coach lines and eating stations belong to the government. In the coach with us was a contractor from Las Vegas, New Mexico, who had not spoken a word to us from the time we started until we arrived at the first halt. When he saw the pleasure it gave the natives to receive us, he went to pay for our meal and was told the station master had his instructions from the palace. When we got in the coach again, the contractor began to ask questions. Among the many questions he asked was: "Can I get in line with these people who are so glad to see you? Are you making a collection?"

"Yes," we answered.

"Let me add twenty to it."

I forgot to mention that while we were at the Palace and had refused the equivalent of $1,500,000 worth of property, one of the group said: "You will not refuse some notable paintings. The subjects are all religious."

"Where did they come from?"

"They are some of the spoils from the Jesuit Church and College."

"It will give me great pleasure to notify the Rev. Jesuit Fathers who are in El Paso that you desire them to get the paintings that belong to them." We told the Jesuit Fathers in El Paso about the paintings. Rev. A. M. Mandalari went to Chihuahua and recovered the paintings which had been confiscated.

§ 5

Aug., 1883.

Dear Sister Justina:

Our unintentional visit to Chihuahua stirred the people of the Territory. The conservative *Revista Católica* made a number of pertinent remarks on the touched consciences of the loyal Catholics of Chihuahua. The enigma to me is how a small minority of freethinkers — and season their number with men of loose passions — can control the government of Old Mexico. But so it is. History is a revolving wall. The bark of Peter is unsinkable. Neither you nor I may witness the end of this farce, but there will be an end.

The Rev. D. M. Gasparri, S.J., is quite enthused about going to Chihuahua. He has been invited to preach for the feast of the Immaculate Conception.

Meanwhile, we are giving our attention to the preparation of a small bazaar, which is to come off the week before Christmas. The Armijo families are taking interest, particularly Mrs. Mariano Armijo. She has a pretty little baby girl, who will be one of several babies to run for a beauty prize.

September 2. The Apaches are doing some damage on the plains. Unscrupulous white men are selling them whiskey. The railroad contractors are insistent upon our going on the railroad works to make a collection. The A. and P. is under construction. Albuquerque is the terminus of the Atlantic and Pacific road.

November 28, 1883. To-day I witnessed a Heaven-stormed

prayer answered. For some months past, the Rev. D. M. Gasparri, S.J., and your scribe have worked to prevent a remarkably virtuous girl from going to her destruction by marrying a man she should not. The reason why she should not marry him is generally known. Here is a case where love is blind on one side and with a seared conscience on the other will make for the destruction of lives. A few weeks since, the Rev. gentleman said to me: "Sister, nothing but a miracle will save that innocent soul; so we must have a miracle. I now go to St. Joseph and will remain on my knees until I get a favorable answer."

Some hours afterwards he came to say: "Sister, I do not know why, but I do know that that marriage will not take place."

To-day, November 28, the groom-to-be sent for Father Gasparri. Here is part of the conversation which took place:

"Mr. Gasparri, I wish you would do for me what you do for your people when they are dying."

"Have you ever been baptized in any church?"

"No, sir."

"Do you believe in God?"

"Since I've studied the lives of your people here, I do."

"Do you believe in Jesus Christ who came to save you?"

"If you believe, I believe."

"Baptism was instituted by Christ to cleanse mortals from sin. Do you wish to be baptized?"

He answered: "I do."

He was baptized, then he said: "Please tell Miss —— that God showed His mercy over my despicable littleness. I have malignant black smallpox, which, in my case, means sure death. Thank you, Mr. Gasparri, for coming to me. I knew you would come, whatever my disease might be."

After a few more aspirations the Reverend gentleman left the sick man to the care of a nurse. He died. I call this a miracle.

December 12. Reverend Father Massa, S.J., came in to say that "Father Gasparri thinks he has smallpox and does not wish to expose the Sisters by giving him any attention."

Every Sister volunteered to wait on him and Father Massa was asked to have the sick man placed in a room where there is no "Inclosure."

This was done. Two of us went in to do for the stricken one — though at once we recognized that he did not have pox in any form. He had a mild apoplectic stroke, followed by a second. By keeping his head raised, he remained conscious. During the time he was delirious he gave us the sermon he thought he was delivering at the Cathedral in Chihuahua. His suffering was devoid of self as his whole life had been.

In one of his conscious periods, he said: "Sister, as you love your soul, I charge you, follow Miss ——, who has been enticed into a life of sin. Do not desist until you save her."

December 18. God took the Man of Faith to Himself. I trust his life will be written for the encouragement of others.

Mr. T. B. Catron, called the legal light of the territory — Protestant — speaking of the Reverend D. M. Gasparri, S.J., said:

"He soared above the best intellects; the peer of orators; the protector of innocence; the father of all the distressed; one who made himself all to all."

We who knew him best could add a list of shining virtues to the above encomium, but do not the majority of Jesuits follow the Model, Christ Jesus?

What I have seen of these religious in this arid country would make me blush ever to complain of any hardships in God's service. . . .

The bazaar is to open tonight, December 19. I sent word to let everything drop, but Mrs. Mariano Armijo came to say how deeply the Catholics feel the loss of our dear Father Gasparri — but that Protestants and Jews, who are much interested in the success of the bazaar, which is being held in New Albuquerque, think it will not take away the respect they feel for the deceased, knowing that the proceeds are to be given to the Sisters.

December 22. Dear Father Gasparri was laid to rest in the side chapel of San Felipe Church, Old Albuquerque.

Sister Pauline marked his grave by a bright piece of zinc. When and where shall we see his like!

February, 1884. We have a Jewish physician here who is a veritable Apostle of Charity. Take this for an example:

Word came to us from New Albuquerque that an underworld woman had been thrown out of a saloon and was lying in the gutter on Railroad Avenue.

We sent a kind native to have her brought to us. Meanwhile, we secured a night's lodging and then rented two rooms, her condition being such that we could not touch her without danger of infection. Our good Doctor came, diagnosed her case, and said: "I will attend to her, Sister, but do not go within ten feet of her. Leave her meals, cleansing linens and bandages in the room she does not occupy, from which room I will also treat her. When the virulence of her disease is under control, we will change our method of attending her."

The woman is from Texas. How long it will take before the doctor dismisses her is based on conjecture.

May 4, 1884. The unfortunate woman has taken a great deal of my time. To-day Dr. Muhl asked:

"Sister, is it worth while to save such a life?"

Rather surprised, I asked: "Why the question?"

He made answer: "Because Mrs. —— thinks our time is wasted on an animal."

"Animal, yes — but that animal contains a soul. If we let the animal part die, the soul still lives."

"Moreover, Sister, she is not of your religious belief."

"Nor of yours either, Doctor. Let each of us analyze the reason why we undertook to raise her from her degraded condition and each will find the basic reason — remote in thought, possibly, but there it flares — a human bearing the stamp of The Immortal."

"Sister, what will you do if I do not visit her any more?"

"Continue as I have been doing."

He quickly answered, "So will I, Sister! And let Mrs. ——'s theory flow down the Rio Grande."

§ 6

Spring, 1884. Father Massa, S.J. — who is minister here — came to say, "I am in trouble. Can you help me out?"

"What is the trouble, Father?"

"Most Rev. Archbishop Lamy and Rt. Rev. Bishop Machebeuf are to be here on the 4 P.M. train, and we have no cook."

"We can solve your problem on one condition."

"What is that condition?"

"That all the Fathers keep the Archbishop and Bishop company. The spread will be served in our music room, at 6:00 P.M. Here is a P.S. to the condition — invite the pastor of the New Town church. Some of us who have heard the Rev. gentleman speak can assure you if you can bring the subject of conversation to pre-railroad days, you will get reminiscences of great interest."

At 7:30 the eight Sisters of us went into the supper room which — as if by magic — was again a music room. The first thing said by Bishop Machebeuf was: "Archbishop Lamy, this little Sister (pointing to me) was to be introduced to me by Father Pinto, S.J., when I visited Trinidad, in 1876, as a hard worker among the Mexicans. Both of us were walking toward a public school house that Sister promised herself to complete without a cent of debt. Father Pinto was telling me how she put the men to work and how the citizens all cooperated in giving nails, paint and brushes; and the carpenters did the carpenter work, and the Mexicans the adobe work, etc., when we suddenly came face to face with that little Sister carrying two buckets of material ready for plastering. I said to Father Pinto, 'The men did not do all the work, as this plainly shows.' You remember, Sister, how annoyed Father Pinto was and asked you why you carried the hod buckets? You told him this day completed the work on the schoolhouse, and all the men had gone home, thinking they were through, which left the plasterer without a server, so you became 'it.' "

"Now, Bishop, that you have brought on the conversation

MUSEUM OF NEW MEXICO PHOTO

Billy the Kid

MUSEUM OF NEW MEXICO PHOTO

Burro alley, Santa Fe, about 1870

Looking east from College Street at De Vargas Street and cemetery, Santa Fe

MUSEUM OF NEW MEXICO PHOTO

about me — give us the pleasure of knowing how you became lame."

"My horse got frightened and threw me with my foot in the stirrup and in this posture the animal dragged me. When the horse stopped, my leg was broken. Of course, I was doing mission work when this happened. My broken leg has not impeded my work."

"What about the time you dined at one of Harvey's restaurants and the waiter told you you occupied two seats, and for that reason you would have to pay for two persons?" remarked Archbishop Lamy. We all joined in "Yes, tell us, Bishop."

"Well, it happened at a period when you could board a train and take advantage of 'thirty minutes for dinner.' All who wanted to dine filed into Harvey's dining hall. Some good man took compassion on my lameness and carried my valise. He looked to see where there were vacant places, spying a table where two chairs were not occupied, he placed my valise on one and helped me to seat myself in the other. The gentlemen at the table were congenial. A few minutes after we were seated, the conductor announced: 'Owing to some obstruction a few miles ahead of us, we will be delayed possibly one hour.' We ate our dinner leisurely. When the waiter came to collect, he said to me: 'You occupied two seats — your charge is double.' The gentlemen at the table looked quizzically at me and I good-humorously said: 'Justice is one of the prime factors of our Constitution, hence I will follow its dictates.'

"Opening my valise, I said to the waiter, 'Bring dinner for one more — this guest does not want anything damp. Bring equivalents in dry edibles.' The men at my table let loose their voices as though a mountain cat were making ready for a spring — the others in the hall joined in the fun, so none of us had any reason to bemoan our delay."

Of course, dear Sister Justina, you have met Bishop Machebeuf. I have often noticed his very kind eyes — eyes full of sympathy which show at a glance his thought is for others. His lower lip has the expression of a good grandmother who fears she never does enough for all who belong to her. His whole makeup is: "You may take advantage of me, but I remain poor, lame Bishop Machebeuf, one of the first modern frontier missionaries of the Southwest."

Father Durante, S.J., has been a silent listener to all that had been said. He broke the stillness by addressing himself to His Grace: "Now, Most Rev. Archbishop, it is your turn to tell us something of your earlier days in New Mexico."

"Well, you all know the Vicar-General Ortiz would not acknowledge me as the rightful person for the See of Santa Fe unless I could show my credentials from the Bishop of Durango. So to Durango I went on horseback. The experience of later years made me understand I was safer in going unobtrusively through New Mexico down to Durango, Old Mexico, than if I had had a large retinue for protection.

"At that time the Navajos and Apaches were constantly on paths of destruction warring among themselves and against our native population. Our Mexican people greatly feared the Navajos and though quite a number of our best families have raised children found on the battlefield after Indian attacks, they still are on their guard against those whom they raised. You would greatly insult a native by calling him a *Chato Navajo* (flat-nosed Navajo) as they do in anger."

Father Massa asked: "Did you administer Confirmation on your first trip to Durango?"

"Oh, no. That took place some years afterwards, when I formulated plans to build a stone Cathedral. The Bishop of Durango kindly invited me to give Confirmation in a number of isolated villages, some of which had not been visited by him for seven years. Those confirmed, or the *Padrinos* of those confirmed make an offering of *dos reales* (25c). The Bishop thought these mite offerings would encourage me in my project of building. The Bishop made my touring from one ranch to another, or from one village to another as devoid of hardships as possible. Most of the *ranchos* or *haciendas* contain many families all depending on the landowner who invariably met us with Spanish courtesy.

"At each stopping place, it was incumbent on us to remain some days to give the Major-domo some time to notify the families who had children to be confirmed and then give the families time to prepare for Confirmation.

"Then came our work of instructing the Padrinos. Very few adults were confirmed, because every child is confirmed at every Episcopal visitation. It took us a few months before we were ready to return to Santa Fe. The Faith of the inhabitants of Old Mexico is most remarkable. The wealthy gave us many *cariños* (love tokens), among them one solid gold brick."

Father Massa asked: "Did you confirm many?"

"Well, yes. In some places Confirmation had not been given for many years, and you know all Mexicans have large families, so there were many thousands confirmed. Since the A. T. and Santa Fe reached Santa Fe our Episcopal visits entail no hardships. But look back from the fifties to the eighties and it meant purgatorial work."

Sister Pauline asked: "How did you make out on meals?"

"I always carried bread, crackers, and a few hard boiled eggs. No greater kindness could be shown than our native population always shows us, but I cannot eat *tortillas,* which is the most used edible in all the ranchos. *Chili con carne* gives one strength and it is no common thing to use meat one month old — dried in the sun, of course. Having spoken of my Durango trip reminds me, Sister Blandina, you went to Chihuahua. Did any of the Church officials mention how the churches are supported there?"

My answer to that and other questions from the Archbishop on the religious situation in Mexico are contained in the record of my trip through that country.

March, 1884. I have been informed that the Presbyterians are going to open a hospital between the Old and the New Town. I am truly delighted. They have rented an adobe house which the ladies have furnished, and have employed a matron,

§ 7

Nov., 1884.

My Dear Sister Justina:

Here are some items I wrote more than a year ago, but over-
looked to enter them in my journal intended some day for your
perusal. You, knowing the injustice constantly practiced against
the Indians, will readily understand that wherever I can give a
helping hand, I do so. Hearing that the Hopi Tribe, near the
Mohave Desert, was being defrauded of what the Government
intended for it, viz.: farm implements, blankets, seeds, etc., and
that those Indians were literally starving through the dishonesty
of the very men employed by the Government to help them, I
took Sister Catherine as companion and started for the Mohave
Desert to get the straight of it. You have heard of the *Jornada
de los Muertos* (the journey of death). When we arrived at
"Martin's Well" where water was lately discovered, and where
you can be supplied with everything necessary for the remainder
of the "Death Journey" the sky gave indication of fair weather.
We were prepared — so we started. Our conveyance was a regular
open jolt wagon. After following the trail for about two hours, a
drifting snow began to fall and we soon recognized that we were
getting the tail end of a blizzard doing havoc somewhere. At the
same time we had lost our bearings. My big dilemma was to
keep Sister Catherine wrapped, for she had had pneumonia a
few months previous, and this was her first trip since her illness;
so using the blankets to cover her, I divided my time between
Sister and the driver, who wore a heavy coat and warm gloves,
but whose ears were exposed. Managing to cover them, I drew
my winter shawl around me, and began softly to sing a hymn to
our Blessed Mother.

We traveled in this manner for some time, when the driver said,
"Sister, we are lost." I replied, "Give reins, let the mules find the
road by instinct," and I used the instinct of self-preservation by
standing while the unseen ruts we encountered kept my blood

in circulation. By sundown our mules landed us at our destination. The Atlantic and Pacific Road was being worked at both ends, namely Albuquerque and the San Bernardino Mountains. The workmen had reached Peach Springs, consequently we were near enough to communicate with the Indians easily.

The next day was Sunday. Sister Catherine was much annoyed that we could not attend Mass. I remarked: "Let us send messages to the workmen as well as the Indians that we will say Mass prayers for the absent, and then say a few words on the love of God for His creatures. We visibly experienced His care of us on the 'Journey of Death.' " This was done, after which the workmen of their own volition began making a collection for us. I asked Sister to attend to that while I had a little talk with my friends, the Indians. It did not take me long to verify the fact that this tribe received nothing that Uncle Sam intended for it. The Indians thought the Chief in Washington had forgotten them. I made them no wiser. The men of this tribe are fine specimens of human beings; tall, with good features, and straight as arrows. I made them understand I would always be their friend.

"Will you put black on white and send it to the Big Chief?"

"Why not? If the Big Chief has forgotten you, he will be glad that someone will tell him about you."

So, as soon as Sister Catherine was ready, we started on our return journey. We stopped at *Laguna* (The Lake). There are Indians at this place. The Indian Governor of the year saw us and walked in front of us several times. I surmised he wanted to know if we were Catholics. I raised my crucifix, the instant he saw it he came toward us. He spoke broken Spanish, asking us to visit the schoolhouse where none of the papooses go. The reason he gave was: the teacher is a broken branch from the Big Tree, the Tree will live, the branch will die. By this process of reasoning, he wanted us to understand that the papooses of his tribe did not attend school, because the teacher was not a Catholic.

Will all the work of the Franciscans be lost because politics and money carry the day? A number of the Indian tribes have teachers who are not wanted.

Two years ago I went to Santa Fe from Albuquerque. When I boarded the Lamy branch to the ancient city, I noticed a number of Pino Indians. Scarcely was I seated when a blanketed chief came to ask me in incorrect Spanish:

"*Tu vas Carlisle, Santa Catalina escuola?*" (Are you going to Carlisle, to Saint Catherine's School?)

"There is no Santa Catalina School in Carlisle."

"No Santa Catalina School, no papooses!"

With this the Indian agent, Thomas by name, came to ask me if the atmosphere was too oppressive, meaning the nearness of the Indian to me. I retorted: "The oppression just now comes from another quarter." Thus by all sorts of deception the Red Man is deprived of the little he desires. . . .

That English phrase, "The survival of the fittest," is being applied to the rightful owners of this country. Let us stretch our imagination and see ten million Chinese suddenly descend on us! Would we not, if given a new chance, be more considerate with the Indians? The money supplied by our Government and misapplied by the agents helps the extermination.

What does the whole amount to anyway? A few more years and we lay our burdens down, close our eyes and carry in our hands the good or otherwise we did during the test of our pilgrimage. There will be no deceptions at the bar of the Supreme Judge.

December, 1883. Sister Pauline and myself have returned without reaching where we intended to go, namely, the San Bernardino Mountains. We started from Albuquerque and reached McCarthy's Camp by railroad. From this camp, we were to travel by an uncovered jolt wagon.

When we arrived at McCarthy's Camp, the whole place was in confusion. Several workmen came to inform us that a man by the name of D— had been selling liquor to the Indians, and he, himself, drank heavily — during which time he killed his father-in-law and another member of the family, and then ran away with a young girl — dressed in man's attire — leaving his wife and children in destitution.

"Will you go see the murdered two?" said a kind Irishman to me. "No, but I will give you a message to his abandoned wife and children. Give this note to show the conductor on any train she may take to Albuquerque. Give her this second note and have her present it to our Sisters in Old Albuquerque — they will supply all her wants — rooms included."

"But, Sister," said the Irishman, "none of them is of our faith."

"A bigger reason why we should come to their aid."

"God bless you, Sister, that is not the way England would treat Ireland."

"We are living in a country where every Christian should be neighborly."

We left McCarthy's Camp in an uncovered freight wagon and had traveled until 3 P.M. before we saw any sign of habitation. This was represented to us by a large commissary tent. Looking at the sun, I remarked to the driver, "We can still travel three hours before camping." While I was saying this, a gentleman left the tent and came toward us. I soon recognized our friend, Mr. Louis Grant, the youngest of the Grant Bros., Bridge Contractors. Mr. Grant looked the picture of a corpse. He cautiously approached and said, "You can go no farther, and neither can you return, the Apaches are on the war path."

Turning to the driver, he ordered him to unhitch and come into the tent. We followed. Mr. Grant, the driver, and Sister Pauline went into the tent. I stood at the opening flap facing twenty-two men with set teeth, each holding a gun, and showing a determination to protect his own life. Soap boxes, nail kegs, etc., were used for chairs. I asked Mr. Grant, "What does this all mean?"

He replied: "The camp ahead of us is a grading camp. At noon to-day a number of Apache Indians galloped in to gather up food that had been discarded by the workingmen. One of the graders said to a group of men near him, 'I'm going to let you see how an Indian kicks the bucket.' He went to his tent, brought out a gun, took aim and shot an Indian through the heart! The Indians looked at their fallen companion, raised him — he was dead, strapped him on his pony and made for their reservation. In less than an hour they returned demanding the man who shot the Indian. They were told he had gone to the Bridge Builders. The Indians came here demanding the murderer. We told them the man had not come to our works, nor had we seen him. The Indians told us, 'We are not an American ball, if he is not here we must go there to get him, he not there, we come back, we not get him we whoop, whoop, whoop,' making gestures with his mouth. This conversation was carried on with one of the Indians who spoke a little Spanish and a little English. We managed to understand what he wanted to tell us."

While Mr. Louis Grant was saying this to me, the men in front of me who could see through the open lapel of the tent, became more tense, if possible. I looked at Mr. Grant, who also could see over my head, and watched his eyes focused on a point.

I asked, "What now?"

He replied: "Scout Indians on the knoll opposite us."

Instantly I determined to go meet them and so stated. Looking at Sister Pauline, I said, "Pray, pray." Then raising my crucifix from my rosary, I turned. The scouts were fully two rods from us. The first sight I got of the Indians my teeth began to chatter and my knees to knock against each other, but my brain worked fast. Twenty-two men and Sister in the tent. If I can make these scouts realize I am the Sister who received the message from their chief to teach their papooses, we are safe. This reasoning had the effect of partially controlling the fright I was thrown into at the first sight of the scouts. Well, I realized that two Indians could not conquer the men in the tent who were prepared to protect all our lives, but the two scouts only needed to give the war signal and our doom was sealed. So bracing myself with prayer, and utilizing my natural courage, I slowly walked to meet them. As I approached, my eyes caught sight of their armor. Each had a gun on his right shoulder, bow and arrows on left shoulder, a belt alternating with bow knives and pistols, as many as could be placed in belt, war paint, red and yellow. Again fear tried to gain ascendancy, but will power won. Holding the crucifix in both hands, and steadily looking at the elder of the two Indians, I said, *"Buenas tardes"* (Good evening). Showing no expression whatever, he answered, in lower chest tones, *"Buenas tardes."*

I added: *"Me conoce?"* (Do you know me?)

He replied, *"No eres tú tata?"* (No, are you a priest?)

I made answer, *"No, yo nana"* and continued, "I am to your squaws and papooses what the priest is to your chief and braves."

He added, "What are you doing here?"

I told him another Nana and myself were journeying to the San Bernardino Mountains, but the chief of the workmen, who is my friend, told me someone has done a wrong to the Apaches, but the one who did the wrong is not here.

"Do you believe him?"

"Yes, because my friend has never told me a lie. Let us go to the tent and I will tell my friend what you say and tell you what he says."

"Do you believe him?"

"Yes, because he has never told me a lie."

We walked to the tent. I asked Sister Pauline for some medals which we always carried. Stringing them, I placed a number around the neck of each scout, then resumed the conversation, saying to the elder Indian:

"What do you wish to say to my friend?"

He responded: "Do you believe him?"

I answered, "I do, because he has never told me a lie."

"Ask him if the American who killed our Indian is here."

Mr. Grant said, "No, he is not here." The Indian looked at me. "Do you believe him?"

"I do, because he has never told me a lie."

"Ask your friend if he or any of his men know where he is."

I put this question to Mr. Grant, who said, "Neither I nor any of my workers saw the man the Indians are looking for."

The elder Indian asked again, "Do you believe him?"

"I do, because he has never told me a lie."

Then fixing his eyes on me, he said, "Tell your friend, the chief, to put his men to work; we will not touch them. We will go to the other camp for the American who killed our Apache. If they do not give the man we whoop, and then we (passing his hand around his head) scalp." Our intensified feeling relaxed. The scouts started on the trail to the next camp. I said to Mr. Grant, "I suggest you send a messenger on horseback to the grading camp and advise giving the wanton murderer over to the Apaches to prevent many complications with the Government, Apaches, and railroad officials. It is plain that, unless the Apaches are pacified, they will break from their reservation and then who can hold Geronimo and his band?" I added, "When you come to Albuquerque, please do not mention this incident to me, or what became of the man. The advice to turn the murderer over to the Apaches is given, as my conscience dictates. I'm not certain that theology bears me out." Mr. Grant is a Catholic. Sister and myself retraced our journey to Albuquerque.

§ 8

April 8, 1884.

I hope, dearest Sister Justina, my vision of humanity is not becoming blurred.

This would prevent me from unjustly appraising the doings of our neighbors.

The Presbyterians have opened their hospital between Old and New Albuquerque.

Yesterday a messenger was sent to me, asking us to care for a woman patient who has typhoid fever. "Our hospital cannot accommodate her," was the message.

The trend of our work here is educational, but not to jeopardize

a human life. We had her taken to the house we use for all cases
not provided for by public administration. In fact, to date, the
town has been unable to consider those in distress, because all
the inhabitants have had more or less to attend to their own
immediate wants — this refers to the New Albuquerque. Our
native people will divide their last crust to help those in need.

The sick woman is a Lutheran. Could that have anything to do
with "Our hospital cannot accommodate her"?

Three weeks later. Our Lutheran patient is convalescing. I
am curious to know why the sick woman was not admitted to the
Presbyterian hospital. Time is a good telltale.

We have a Doctor Russ in Old Albuquerque who competes
with Dr. Muhl in giving service to non-paying patients. He was
introduced to me by the Superior of the Jesuits as "a man who
does not believe in God."

I looked at him searchingly and read through his eyes a golden
heart and I answered the introduction by: "I'll see the day,
Doctor, that you will claim God your Master." His look at me
was an inquiry. One thing is certain — Doctor Russ is the essence
of kindly attention to the poor, and he never neglects to notify
the Jesuits when a patient is in danger of death. Nor does he
let an infant die without baptism. He laughs the subject off by
saying: "If, Rev. Sir, you believe in infant baptism, knowing you
could not reach the place in time, I use your formula."

The heart of man is less readable than that of woman.

To illustrate: Mrs. —— walked into my music room this morning. She said: "Sister, we have a pathetic case, and I told the
ladies of our committee I was sure you would help us out.

"We engaged an organist to conduct our choir — (Mrs. —— is
leading soprano —). The conductor and his wife have only been
here a few months. His wife took sick and died last night of
typhoid fever. As you know, I have three children, and the other
ladies of our committee have family responsibilities. I told the
committee I felt sure you would not mind preparing the corpse
for burial. The couple are poor and newly married."

Smiling, I asked where the departed was. Having been told, I arranged to postpone some of my lessons, and with a companion, went to the place of sorrow.

Father of us all! May I not again see such pain as was portrayed by the young husband bowed, yet guarding, the Angel of his life. Two chairs in the room, and his dearest on two planks, waiting for what I know not.

I approached the sorrowing man and said: "My heart's sympathy to you in this your hour of trial and darkness."

He looked at me, dazed; then looked toward his beloved. Bringing his gaze back to me, he asked: "Are you not the music teacher at the Convent? And are my own people afraid to come near because my wife died of typhoid?"

As soothingly as possible, I said: "Rest assured, my friend, I will do all in my power to lighten this heavy weight."

Sorrowfully he spoke. "The Presbyterians where I came from would not do this to me."

I prepared his wife for burial and left the husband in his grief — to report to Mrs. ——.

This incident made me soliloquize thus: To add any annoyance to one's sad condition by reason of his religion or no religion, is irreligious — not Catholic.

Living in a rush frontier railroad town where no one can foresee what the next misfortune may be, we find it is incumbent on us who take life more seriously to help alleviate every adversity that may befall our neighbor. . . .

Do you remember, dearest Sister Justina, when in 1866 the cholera was raging in Cincinnati? You went to a drug store to purchase a disinfectant — half an hour afterwards I entered the same place to make a like purchase. The clerk said to me:

"Your sister was here a short time ago and asked for a disinfectant. What's up?"

"I want this as a sort of preventive, for, wherever I see a yellow flag I'm going in to ascertain if I can be of any service."

When we met, both of us had a hearty laugh over the fact that we were doing the same thing without each other's knowledge, and both had forgotten, after visiting a few patients, to use the disinfectant!

No case out here has ever been as strenuous as when our Italian teacher took the cholera and asked me to get a priest for him. His daughter and myself went to St. Patrick's, where Father Cubero was assistant, and spoke Italian. We rang the bell, and the housekeeper raised a second story window to know what was wanted.

I said: "Father Cubero for a dying man."

She answered, "No priest here," and in her fright slammed the window. My companion caught the fright and said: "Rosa, I'm going home to my mother," and with the saying, literally ran toward her home. I thought, "The next nearest church is Holy Trinity." When I got there every priest was out attending to the sick or dying. The housekeeper said, "Wait a while, a priest may come at any time."

I waited for about an hour, then went to the Cathedral. No priest to be had, all out on sick calls. I went to St. Thomas and was referred to St. Xavier, no resident priest at St. Thomas. At St. Xavier all priests were out attending the sick and dying. The Brother saw my great distress and asked me to wait a while, hoping someone would return. "For," he added, "not one of our men waited after Mass to take a cup of coffee, and it is now 2:30 P.M. Is this the first place you applied for a priest, Miss?"

"No, Brother. I've been out since eight o'clock this morning. I'm going to make the rounds backward. Good-bye."

By the time I got to Holy Trinity it was three o'clock. A priest was going toward the vestry. I caught up and said: "Father, please come. A gentleman is dying and wants a priest."

He looked at me with the most worn-out look I had ever seen, and said, "I doubt if I can drag myself to another sickbed."

I caught hold of his cassock sleeve and said: "I've been out since eight o'clock this morning and you are the only priest I've seen, so please come before the patient dies."

My earnestness seemed to have put new vigor into his tiredness. He said: "Come, Miss, show me the way."

The priest got there in time to hear Mr. Ligori's confession. Very shortly after, he went into delirium. You remember the scene that followed. Don Carlo and Brother Bartholomew, read the prayers for the dying in Latin, and each became more religious for a while. I gave more words than I intended to old reminiscences. . . .

The people here are dreadfully afraid of typhoid. The natives are not. Their faith in Divine Providence calls to mind the trust of the first Christians. Those outside of the Church call the natives "Fatalists."

It were better for our natives, had they not been so trustful, for dishonest people took advantage of this trait and despoiled many of them of all they possessed. As these talks and impressions are only to be read by you, I feel free to jot down what otherwise I would not do.

§ 9

We have sprouts of bigotry which are plainly seen. These are nourished by new arrivals from different parts of the United States, who simply take a bird's-eye view of conditions as they find them at present, and judge erroneously of our native population.

Some months ago a press agent from the East looked up Colonel Chavez for the sole purpose of asking these questions:

(a) Why are the natives of the Southwest so backward in education?

(b) Is it true the Catholic Church is to blame?

Colonel Chavez told him: "Being a native myself, I'm going to introduce you to one who is not of us, but who is working disinterestedly among our people. Ask her any question on the subject of our natives."

The above dialogue took place in Santa Fe. Both gentlemen came to Albuquerque.

I was somewhat surprised when Colonel Chavez turned the press agent over to me.

These are the first questions he asked:

(a) Why is it that the native population is so densely ignorant?

(b) Why so superstitious?

(c) Why so backward in the present progressive world?

I said: "My surmise is you are gathering information for the public press."

"You are correct, Sister," he responded. "North and East, we get news from persons who lately have been in these, our recently acquired possessions, and the information given is so conflicting that I was instructed to gather my data from reliable sources, or leave the subject untouched."

"You will get the truth, but will the press publish it?"

"Why not, Sister?" This was a quick response.

As quickly, I answered: "The press will answer that."

He resumed, "I was referred to you as the one person who had impartially studied past and present conditions of the inhabitants of the Southwest, and from whom I can obtain reliable information."

"Thank you. I'll answer your three questions in one. Any other class of English-speaking Caucasians (not Catholics) living under the same conditions from the founding of Santa Fe, 1610, to the peaceful surrender of the inhabitants of New Mexico to General Kearney, August 18, 1846, would have become brutes and would not have retained any semblance of Christian civilization."

"Why, Sister?"

"Because their existence was daily menaced by the different roving Indian tribes, who often had as allies some of the Pueblo Indians. It was the people's great faith in God — morals followed the trend of that faith — that sustained them."

The visitor was doubtful and asked: "Why did the Indians, who were Christianized by the Monks who accompanied the first discoverers of those regions, rise against the Monks?"

"Ah! Not against the Monks in a literal sense, but against

those who governed and ill-treated the Indians, notwithstanding the Monks' advice and pleading.

"How could the illiterate aborigines distinguish between those whose sole aim was to do good and those who might have had a sprinkling of the same aim in the beginning, but lost sight of it when told of the fabulous wealth, here or there, and following the directions indicated and finding disappointment, did not relinquish the desire for riches? The consequence was, some Indians were made slaves, others were given more work than any human being could perform. The Indians' allowance of food was not sufficient to sustain life.

"When the Indians daily saw the Monks mingling with those who were treating them unjustly, how were they to comprehend that the Monks had nothing to do with the treatment they were receiving?

"If you go to the archives at Santa Fe, you will discover the Monks were the only constant friends the Indians had."

"That gives me light upon the first series of warrings, but what about the massacres that took place at different periods since?"

"With more reason the same question could be put to civilized nations, where culture should restrain them," I replied. "Does it? What then are we to expect from natures who have enjoyed the freedom of earth and air, but see themselves deprived of what they love best? In judging the uprising of the Indians, these facts must be kept in mind:

"(a) Every tribe had its medicine man, or sorcerer. From times unknown to us, his influence had been exercised in his tribe. Will he easily give it up?

"(b) Malcontents are found in every group of humans."

"Sister, your comparison between cultured man and the free roving Indian has driven the cloud from my mind."

"The injustice against the Indian is so great to-day that I marvel war implements ever rest. Here is a late sample of man's inhumanity to the Indians:

"Last week a prominent lawyer from New Albuquerque, who

is to represent Bernalillo County at the next session of the territorial legislative assembly, came to Old Albuquerque to see me,
ostensibly to ask the pronunciation of some French words ('My
wife is going to have a *soirée*'), but in reality had another reason
for his visit. After the pronunciation was given, he commented
on the weather, blue sky, fleecy clouds, then said: 'By the way,
Sister, have you noticed the fine herds of cattle the Isleta Indians
have? And it is said they are quite rich.'

"The response was, 'So I have heard, as well as that their knowledge of how to increase their herds and hold their money was
taught them by the Monks, who knew something more than
their catechism.'

" 'Do you not think the Isleta Indians ought to be taxed?'

"I said, 'I can suggest something better than that.'

"Quite interested he asked, 'What, Sister?'

" 'Tax the atmosphere they breathe.'

" 'Is that your attitude?'

" 'Complete, sir.' "

"Let me cite an incident which is not generally known:

"At the American occupation of the territory the officers were
entirely without funds, owing to the lack of rapid communication
with the East.

"The person from whom they secured money for immediate
relief was Ambrosio Abeyta, governor of Isleta. He furnished
the American paymaster $18,000 merely taking his receipt.
Twelve years passed and no action was taken to return his money.
He went to Washington, accompanied by a former governor of
Isleta, Alejandro Padilla, and John Ward, U. S. Indian Agent.

"Through the interest of General Grant, then President of the
United States, he received the amount with the thanks of the
government. Our friend, Don Amado Cheves, holding a clerical
desk at the White House, was detailed to escort the two Indians
to Isleta. And these are the Indians the lawyer wished to tax!

"Of course, you are conversant on the subject of spoliation, and
'Move on' that has been practiced on every Indian tribe?"

§ 10

We received an invitation to a meeting called by the Superintendent of the Presbyterian Hospital — closed since — for the purpose of discussing the admission of a patient into the hospital.

I will copy the proceedings of that meeting as I took them.

First, the invitation which came through the mail — name of Superintendent omitted.

"To Sisters of Charity,
    "Old Albuquerque.
"Dear Sisters:
    "The Superintendent of the Presbyterian Hospital is calling a meeting to discuss a case which does not come under the provisions made for the admittance of patients into this hospital. The Superintendent will be pleased to lay the subject before the Assembly — receive opinions, and in conclusion do the best our hearts will dictate. Please attend to-day at 3 P.M. — 1885.

                                        "——, Superintendent."

Sister Mary Josephine and myself concluded that some vital point was to be discussed, so we put aside every other consideration and found ourselves at the Presbyterian Hospital at 3 P.M. I particularly noticed a large group of physicians which increased my appreciation of having come to the meeting — their presence, to me, indicated that something of unusual interest would be discussed. With regret, I noticed the absence of Drs. Muhl (Jewish) and Russ (supposed atheist) on whom the Sisters could call any hour of the day to attend to indigent patients. Keep in mind, Sister Justina, our work here is educational, but who with any sense of suffering or humanity would walk into a rut and tie himself there? Surely not Sisters of Charity.

The Superintendent (Chairman) opened the meeting.

"Ladies and Gentlemen: We meet to exchange ideas on a sad case. A stranded man, sick, a stranger in a strange land, needs hospital care. Now the question is, either we abide by the Constitution or we do not. If we abide by the Constitution, someone has to be responsible for him."

Dr. Wells, County Physician, asked: "Why wait for any discussion if this man is so ill?"

"Because," answered the Chairman, "someone has to be responsible for him."

Mrs. Burke, the School Superintendent's wife, rose to say:

"I understood when we collected, rented, and furnished the Presbyterian Hospital that it was to meet just such cases as the Chairman speaks of to-day."

Another lady took the floor:

"I was Treasurer at the time the ladies of this town inaugurated the movement to open this hospital and we ladies all agreed to make provision for the sick poor or sick and indigent strangers and not leave the whole burden to the Sisters in Old Town, whose principal work is teaching."

"And I repeat," said the Chairman, "someone has to be responsible for him."

Some doctor I only know by sight who sat next to me, leaned toward me and said: "Please do not think my ideas are made of the Chairman's stuff." Sister Mary Josephine whispered: "Are you not going to say anything?"

"Wait a little, Sister," I whispered back.

One physician abruptly asked: "Suppose a man took suddenly sick, or met with an accident — would you have to call a meeting before admitting him into this hospital?"

The Chairman replied: "The Constitution reads someone will have to be responsible for the patient."

Another voice asked: "Is not the hospital responsible?"

The subject of constitution and responsibility occupied fully twenty minutes. The indications were plain — everyone at the meeting was surfeited with the Constitution and responsibility except the Chairman. I arose.

"Mr. Chairman, I will make a proposition. Give the sick man

a bed here, and we will supply all medicine, nourishment and care. Our eighteen room house for emergent cases is filled to overflowing."

The Chairman answered: "Someone has to be responsible."

Dr. Wroth, our Convent physician, said: "Who is more responsible than the Sisters?" The Chairman fell back on the Constitution and the wrangle continued. I had two heartaches: One for the sick man and the other for the ladies. The darts between the Chairman and physicians continued, and I waited for a breathing space. The lull came. I arose and addressed the assembly.

"Ladies and Gentlemen: Here is my second proposition. If you cannot dispose of the stranded sick man — a stranger in a strange country — please let me know before the next train leaves for Santa Fe, and I will accompany him to our Santa Fe hospital."

With these words Sister Mary Josephine and myself arose to leave. We had not reached the exit when the Chairman sent his dart: "That would be a disgrace to Albuquerque."

I darted back: "And I think you are going to let it be. Good-bye."

Next day at 5:10 A.M. the door bell rang and I answered. A Mr. Patrick ——, who had attended the meeting, stepped in and began his conversation.

"Sister, I do not want you to think my backbone is made of the jibes that came from the Chairman yesterday. Moreover, I want to inform you I have sent in my resignation as a minister and educator for the Southwest, especially Old Albuquerque. The most important event of this early visit is the subject of yesterday's meeting: he is won over to you."

"Thank you, Mr. —— May I trouble you to have the patient at the station at ten minutes of seven? I have transportation for myself and one, hence will not have to lose time."

Mr. —— said: "The patient is attended to by Dr. Wells, county physician, and he will have him at the station on time!"

"So you have sent in your resignation?"

"I have, Sister."

"Mr. ——, would you mind telling me how you with the name of Patrick —— assumed the responsibility of a minister?"

"Well, Sister, many times have I wondered at it myself, but the facts are these. I am one of the many boys who under the shadow of the law, were put in a railroad car and delivered to farmers to be raised by them. The farmer who adopted me treated me well in every way except religion. I knew I was a Catholic; I knew the prayers we children said every night — the Our Father, Hail Mary, and especially a short act of contrition. So the first night after being shown where I was to sleep, I knelt to say my usual prayers, by first blessing myself. The son of the farmer, who was to occupy the same room with me, said: 'Do not make those figures — it is wrong.' Then added, 'Let me hear what kind of prayers you know.'

"I said the Lord's Prayer and began the Hail Mary. He said 'Stop — that is not in the Bible.' I began to cry and he told me to go to bed. This scene was burned into my memory. I attended a country school until I went to Topeka to one of the farmer's relatives who sent me to the Town School. When ready for college I was told it was a college to prepare young men for the ministry. You may wonder why I did not rebel? It would be difficult to describe how I felt. For the first years on the farm I did not know where I was. Then time began to obscure memory. The farmer, his wife and children were all kind to me and ever treated me as one of the family.

"After I was ordained, I was commissioned to the Southwest and Old Albuquerque was to be my place to teach the Mexicans to love Jesus and the Bible. As you know, I rented a house and surveyed my surroundings, visiting as many families as I knew had children of school age. I succeeded in getting four girls to come to my school for one week; at the end of the first week they told me they would come no more. I also know you had gone to the mothers of the pupils I had induced to come to my school; moreover, I was fully informed that you do not proselyte, but strongly work so that no one like me will destroy the faith of the natives. Knowing what you have done with your eighteen room house which shelters more of other denominations than Catholics, I marveled yesterday when you did not say some plain truths to the Chairman."

"I differ with you there. The people here do not consider him their representative. That was plainly shown at the meeting. There must be some undercurrent working that has not come to the surface. However, the stranded sick man will be taken care of."

"Yes, Sister, that reminds me, I'm keeping you too long. Good-bye."

Two Sisters accompanied me to the station where I met Doctor Wells and the patient I was to see safely to our hospital in Santa Fe. Having made him comfortable by turning a single seat into a double one, I asked: "How do you feel, Mr. ——?"

"McKenzie is my name. I feel rather dubious."

Seeing a suppressed, amused expression flit over his countenance, I was at bay. I could not diagnose his illness, but anyone with less experience than myself would at once place him in a chair of gentleman and culture.

When we were nearing Wallace — named after ex-Governor Wallace — I remarked: "At the first stopping place we are apt to see Indians from the pueblo of San Felipe, who come at train time to sell turquoise and Indian pottery. Perhaps you would enjoy a cool drink of mineral water?"

"Do you think you could order some mineral water that would take the cobwebs off of my brain?"

He said this with a broad, amused look and I entered into the mood and spoke of the Pueblo Indians and how little they cared for the white man's luxuries. Meanwhile, the cool drink I had ordered was brought. He drank and enjoyed its coolness. Again the amused look came into his face. Intuition told me there was much hidden under that suppressed smile, but I could not imagine what.

We arrived at the hospital and I pleaded for the best care that could be given to a patient. Not mentioning the meeting or the stranded sick-man-story, I took the next train for Albuquerque. Twelve days after the above trip a group of tourists landed in Albuquerque, were driven to the San Felipe Hotel, secured rooms and asked the number of Mr. McKenzie's room. The register was examined, but no such name was found. Dr. Wroth, who had happened to hear one of the tourists ask for Mr. McKenzie's room, at once associated him with the man who had been the cause of the meeting at the Presbyterian Hospital and who had been sent to Santa Fe. The doctor slipped toward the inquirer and said, "I believe the gentleman you desire to see is at St. Vincent's Hospital, Santa Fe."

Two of the party volunteered to go at once to Santa Fe, but as there was no train until the next day, the tourists unfortunately were told of the whole sham of the called meeting to act upon Mr. McKenzie's case.

True, he had gone to the San Felipe and asked to be shown a suite of rooms at once, as he was not feeling well. "My party will be here within the next two weeks. I detached myself from my friends, fearing a fever." The clerk asked him to be seated for a few minutes and went to ascertain if any banker's identification had come for Mr. McKenzie and was told "No." The clerk then asked Mr. McKenzie if he would deposit cash for the rent of the rooms, as no identification had been received. Mr. McKenzie asked: "Is there a hospital in this place?" He was answered "yes" and told, "I will get in touch at once with the Superintendent." Which the clerk did, and the result was the muddle we listened to at the meeting. Mr. McKenzie paid his bill at the hotel as he was asked, but was quite taken by surprise when he was made to feel comfortable in a train instead of being brought to a hospital. Picture a rich man, and a Scotch Thistle at that, riding on a pass reading: "Pass Sister Blandina and one."

His friends found Mr. McKenzie in a room furnished to his taste and apparently quite jovial for a Scotchman. When asked,

"Are you ready to join the tourists?" he answered: "Not yet, my friends. Follow our itinerary to San Francisco. I will be there in time to start for China."

In justice, I must add the Superintendent of the Presbyterian Hospital did not represent the ideals of the citizens of Albuquerque, and when, the following year, the hospital was closed, those who were well informed said that by ways and means known to the Superintendent alone, the hospital was brought into disrepute, and the failure of its purpose caused. His supervision also accounts for the indigent Lutheran woman with typhoid fever being tilted to our care.

Sister Magdalen (in charge) told me (very much to my disgust) that bit by bit the whole proceedings of that hysteric meeting were narrated to Mr. McKenzie. I cannot think any of our Albuquerque citizens so wanting in civic pride. The strangest part of the whole thing is Mr. McKenzie remained at the hospital until he made his profession as a Catholic. *Omne malum bonum.*

§ 11

Feb., 1885.

My own dear Sister Justina:

So many incidents have occurred since I wrote in this journal that it makes it difficult for me to choose the most interesting.

Syllogisms have very little use here; you have your premises, but the logician who can work out a conclusion has yet to appear. Illustration:

Here our New Albuquerque is a town of intense mushroom growth. The activity of every family coming here was directed to securing a home. Heads of families were helped by their wives and older children to build such a home. Citizens encouraged each other to "Build Albuquerque." We secured sixty-four lots to do likewise. We fully realized that Old Albuquerque would remain in *status quo* and New Albuquerque would progress. Meanwhile, dwellings, stores and churches and our "New Town" school were in course of erection.

Suddenly in the manner of our thunderbolts from skies of blue, a firm by the name of Stern and Douglas claimed the land whereon the whole of the New Albuquerque was being built.

Picture the consternation of those who, by economy — even unto sacrifice — exerted every power to make a home!

During this time of alarm I was superintending the building of our "New Town" academy. We are building one-third, or one wing of what the structure will be when completed.

The dwelling in Old Town, which we were to occupy, but could not on account of a lease held by the occupants, has been at our disposal for a little over one year. We use the house for emergency distress cases. Some two months ago, a lady came to ask assistance. "I have no money to pay for my room rent — not ten cents to buy a loaf of bread. I have a daughter who ought to be in school, but —"

"Where is your husband?" I asked.

Sadly she responded: "He is living, but is of no assistance to us."

"Take heart, you may have a room for yourself and daughter, and if you have not enough furniture for it, let me know what you still need, and we will supply it. Until you find employment, you and your daughter may come to the Convent for your meals. Meanwhile, your daughter may attend school."

A look of alarm came over the woman's face. Then she spoke.

"Sister, I am not a Catholic."

"Christ was never known to ask 'Are you one of My disciples?' so, Mrs. ——?"

"Douglas is my name."

The name impressed me; yet I did not connect it with the firm that had all the inhabitants of New Albuquerque in a ferment of anxiety.

One sunny day, while measuring space to plant fruit trees, hedges, etc., a man on horseback rode up to me and asked: "Are you Sister Blandina?"

"I am."

"My name is Douglas, of the firm Stern and Douglas. Does it mean anything to you?"

I answered as I felt. "Not much."

He sat stiffly on his horse. "Then you have not heard that the grant upon which New Albuquerque is built is not confirmed and my firm claims the grant?"

I stood looking at him, mentally weighing the prudence of answering or keeping silence. I determined to let him talk.

"Sister, I came to tell you our firm does not intend to annoy you in any way — you look as though you do not believe that Stern and Douglas are the owners of the grant."

"I am looking to the future, and I read the day is not distant when I will have to attend to your physical wants."

He looked at me seriously, but made no remark. While Mr. Douglas was speaking, I had studied his actions. His face twitched at every sentence he spoke — his whole person indicated extreme nervousness. A near paralytic stroke was plainly written on his face.

Remarking, "We are not going to disturb you in any way, Sister," he galloped off.

One of the firm of Stern and Douglas went to Washington, and those who worked honestly to build a home were represented also. Washington, not as fast as our generation, pronounced its sentence in more legal terms than I write, but it meant, "Let the case stand for full research." Legal minds here, who have studied the question of "Grants," know that it will take time before a final decision can be given. This clipped the wings of the firm of Stern and Douglas.

Two weeks later, Mrs. Douglas, whose daughter and herself we were protecting in every sense, came to ask if she might occupy an additional room, as her husband was very ill and penniless. "Sister, he is one of the two lawyers who tried to claim the land upon which the New Town is built — to this end he neglected everything else, used up what money we had, and now he is a hopeless invalid."

"Mrs. Douglas, let him occupy the room next to yours, and let me know what you need to make him comfortable. At the noon hour, I will be over to see him."

12:30 same day:

"Well, Sister, without mincing words, here I am at your mercy."

"And as I hope for mercy at Mercy's Throne, so will I mete it out to you in the name of the New Town people who, though of many denominations and nationalities, I feel have the generosity not to trample on a fallen enemy. So be easy in mind. If the care we can give you here is not sufficient, I will see that you are received at our hospital in Santa Fe."

Six days later: Mr. Douglas is under a great mental strain. Of necessity he will have to receive better medical care than we can give him here. No one of his church affiliation has come forward to assist him, hence Saturday I will accompany him to St. Vincent Hospital, Santa Fe. I have an annual pass which reads, "Sister Blandina and one." This "and one" has done good service for many physically ill and distressed souls.

In connection with this annual pass, I must tell you of a strange experience. Mr. A. A. Robinson, General Manager of the A. T. and Santa Fe, came to me in Santa Fe and asked: "What can I do for you in the way of transportation, etc.?"

I answered: "I may want to freight from Trinidad. My urgent need now is to pick up sick persons on the plains and land them safely at the hospital; as well as to send back to the States men who have convalesced, but cannot endure the altitude of this climate. These, of course, were men imported to work on the railroad."

"You may use your annual pass for anyone you wish. Mr. Conant, the station agent, has orders to pass any man or men as far as Kansas City when the request bears your signature."

I had to go to Las Vegas. Not being able to take a Sister, I took a native woman. When the conductor came to collect I mentally remarked, a new man. He looked at my pass and I said: "This lady is with me."

He answered: "She has to pay her fare."

I called his attention to the wording on the pass.

"That has nothing to do with me. She must pay her fare."

I told him: "My name is on that annual pass. Please give me your name. It is your privilege to report to headquarters. She is not going to pay any fare. She is my 'one.'"

Having transacted the business in Las Vegas, we both went to the station. The first object that drew my attention was a group of travelers looking at an order headed, "Topeka, Kansas."

It read: "Honor Sister Blandina's pass," chalk-written on a blackboard. "This order has been sent all along the line," said the station agent to me. "Has any conductor been discourteous?" I smiled and said nothing.

So you see, dear Sister Justina, we can have deviations from the quiet life of a religious.

Mr. Douglas died at our hospital in Santa Fe.

Here is another incident I consider worth while to record. Our Sister Magdalena, of Santa Fe, sent me a physician in the third stage of tuberculosis, and the last stage of inebriation, and of no religious affiliation to work on. I sent for my standby, Dr. Muhl. Remember he is a Jew.

I said: "Doctor, I hardly know how to place this case – a physician – last stages of tuberculosis – a gentleman, no money, very fond of drink. He is welcome to come here for his meals, but I cannot think of associating him with the rough crowd who usually occupy the rooms kept for penniless men."

The doctor looked at me seriously, then amusedly, and said: "I venture to say your last case is not a Catholic, and yet you seem to hesitate to ask me to do my share to one of my profession."

"Of your profession, yes, but not of your faith."

"Well, Sister, he can share a room in the rear of my office. Moreover, I have steady practice, and have been offered the position of railroad physician on the route from Albuquerque to Los Cerillos, about two hours' daily work – the job pays about $100 per month. I can turn this over to him."

"How can I ever thank you as you deserve?"

"Tut, tut, Sister, where do your thanks come from?"

I write this to let you see the unselfishness of Dr. Muhl.

§ 12

July 19, 1885.

Dearest Sister Justina:

You will not be surprised if I state we need an addition to our New Albuquerque Academy building. This extension will have no connection with the Academy blue prints of the main structure. No, because José Apodaca, a Navajo Indian, who was partly raised by a native family, and your fit-in-to-any-assignment sister are to be the architects and mostly builders.

The addition will be an adobe of four rooms, tar and pebble covered roof. This second item is going to make the Navajo look at me and think:

"You are like the squaws of our tribe who think they know, but you will find out that only a mud roof will protect an adobe house from rain and snow."

I anticipate some amusing scenes when we measure space for windows and doors, but particularly for joists for floors and roof. He will advise projecting joists for his kind of roof. I will say: "Why project the roof joists?" With one inch turn of his head toward his left shoulder (he likes to imitate) but finds iron clad norms holding him tight: "Because that is the way adobe houses are put up."

"Yes, José, but we are going to use sawed joists instead of barked trees. We will need no projections."

Poor Indian! With generations of customs pressing on his stagnant brain, how can he look favorably on changes which, though here are gradual to our fast growing people, are new and too fast for him?

The Navajos feel they are conquered, but the Apaches are still on the road to conquer, or know why.

Unfortunate aborigines!

What can a few sympathizers do to stay their extinction! You know, dearest, my policy of action has always been: Do what you can for others in the position you find yourself. Leave the rest to God.

July 31, 1885. Feast of St. Ignatius.

Big preparations are being made to celebrate. Fireworks, singing, and several speeches — not to say sermonettes — will take place in front of San Felipe Church this evening. Father Carlos Personé, S.J., is in his element, when young or old, straight or decrepit, are gathered together, and he, in the midst, to speak, chide, or praise them in his own inimitable way. . . .

It will take many years to efface the scandal given by a former parish priest who unfrocked himself to gain the position of Delegate to Congress. The loss of Catholic piety and looseness of morals began with his loss of interest in his parishioners. The sliding down was an easy accomplishment, but the Jesuits here have the drudgery of assisting them to mount, which is slow work. The old Spanish families remained true to Catholic principles. Wise St. Ignatius provided in his constitution that no Jesuit is to aspire to any honors, ecclesiastical or otherwise. Three different Jesuits have been slated in this territory at different times for Bishoprics, and how they did fight against the honor! And to date, have succeeded. Of course, you know their fourth vow is Obedience to the Sovereign Pontiff — should he command the acceptance, they obey. Out here we call the Jesuits "The Vanguard of the Church."

August 8. Our adobe addition looms good — at least in my estimation. A gentleman, who holds a responsible position in New Albuquerque, came to me last week and said with apparent anxiety: "Sister, you are building on a public road. I looked at the Armijo plat, and it shows a road between your two squares, and you are building on the road."

I remarked: "It is very kind of you to take so much interest, but we had the road condemned. It had never been used either by pedestrians or by wagons."

He said: "In that case, the land of the road reverts to the original owners and you must clear your title through them."

"That was done before we began to build the adobe," I replied. "The plea, and proceeding of the grant you will find in the Commissioners' County Records."

He seemed dubious. This incident did not annoy me, because I had taken every precaution to comply with the building and land laws. Subsequently, I found out the gentleman's anxiety was not to safeguard our interests!

§ 13

August 13. Sister Mary Josephine, who stays at the Old Albuquerque School while the adobe is being built, asked me to meet a Sister who is expected on the incoming train. I went to the station, and whom should I meet but Sister Mary Thomas, who was surprised to find me still in Albuquerque and said: "I thought you had gone to Pueblo." I told her I had not been to Old Town for some days. All our mail is sent there. We both went to Old Town and found Sister Mary Josephine ill. She remarked: "There is mail for you." Opening a letter from the Motherhouse, I read:

"Dear Sister:

"You are missioned to our Pueblo Hospital. Your first attention will have to be given to a three thousand dollar note due the first of September."

Unconsciously I whispered: "From one fire into another." Sister Mary Josephine said: "I, too, received instructions. Please write and ask to be allowed to remain until at least you get through with the adobe."

My full attention was now given to Sister Mary Josephine's physical condition. Dr. Muhl came and at the first visit looked serious. He tactfully asked: "In case I find it necessary to have a consultation, whom do you wish?" At once I replied, "Doctor Longwell of Santa Fe and Doctor Wroth of New Albuquerque," then said, "Please let us wait a few hours." None of the Sisters except myself were alarmed. Since the opening of this mission, I had studied every trait in Sister Mary Josephine's character. She possesses a combination of the most unique characteristics in any one person I have ever met.

August 18. Sister Mary Josephine became quite ill. Doctor Longwell had come several days before and remained. A number of consultations took place. My own fears from the beginning were that she would not recover. At the noon hour to-day I was alone with Sister. As I looked at her she caught my gaze and thought, too. In mind I was saying: "It is time to call our confessor." She said, as though I had spoken: "Yes, Sister, call Father Durante."

Hearing footsteps, I went to the door. There stood Sister Agnes Cecilia with ready wit to make Sister forget she was ill. One look at me changed her whole demeanor. "Is Sister worse?" she asked.

"Yes, Sister. Take a companion and ask Father Durante please to come at once and bring his stole."

In a few minutes he came and heard her confession. When he reached the outside of the door I asked: "Was she lucid?" "Perfectly, Sister."

I went in. Sister said to me: "I'm going to receive Holy Viaticum." The Sisters came and knelt while waiting. Presently we heard the first signal of the priest's coming. She softly exclaimed: "My Lord and my God!" and quietly arose and knelt at the bedside. After making a short and prayerful thanksgiving, she began: "Oh! What could my Jesus do more, . . ." and softly sang the first stanza, then said to me: "Finish it, Sister. I feel tired."

A short while after she became delirious. She had lucid intervals at which time she spoke of subjects which will always remain sacred to me. From my first introduction to Sister, in my estimation, I placed her on a very high pedestal. In daily work with her for four years, not only did she not descend, but soared many degrees above my first estimate. I have seen that lofty soul under fire which would have discouraged many, many others. Her charity was only limited by the funds of the convent, her prudence noticeable, her judgment sound, her impartiality admirable, a lady perfect and, above all this, a religious of rule.

You, dear Sister Justina, can realize how I admired and appreciated her. We placed her body to rest in Santa Barbara Cemetery. The stone over her grave reads:

> *Sister Mary Josephine Irwin*
> *Called Home August 22, 1885*
> *Aged 33 years.*

Sister Sebastian and a number of Sisters came down from Santa Fe for the funeral. I feel like "the last rose of summer."

Sister Victoria is daily expected. She was detained in Denver. The two houses, Old and New Albuquerque, will be entirely separate. I remain in Old Town. Sister Isadore takes charge of the New Town school.

Sister Mary Josephine's passing has left us all more pensive.

Here is a clipping from our Albuquerque paper:

> *Sister Josephine*
>
> *Another noble heart is stilled forever,*
> *Another spirit freed from earth's sharp stings;*
> *Another soul has crossed the silent river,*
> *On angel wings.*
>
> *She turned her back on all the fleeting pleasures,*
> *That lure the young in fashion's giddy whirl,*
> *And shone for years, 'mid all religion's treasures,*
> *The fairest pearl.*
>
> *Her mission was to banish care and sorrow,*
> *To cheer the sick, and comfort the distressed —*
> *She trod the path of duty, thorny, narrow,*
> *And knew no rest.*

No snowflake ever fell from heaven purer
  Than was the soul just called from earthly scenes,
No hope of heavenly bliss was ever surer
  Than Josephine's.

Within the shining gates of heaven o'er us
  Her spirit pure has joined th' angelic band,
Her low, sweet voice now swells the rapturous chorus,
  At God's right hand.

There Jesus, with the hands once pierced and bleeding,
  Placed on her head the crown so nobly won,
And whispered in her ear the welcome greeting:
  "Well done. Well done."

§ 14

Feb. 2, 1886.

Dearest Sister Justina:

The Apaches are leading our soldiers a fine chase. Not only is Gerónimo riding at large, but Victorio and other captains also.

Last week Sister Catherine and myself visited one of the grading camps and stood on a mound where, the day before, Victorio had scalped two of the working men. Everyone in the camp was as quiet as though nothing had occurred.

Now that the warriors of the Apache tribe have broken their Reservation, it is the general opinion that Gerónimo will not stop his depredations until he is captured, dead or alive.

Poor savage breasts! How overflowing with injury and anger! Away from their Reservation, they still feel the atmosphere is theirs to breathe. Company after company of our soldiers are following the Apaches' trail. What our government wants most is to capture Chief Gerónimo. As the Apaches know this is their last chance for war, it will be some time before the tribe submits — at all events, not until Gerónimo and his warriors are captured. . . .

I have often compared what the secreted feelings and thoughts

of Indians and the congenitally deaf must be like. Each receives
a definite impression. That impression remains until an over-
powering one removes the first, and it is the last impression which
causes unlooked for consequences. The congenitally deaf have
much in their favor, being surrounded by some care and culture
which, to some extent, react toward the good, while the Indian
has naught but savagery to influence him.

Feb. 11. To-day, while waiting at the station for the Santa Fe
train, a well-muffled gentleman entered the waiting room, glanced
around, then fastened his look on me. His next move was to come
toward me, saying: "You do not recognize me?" He lowered his
muffler and, as I caught sight of a heavy scar, memory rushed
to my aid and the tragedy of the Estancia Ranch with its melancholy ending was laid before me.

The Estancia Ranch has been claimed by the noted Otero
family for generations past. No doubt ever entered the mind of
the family as to their rightful claim. A well-known New York
City millionaire financed a brother of his to claim the land grants
that are not confirmed.

This question of unconfirmed land grants has been pending
for a number of years.

Manuel B. Otero (who is half-brother to our Sister Mary
Teresa Otero de Chavez), previous to this time, had been sent to
Europe to finish his education. He returned well versed in a
number of languages, particularly German. On his return from
Europe, he married Miss Eloise Luna, unquestionably the most
beautiful woman in the territory. To see Miss Luna and her
brother, Tranquelino, together, would at once transport one to
a "Beauty Court of Europe." Miss Luna is as good as she is
beautiful, and comes rightfully by goodness on her mother's side,
who is a living model of Christian virtues.

Mr. Otero turned over all his business to his son, Mr. B. Otero.
Being young (22 years old) and understanding the temperament
of ranchmen and naturally generous, he was like a good monarch
among his subjects. He loved his ranchmen, and they would go

through the Mohave Desert without provisions if he said: "Go."

His home life was earthly happiness. On one memorable day he and his men returned from the Estancia Ranch, having left some cowboys to safeguard the interests of the ranch and herds of cattle. While Mr. M. B. Otero and his retinue were enjoying a few days' rest and making the best of Mrs. M. Otero's hospitality, a messenger like a whirlwind, launched himself off his bronco and without any preamble rushed to Mr. M. B. Otero's side, said a few whispered words, when, lo –, all the merriment left Mr. Otero's countenance.

His men gathered round him. "What is it, Señor, what is it?"

In positive tones he announced: "Some Gringos are trying to jump La Constancia."

The men laughed derisively – not so Mr. Otero who, in an instant, was ready for action, but who had to give the reason for suddenly cutting short the merry-making. He went to where his wife was seated, took a place near her and said: "*Alma mía*" – (my soul) – "we have to return to La Constancia."

In alarm she replied: "But why?"

"*Eloisa mía*, a messenger came to say that some Americans are trying to claim the ranch and have taken possession of our ranch house."

She replied: "*Querido* Manuel, I do not understand why the Americans are intruding, but I intuitively feel there is danger for you. Do not go. Cannot you at once give the case over to the Court?"

"The Americans will claim it by possession if we do not resist them," he made answer.

So Mr. M. B. Otero and his men left for the ranch. On the way they chatted merrily, Mr. Otero remarking: "If they are real Americans, our first parley will settle the question of ownership."

When, within sight of the ranch house, Otero's party plainly saw the movement in the ranch house showed resistance. Still the party continued toward the house. When within hearing distance, some voice spoke: "Halt, or we fire!"

Otero answered: "Two can play the game. Had we not better have an understanding?"

"Nothing to understand. We claim the ranch." Firing began on both sides. Mr. M. B. Otero became the target and was shot by the New York financier's brother — so the report came — and he, himself, was shot on one side of his cheek.

At this time I had accompanied Sister Mary Teresa Otero de Chavez to Santa Fe. She had to consult a doctor. While at the hospital, the New York financier's brother was brought in wounded.

As soon as I knew he was in the hospital, I asked Sister Mary Teresa if she were ready to make an unusual sacrifice. She asked if it concerned her brother Manuel. I answered "Yes," then added, "Are you willing to visit him as a patient and during your visit make yourself known and say 'I forgive.'"

Her response was slow, but deliberate.

"I will visit him as a patient and will say: 'I forgive you, as I hope to be forgiven. I am Manuel Otero's sister.'"

So she did.

That same night the patient was spirited out of the hospital and from that time to this, I had not seen him. The ranch is in litigations. . . .

The United States Government is giving full attention to the Apaches — Chief Gerónimo and all the petty chiefs of his tribe are doing all the depredation they can to any obstacle which impedes their furious raids. At present Gerónimo has broken through the United States line and is skirmishing in Mexico, which makes this outbreak, in the manner Gerónimo is working it out, an international case.

Poor, poor Indians! They are doomed to lose. Then will come strict adherence to reservation rules — then diminution of numbers, and then extinction.

Often have I pondered over the amount of money expended by our government to civilize the Red Man, and how ineffectually that money has been expended.

Charles Loomis, who is now studying the characteristics of the Isleta Indians thirteen miles below Albuquerque, and who lives among them, would make an impartial judge in giving to the United States Indian Department his opinion as to what would benefit the Indians and show results for money expended. You know, dearest Sister Justina, I am not indifferent to the rightful owners of this continent. Here is a little episode concerning the Isleta Indians. It was reported to me that a Government teacher was drawing $75.00 monthly salary for teaching the children of the Isleta pueblo, but that he did not teach them.

Taking a companion, we boarded a freight train that had a caboose attached to it, had ourselves dropped at the pueblo, went direct to the schoolhouse, found it empty, directed our steps to the Post Office, kept by a Mr. Ray, whose daughter is one of my music pupils.

After the first greetings, I remarked: "We are interested in the school of this pueblo. How can we visit it?"

We heard a movement behind the portiere separating the office from what we supposed was a sitting room and, presently, we heard a bell ring. Meanwhile, Mr. Ray was keeping us interested in things Indian. In about ten minutes Mr. Ray said: "May I show you where the schoolhouse is?"

So to the schoolhouse we went and lo! we found about twenty urchins with soiled faces and hands and no books in their desks. The sham was so apparent that I made no comment, but went direct to the priest's house and asked: "Are you aware that Mr. — is receiving money for teaching the Indian children, which he does not do?"

"I know he receives a monthly recompense for what he is supposed to do and is not doing."

"And you tolerate it?"

"Sister, I have the interests of my Pueblo Indians at heart, and, until I can get Sisters to teach my people, he does less mischief by not teaching the boys and girls of this pueblo than if he taught them."

"Thank you, Father. The explanation is satisfactory."

The next month failed to bring the teacher's salary.

We have the son of the Governor of this Indian pueblo at our school here in Old Albuquerque. While speaking (rather writing) of Indians, I will tell you of an incident which occurred at our Santa Fe Hospital. Possibly you know Sister Mary de Sales;[4] if not, I will describe her as strong, tall, and a very matter-of-fact individual. She can easily discipline a score of undisciplined school boys by a look or gesture, and this characteristic accompanies her in her daily work in the men's ward of which she has charge. Among her patients, she had an Indian, who suffered a great deal — which made her more attentive to him, as he never complained, nor even groaned.

When he began to convalesce his progress toward health was rapid. Then came the day he was discharged. A number of Indians came to escort him home to his pueblo, the Santa Domingo, but he hesitated. He waited until Sister Mary de Sales[4] came. He took her hand and she, thinking he wanted to say "good-bye," shook the hand American fashion, but he held on. She was puzzled until an interpreter explained he was waiting for Sister to go with him to his pueblo. The go-between explained that Sisters do not accompany discharged patients. "But why was she so good to me and cured me? Does not that mean she would live with me and my people?"

As soon as Sister realized his meaning, the answer was one between Irish indignation and Irish wit — the modification was: "Tell him if he injures his spine again, he can ask one of the squaws of his pueblo to nurse him to health." I narrate the incident as it was told to me.

The Apaches are leading our soldiers the most strenuous chase made in the Southwest. General Miles is now in command of the troops. For a good Indian scout, he has Santiago Valenzuela, who knows every Indian tactic and who can detect the slightest bronco hoof on any trail or no trail.

§ 15

1886.

Dear Sister Justina:

Gerónimo was captured by General Nelson A. Miles, but the prime mover in the capture was Santiago Valenzuela, the Indian Scout. Gerónimo's bronco is now in New Albuquerque, and as our native people here say: *Todo el mundo* (everybody) has gone to see it.

It stood on exhibition on Railroad Avenue, and having to go to one of the stores, I was stopped by some friends who remarked: "You surely must take a look at the Chief's bronco," which I did. As I looked at the animal and recalled the many super-flights it had performed by only a word from Gerónimo, I wondered at its apparent demureness. A connoisseur of horses walked in front and both sides of the bronco, and while doing so, he said: "Watch the expression of the beast's eyes." They were live coals and ready to fly — but had not its commander to give the word or signal. Everybody agrees the Apaches have made their last fight. . . .

August 10. I answered the doorbell and ushered into the reception room a woman whose head was all bound with white bandages. She roughly said: "I want to see Sister Margaret."

I replied: "We have no Sister by that name."

"Well, then, I want that Sister who gave my baby to the Armijo family. John Kirby is my baby's name."

I comprehended. "I am that Sister."

"You are, are you? I am John Kirby's mother. I am just from the Texas penitentiary for killing three men" (looking at me fiercely), "and I want John Kirby, my boy."

I replied: "If you are John Kirby's mother, yours is the first right to him. Yet before that right can be acknowledged, you will have to prove your right! Why did you have yourself published as having died of smallpox? Why did you abandon the child for so many years? Now that you claim him, you will have to prove that you are the proper person to raise him."

"I say, who can raise him better than his mother?"

"That you will have to prove."

She went direct to Mr. Field's law office in New Town. Here is what Mr. Field told me:

"A woman came to my office to say: 'I want my baby boy who was stolen by someone who lives in Old Albuquerque, and that someone gave him away (for money).' Though the claimant's personal appearance had everything against her, yet if it was the case of a stolen child, it was sufficient to raise my interest. I asked: 'To whom was the child given for money?' She replied: 'To a family by the name of Armijo.' 'How long ago?' She reluctantly replied: 'About four years.'

" 'Why did you not claim your child before this time?'

" 'I had no chance to, besides the one who gave my child away has many friends who think whatever she does is just right.'

" 'Who is that one?'

" 'They call her Sister.'

" 'Can it be Sister Blandina?'

" 'That is the name.'

" 'Your name is?'

" 'Never mind my name — the boy's name is John Kirby, and I want him because he is my boy.'

" 'Mrs. Kirby, your case is clear to me.'

" 'Well, then, get me my boy.'

" 'I do not apprehend any trouble whatever. Pay for the time the Armijo family cared for John Kirby, and I know Sister Blandina will acquiesce in the arrangement.'

" 'How can I pay? I was in the penitentiary nearly all the time.'

" 'I see clearer than at the outset. You better get someone else to take up your case, if you think you have a case. Good-bye.' "

You are aware, dear Sister Justina, that no provision has, to date, been made here either for the sick, orphan or abandoned child, so we do what we can in every urgent case. . . .

September. I have been missing Doctor Russ, so I asked one of his poor patients if she knew where the doctor had gone.

"Gone? Nowhere, Sister, he is sick and will not allow anyone but me to enter his room. He has been in bed for more than a month."

This is the doctor who was introduced to me as being an infidel. All these years that I have known him he has attended to the poor — under any condition, free — often giving the necessary medicine. We went to his adobe room — the door was ajar. We rapped. "Stay out," came the answer.

"It is only I and my companion, doctor. I came to make arrangements to bring you to our hospital in Santa Fe."

"Why not let me go off quietly from this room, Sister?"

"After all the good you have done our native people for both soul and body! It is time some of us do something for you."

"Sister, I have cancer in my foot."

"So I surmised. Dr. Muhl will drive you to the station to-morrow morning, and I will accompany you to our hospital."

"Now, Sister, I'm not worth all that trouble."

"Let others be the judges, and at least give me the pleasure of doing a wee bit for the many, many prompt responses you gave to my requests to attend our cases of sick poor."

Dr. Muhl gave his heart and time to Doctor Russ and had him at the station for the first morning train to Santa Fe. A more patient person could not be imagined. I pleaded for particular attention for the doctor who had given many of his best years to persons who could never remunerate him.

After the doctor was in the hospital for a few weeks he asked to have the Vicar-General visit him. They remained in private conversation for several hours. The next day the Vicar-General brought the doctor Holy Communion, and this was the man who was introduced to me as "One who did not believe in God." At last he came unto his own. . . .

Here is another unique case. A well dressed young white woman asked for me and greeted me by: "I would like to have you find a place where I can board my child. He is two years and six months old, has hernia — is colored, and I feel disgraced."

I thought, "And you have disgraced his life!" With this in mind, I looked at her with the pity I felt in my heart. She seemed to realize my feeling, and a rush of blood overspread her whole countenance, then she asked: "Do you think you can find someone to take care of the boy if I pay for him?"

I replied: "I will ask a good widow to care for the child."

She left twenty dollars for the boy over one year ago, and that is the last I have heard of her. Of course, we have been paying the widow for her work and clothes the child needed. There is great need of a Children's Home here. . . .

Yesterday Mr. Amado Baca's younger brother came to see me and opened his conversation by: "Sister, I have something against you. It is several years since I left my application for any abandoned boy, and you have not given me one."

My thoughts instantly went back to the widow's home (Mrs. Banks) where the mulatto boy was being cared for, so I replied: "The only boy that we can dispose of is a mulatto, but it did not occur to me to tell you so."

"A mulatto! That would just suit us. Can I see the chap?"

"The child is under a doctor's care."

"I'll have our doctor care for him."

The little fellow was brought in by Mrs. Banks. I asked, "Would you like to have a new papa?"

"Yes, Sister."

"Very well, dear, you can go with him," pointing to Mr. Baca. I drew a long breath of relief, for it had never occurred to me that I could dispose of the child except to some colored family, and I have not seen one in New Albuquerque since its mushroom growth. . . .

§ 16

Cosmopolitan truly is our Wayfarers' house of eighteen rooms. The distressing cases in it at present are: One woman with typhus fever, who has the best and sunniest room in the house; a woman and daughter, whose father is quite ill, two rooms; a man just out of the penitentiary and his family, which consists of wife and three children, three rooms; a discharged prisoner who married a Mormon woman with one daughter, three rooms; and a sailor and a carpenter who had saved three hundred dollars and had agreed to go on a spree and continue it until the money would be spent — which they did spend.

One day at 8:30 P.M., when the thermometer registered 5 below zero, the doorbell rang. I asked: "Who is there?"

"Two hungry and very nearly frozen men."

No trouble to realize the last part of the sentence. I opened the door and in walked two men, entirely different from each other. One man was tall and dark complexioned, the other, a small sized, cheery man, who said: "Besides being nearly frozen, we are nearly starved."

I replied: "You can thank the thermometer for your entrance here at this late hour."

Sister Eloisa and myself started a fire and prepared for the two men what was intended for the Sisters' breakfast — a pot of coffee and hash. We cut one loaf of home-made bread and in a few minutes it disappeared. We sliced another loaf — it met the same fate. The little man said, "I told you we were hungry," so we used up another loaf which was also eaten. We did not offer the fourth loaf, since it was all we had for breakfast.

So the men arose from the table, and the little one remarked: "We can now walk briskly to save ourselves from freezing."

"Walk to the corner," I told them, "then turn to the right, and when you reach the next corner walk straight across the street. Open the door in front of you. There you will find matches, kindling and coal, two beds and plenty of covers. Return in the morning and I'll see what can be done for you." These two men presented a study for me and I concluded to make the experiment.

Both men returned the next morning and asked: "What can we do to show our gratitude?" The tall man said, "I am a carpenter. I'll gladly do anything in my line as long as you need me."

The little man said: "My name is Jimmy Burns. I've been a sailor all my life — which means I can do more than turn somersaults."

"I feel grateful to note how appreciative you both are for what has been done for you."

The little man answered: "If we are here to-day, it is due to you having fed and sheltered us, so now we are ready to do anything we can for you."

The carpenter was given some repair work, but I kept him in view when possible. I sent Jimmy Burns to help unload a car of coal and to see it properly consigned. The first opportunity I had to speak to Jimmy I asked: "Have you and the carpenter been together long?"

"No, Sister. I met him two weeks ago at the Gulf. He said he had money he wanted to spend, and I said I had too, so we agreed to spend what we had together. But I kept my weather eye on that dark face and, Sister, I'll tell you the truth — I don't like to see him around here."

"Perhaps he will make up his mind to go soon," I told him.

"Trust me. I'll watch him and give him a chance to go soon," he replied. The chance came sooner than he anticipated. The two-sheet paper of New Town gave a description of a man who was very much wanted in New Orleans and the description tallied perfectly with our carpenter. Jimmy mentioned this to the carpenter when both were in their room. The carpenter took a flyleaf from one of the books left on the table of the shelter room and with a pencil wrote on it, then retired. So did Jimmy — but not to sleep. In an hour or so the carpenter rose quietly and left for parts unknown. Jimmy fastened the door, fearing he might change his mind and return. The next morning Jimmy brought the writing the carpenter had scribbled on the flyleaf. Here is what it said:

"Sister — you have saved my blackened soul from additional crimes. Had I twenty years ago met your manner of trusting faith instead of a number of men of the 'Devilish Cult' I would not be what I am to-day — the dung outcast of all society. I opine it will never again be in your power to avert the great catastrophe that had been planned by the 'Devilish Cult,' which was to be put in execution by this outcast, but which you prevented by the treatment you gave the two men who were hungry and nearly frozen. The companion you fed and sheltered with me knows nothing of me or what I was to do. If ever I regain my manhood, I will find some way of informing you — if you do not hear from me it will mean I went to the depths alone.

"The Outcast."

When and where, dearest Sister Justina, will you read this journal? And when and from where will I hear from the "Outcast"?

Jimmy is here endeavoring to prove his gratitude for having saved his life — so he says. The thing that pleases Jimmy most is that the "Outcast" has gone. Jimmy is one of the most superstitious sailors I have ever met.

"Sister," he said to me yesterday, "you don't want to believe it, but I can tell you I have seen more than twelve men come on board our ship at one time and not one of those men had a head on his neck!"

"Of course, you saw the headless men when you returned on shipboard to sleep, after being on land for a few days," I replied.

He was confused.

"Did you never reason that the unreal things you tell me were always seen by you after some days of hard drinking?"

"Ah! Now, Sister, did you ever cross the ocean?"

"I did, but never saw men without heads, nor men walking by their tongues, nor men flying by the stumps of their arms and eating with their feet."

Jimmy tells me he was born a drunkard. "I tell you the truth, Sister, before you took me in that cold night, I would have been willing to go through blazes of burning coals if I saw a glass of whiskey on the other side — now I don't want it."

I am wondering how long his will will say: "I don't want it."

The Presbyterians have closed their hospital. We can only surmise the reason. Aside from our eighteen room house which we use for cases of evident distress, we keep at the convent a table for those who are hungry and have no money. The natives seldom apply for food.

We make regular visits to the jail (which is quite near our Wayfarers' house) for those in need. To-day for the first time we saw Indians receiving the punishment of white men — with this difference: The Indians were allowed to sit on top, outside the iron cage, while the white men were locked in the cage. I have never seen a native woman in jail here.

Lamentable is the condition of a portion of New Albuquerque. The Mayor has issued orders to do away with a certain public nuisance and allowed the denizens a limited time to close their houses or leave town. What do you think they did? They made a collection of old bells, gongs, tin pans, and any object that would produce noise, and, the night before the day appointed to either close their houses or leave town, all went pell-mell to the front of the Mayor's residence and serenaded him!

This is still a frontier town — how long it will remain such, no one can predict.

A mutual friend of our present sheriff, Don Santiago Baca, came to see me. Here is most of his conversation:

"Sister, Don Santiago has many friends due to his big heart and trustfulness in humanity, but his friends are positive the bookkeeper handling the public money for him is squandering money here and there in excess of the salary allowed him. Will you as a friend, call his attention to what many persons have observed?"

Don Santiago is the son-in-law of Doña Nieves, who was determined to give us her house and land which were very

desirable for a convent and which gift she wanted me to accept.
But I refused it, knowing that her daughter and her children
would, by this surrender, lose much of their expected inheritance.
This fact made it somewhat easier for me to broach the unpleasant subject of his bookkeeper to him.

At my first opportunity I told Don Santiago some of the
rumors in circulation concerning the public money handled by
his bookkeeper. He looked so hurt to think that anyone would
have so low an opinion of the man he himself trusted. I said
all I could to put him on his guard, but could not surmise
what effect my conversation had on him.

A few weeks later, Don Santiago came to the convent. His
face was flushed; he did not lose time making many explanations.

"Sister, financially, I'm a ruined man. You placed nine hundred
dollars of school warrants in my keeping — I must make that
good. I have fifty acres of fenced-in land in Atrisco, which I
beg you to accept in lieu of my indebtedness to you. This parcel
of land is the only thing I can control. I will be left penniless
and the only shelter for myself and family that remains to us
is the house and garden you refused to accept from my mother-
in-law."

"Thank God, you and the family have that."

The general public sympathizes with Don Santiago Baca —
but the added phrase is "Business is business." So the good and
the bad become submerged, and the world goes on the same. . . .

Our sailor lad, Jimmy, told me shortly after we had sheltered
him: "I can do more than turn somersaults." He is proving his
assertion. He rises two hours before any working man, begins
his daily routine and does odd jobs here and there. He has
established a regular chain of early jobs, collects his wages,
and places it where I must see it. When called to an account,
he remarked:

"Don't I see that it is the likes of me and others who have
many to provide for that is all the time taking from your
pocketbook, so I work before working time to help you."

"But, Jimmy, I'm not paying you any wages."

"What did I ever save when I got wages? Only a sailor suit, and I have now more clothes than I can wear, so, Sister, be aisy on me for the little pleasure I take in helping you to help others."

Now, dear Sister Justina, is not that a most gratifying speech from an illiterate sailor?

§ 17

To untwist twisters seems one of the many oddities that fall to me.

The Superintendent of our Public Schools engaged a staff of teachers for the New Town public school. The Superintendent remarked: "The funds are low, but money will be available when taxes are collected." Both New and Old Town public schools are taught by our Sisters.

The school warrants are issued to us every month, but not one can be cashed. Meanwhile, we were paying interest on borrowed money. The face value of warrants on hand exceeds $6,000. The Territory was preparing for the Legislature. A young lawyer, newly admitted to the bar, was to represent Bernalillo County. Since he was young and aggressive, I feared to entrust him to have our unpaid school warrants legalized by the "Law Makers." So I consulted Mr. T. B. Catron,[5] who has been from the beginning our counsellor-at-law, besides being considered the "Legal Light" of our Territory.

But, lo! This act of mine was resented to the fullest by the young lawyer who wrote me one of his characteristic effusions. Among other things, he said: "Having ignored your representative, I will see that the Bill legalizing the school warrants will not pass."

My best security for its passage was to mail the wrathful communication to Mr. T. B. Catron, mentioning to him that the town of Bernalillo as well as Santa Fe was in the same predicament as ourselves; then I stated, "I'll be in Santa Fe one week from to-day."

When a week after I went to Mr. Catron's office in Santa Fe — a few minutes after we began to speak on the subject of legalizing the school warrants — in walked every lawyer in the building, each with an amused look and suppressed laughter. Mr. Thornton, one of Catron's firm, wanted to know if I had not been intimidated by that threatening letter. Mr. Clancy said: "What are you going to do about it?" All seemed to enjoy the "threat." I did not enjoy the laugh on the young barrister and remarked: "Is there one of us who would not undo some things we have done?"

"Even to kill a double just claim?" said one of the lawyers.

Mr. Catron took up the conversation: "Sister, even had I been indifferent to your claim — which I was not — that offensive epistle would have brought out every fighting nerve in my anatomy. So now rest assured those school warrants will be legalized. It was one of two things — either close the schools or issue warrants. We did the same here in Santa Fe and all teachers who possess school warrants are entitled to their face value."

Now comes the comedy part of the subject. Sister Victoria, in charge of our hospital in Santa Fe who has never been known to swerve one iota from her daily routine work, was asked by a lawyer, who surmised I was in Santa Fe in the interest of our school warrants (and whose politics are not the same as Mr. Catron's), to speak to me on the subject of drafting an omnibus bill which would include expenses incurred for school furniture not authorized to be purchased, adding: "I have every guarantee that an Omnibus Bill such as I have in mind will be read first, second and third time and unanimously passed. So speak to Sister Blandina and ask her for her own interest to consider my proposition."

Sister Victoria gave me the entire conversation as it was spoken to her by the lawyer. Sister urged me to join our interests. I told our dear Sister I preferred to take my chances in the way I went about it in preference to making a change.

"But, Sister Blandina, Mr. — assured me you are going to lose."

So the conversation dropped. But the lawyer came and began his talk. "I cannot understand, Sister, why you are coming to draft a bill that will be tabled. Do listen to a lawyer who has your interest in mind as well as the cause he represents here. Do let me persuade you to agree to an 'Omnibus Bill.'"

I told him: "I am satisfied with the way the bill is drafted, viz.: to cover the face value of school warrants issued, proving the fact that schools were maintained in session during the period the school warrants were issued."

So the conversation ended.

Incidentally, Governor Edmund G. Ross[6] (our present Governor) and I met. He remarked: "I understand you are doing some lobbying."

"I am only explaining why we have been paying interest on borrowed money to meet the expenses of the public school in Old and New Albuquerque, and how warrants were issued for services rendered. But when these school warrants were presented for payments, we were told 'There is no money in the Treasury.' So I am here to have these school warrants legalized."

"Fear not, Sister. Your claim is just and you shall have the pleasure of seeing me sign the bill."

"Thank you, Mr. Ross. I imagine it will give the people of those towns — Santa Fe, Albuquerque and Bernalillo — a great satisfaction to feel their disinterestedness has been appreciated. Have you remarked how uniquely you are taking action in two transition periods?"

"In what way, Sister?"

"Did not your vote prevent President Andrew Jackson from impeachment in the Reconstruction period after the Civil War? And now you are doing the act that will prevent a great amount of discontentment among the old residents. Yet you will be criticized by the late incomers who will not take time to study conditions as they were and as they find them."

I waited until I saw the bill signed by Governor Ross and then I returned to Albuquerque to find that one of the Jaffa Brothers, who is on the School Board, had left for Trinidad from which place he would go on to New York and Europe. I needed his signature — on the warrant affair — so I took the first train for Trinidad, arrived at 4 P.M., saw Mr. Jaffa the same day, and took the train for Albuquerque.

At Lamy Junction — the Santa Fe branch, I found a wire telling me: "Come to Santa Fe, or your bill will be tabled." Also a Santa Fe gentleman met me at Lamy Junction trying to persuade me to return to the Ancient City on the branch line. "Else, Sister, your bill will die a natural death. Only three days and the session closes."

I replied that I was on my way to Albuquerque and did not find it convenient to change my route. Arriving at the convent, the Sister who had received the wire addressed to me and had repeated the contents at Lamy Junction, could not be persuaded that "all is well."

Personally, I was curious to ascertain why so much confusion. The cause was the "Omnibus Bill" man who still had hopes of incorporating our bill into his "Omnibus Bill" which he knew would be killed.

You see, dearest, I had to act so quickly that it gave me no time to think except to make a success in having our school warrants legalized. All this may not be of much interest to you only inasmuch as it relates to me.

Later: The bonds were issued with coupons attached, bearing 6 per cent interest.

§ 18

1886.

"Vanity of vanities and all is vanity."

Fortunately for my peace of mind, dear Sister Justina, neither praise nor unjust criticism affects me. At this period, it is praise. What does it all amount to? If the laudation is given actions performed and those actions are accompanied by single-mindedness, and the direction is straight to God — He will be the recompense. If flaws are found — may the mercy of Christ cleanse them.

As complicated as is the frontier life (and I've lived it fourteen years — from Kit Carson to Trinidad, Colorado; to Santa Fe, New Mexico; to Arizona — by trips) yet I have never turned aside from the purpose for which I was missioned to the Southwest, viz.: to teach and meet emergencies as I saw them. "To meet emergencies as I saw them" is my interpretation of the Superior's wishes.

If ever we meet and have time to review the many serious, humorous and ludicrous situations I have found myself in, our health will receive 100 per cent to its credit by laughter.

Rev. Father Stephan, of the Catholic Indian Bureau, Washington, D. C., has given us two section houses to be used to instruct the Catholic Indians attending the government school near Albuquerque. Mr. McGinnis (ex-editor of a daily) and myself (don't laugh) erected them.

Our José Apodaca (Navajo Indian) did the foundation in cobbles under my direction! I foresee that it will not be long before these Indian students will have to attend Mass in the New Town Church — San Felipe in Old Town cannot accommodate half the number that come to our instruction classes.

The New Town Church is much larger than San Felipe. Both churches have Jesuit pastors.

It is a pleasure to work with the S.J.'s. As a whole, they meet any emergency and never shirk duty, though death may stare them in its performance. How could any of us be less generous toward God?

Often have I wished that our Most Reverend Archbishop would designate some energetic, talented priest to keep at least a synoptic record of what has transpired and is taking place in the Territory. In years to come it would make a good history of the Church and its struggles in the past and present, noting the efforts of our natives to adjust themselves. During my stay in Santa Fe, I read an article written by W. G. Ritch, a former secretary of the Territory, who stated that no thought had been given to education until the Americans took possession.

That pronouncement is inconsiderate. What has any government ever accomplished among uncivilized people without the aid of missionaries? From notes taken at different times, you may read some facts. Here are some of my findings: Rev. Brother Baldwin, Vice-President of St. Michael College, Santa Fe, was a substantial help to me in taking notes.

Education in New Mexico began in 1599 by the Franciscans who had accompanied Onate. The Spaniards were expelled in 1680. The Franciscans had no possibility of continuing this branch of their work until after the reconquest by De Vargas 1692-1693, at which time the Franciscans used educational methods among the Indians, opening every avenue to Spanish children. In 1721, the King of Spain ordered public schools to be established. From 1721 to 1822 many efforts were made to maintain schools, but the results were meager. Even an attempt to teach in those periods was heroic. A law was passed in 1823 to establish a high school in El Paso del Norte (Juárez). Two colleges, one in Santa Fe, the other in Taos, were established in 1826. This was done by Vicar-General Fernandez of Santa Fe and Padre Martinez of Taos, who shouldered the expense. From these two colleges good results were obtained. At this time (1826) there were also seventeen schools scattered here and there. By 1844 schools had been opened in all important places. Governor Mariano Martinez, 1844-1845, had two professors come from Europe and helped with his own money to carry on public schools, adding military instruction in the school at Santa Fe. Governor Francisco Xavier Chavez gave $1,000 to help pay the teachers. Governor Xavier Chavez was our Hermana Dolores Chavez de Guiterrez' father.

Who can recount the hardships endured by the natives before New Mexico peacefully surrendered to the United States? Hermana Dolores often kept me spellbound narrating the losses and narrow escapes her family had on account of invasions and raids made by Apaches and Navajos; the medicinal use the natives made of camphor and cinnamon; the method employed once during the year by some Indian tribes to care for their health, but — all her talks and traditions in the family pointed to the undeniable fact that the natives were in constant danger of their lives as well as in danger of death by starvation. Our backwoods Missourians and Kentuckians have not many obstacles to encounter, yet their illiteracy is marked. I make these statements to you because of the oft repeated taunts of incomers who find fault with almost everything our natives do.

Last year we invited Hermana Dolores to spend a week in our Old Town mission. This was the first time she rode in a train. Coming down the Rio Grande she missed the burial stops. Fearing you may not know what a burial stop is, I will explain. Suppose a person died five or ten miles from Bernalillo or any other place and the family of the deceased wished to bury the lamented from the Bernalillo church. Every time the cortege makes a stop, the place is marked by a mound of stones or boulders surmounted by a cross. Hermana Dolores missed the mounds, but saw the telegraph poles which, when the train moves fast, look like so many crosses. I saw her bless herself and turning to me, she said: "Thank God, my people do not forget their religion." Beautiful faith — yet it reminds me forcibly of many who express their opinion on subjects they do not understand.

I missed the jail-keeper and to-day I was told he is very low and wants to see me.

I took Sister Pauline to make a visit to see the sick man. When we got near the adobe he occupied, a man was on guard with a large bottle of disinfectant which he used to sprinkle in the room. He cautioned us: "Do not go near him." Wondering why, we entered. The man's scalp was slit open and infection, in its most terrible and repulsive form, had set in. His right arm and hand were in the same condition. The patient told me he had been a Catholic, but had joined the Masons to better his condition. Every Mason I've met here is a *good* specimen of humanity, and I do not see that they can do any more for him than they are doing. . . .

I was called to the music room and greeted by Mr. Adolph Bandelier,[7] which visit was a pleasant surprise. Here is a big man — very big — but biggest is his modesty. Among other things he told me he was going to live in a village where the Indians are supposed to worship snakes, and he will remain in that village or pueblo until he ascertains the truth or otherwise, of the supposition. He added: "When I return I will come to see you the first one." I cannot realize why he has given me the pleasure of a visit and promise of a second one unless he has heard that anything appertaining to Indians has interest for me.

You may not know that Mr. Bandelier is a scientist employed by the newly-formed Archeological Institute of America. With the general aim of the new inhabitants to reach goals — land, home, gold mines, turquoise mines, coal mines, lost mines, etc., I doubt if the object of this sincere man of science will receive much attention, except perhaps by such characters as Judge Prince and Charles Loomis. Mr. Loomis would be more to Mr. Bandelier's mind. Judge Prince — though he has been making historical researches, these are as preludes to Mr. Bandelier's correct aims.

There is another man whom I have met and who might have achieved wonderful results by his researches had he kept his theology in mind and worldly ambition at miles' length, but — to his misfortune and my chagrin — he is satisfied with the "husks the swine did eat." This man's mind is expeditious in reaching at results (in all but his spiritual life) but not near as enduring as Mr. Bandelier's. The latter may not soon make a name for himself — the former has given his name to several places of prominence and leads men in prospecting and researching groups, wherever he is. And the end? "What doth it profit a man if he gain the whole world and suffer the loss of his own soul?" Fortunately, dear Sister Justina, this criticism is sacred to us.

I received a short note from the "Outcast" which says:

"Sister, I have done nothing wrong since I left Albuquerque. The impulse to carry out instructions given me by the Head of the 'devilish cult' has been strong. Your sincere kindness drowned the impulse.

"The Outcast."
Oct., 1886.

The last time I scribbled in this journal, mentioning incidents above the ordinary, was the day I received a few lines from the "Outcast." Today a partial letter came from him. The contents follow:

"Sister:

"Life is a tragedy, a complex beyond my comprehension in its smallest detail.

"From Albuquerque to the Atlantic Coast have I traveled, holding strongly to the seed sown by kindness and smothering the seeds which began to sprout some twenty years ago.

"I ship for home where I will resume my name. You may never learn who I am, but of this be convinced: no greater disasters have ever been prevented than you did by the reception you gave the sailor and myself on that cold winter night. The gleamings of Faith are returning.

"The Outcast."

§ 19

January 22, 1887.

To-day Sister Mary Teresa Otero de Chavez was called to her reward. January 22, 1872, will bring to your mind another call — the Rev. William Bigelow, who left his earthly toils possessing $3.50, but whose purse was ever open to the needy. This will also call to mind the brilliant young lawyer (his brother), who came to the funeral and to attend to the business end of Rev. Bigelow's affairs.

Some years after, we heard the lawyer had gone to the Holy Cross Congregation. To that I can add a colorful sequel.

Last year I received information that a Holy Cross priest was in Socorro in the last stages of tuberculosis. The altitude of Socorro was better for his disease than that of Santa Fe, but the care was not. So I insisted that he be brought to our Santa Fe Hospital, where I visited him as often as possible. The Rev. Father Zahm happened to be in New Mexico with a chartered car registering students for the Notre Dame University. Father Zahm came to Old Albuquerque to see me, hoping I could give him information of Rev. Father Bigelow's whereabouts. Father Zahm went at once to Santa Fe. Imagine the meeting! One on the verge of the grave — among strangers — the other all equipped to bring him to die among his own! The invalid was carried to the chartered car, and Father Zahm wired Mrs. Bigelow to be at the University when Father Bigelow arrived in as fair condition as could be expected. Mother and son had a short interview after which he went to God, so Father Zahm's brother wrote me.

Rummaging in memory's storehouse reminds me of a day in 1871, when Rev. William Bigelow received a visit from Mr. Seward, Lincoln's Secretary of War, who had come to visit a member of the United States Cabinet, Mr. Stewart, who was ill. Father Bigelow brought Mr. Seward to my schoolroom door. I went to meet the visitors. The Secretary was introduced, and presented his hand, which I refused to see, saying: "I cannot touch the hand of the man who signed Mrs. Surrat's death warrant." You remember, I always claimed Mrs. Surrat was innocent of the charge of being in the plot to murder President Lincoln. What plotters of such a plot would take a rooming house — or boarding house — woman into their secret! You, dear Sister Justina, never approve of my abruptness, but did I not act in this manner, I would be false to my principles. The one treated uncivilly can never feel the torture I do after the uncivil act is done. Yet, with my temperament would I not be a hypocrite, did I act otherwise?

April 14, 1887. Hermana Dolores Chavez de Guiterrez winged her flight heavenward. A long obituary was published in the *Revista Católica*. This dear Sister I've mentioned several times in my journal — which I hope you will enjoy when it comes into your possession. Through respect for his aunt (Hermana Dolores) Colonel Chavez followed the funeral cortege walking and bareheaded to the cemetery. Hermana Dolores was sixty years old when she was received into the Community and lived twenty-one years the life of a Religious! Think of the sacrifice this must have entailed!

Mr. Bandelier has returned from the clan that worships snakes, and has verified the fact. When I went into the reception room and saw a sun-burned, emaciated man rise to greet me, it took a few seconds before I could say: "Mr. Bandelier!"

"Yes, Sister, but you did not recognize me when you came in."

"Perfectly true, Mr. Bandelier, which leads me to think you have borne many hardships since you left Albuquerque for your present quest."

"I told you, Sister, when I was about to go to the Indians, who were supposed to worship snakes, that I would remain with them until I could prove the truth or falsity of snake worship. Here are my proofs (unfolding sketches of an *estufa* and some snakes) — no doubt whatever, these Indians are snake worshippers."

"Knowing the Indians' tenacity to hold secrets, I am curious to know how you managed to get into their *estufa*" (Council Chamber).

"I will tell you, Sister. The first day I approached these Indians they gave me plainly to understand I was not wanted. They saw I was not armed. I only carried my whittling knife, water colors and material for sketching. I made sketches of my own surroundings, which pleased those who saw them and who were trying to find out why I came among them.

"The day passed and night came. I made a bed of leaves and cedar and was content. The next day other Indians of the same clan came and treated me about the same — only I spoke more in order to get them to answer as I wanted to familiarize myself with their particular language. The interchange of speech pleased them, but their attitude toward me remained the same. In a few days the small amount of my edible provisions gave out, so I ate what the Indians threw to the dogs — after the dogs were satiated."

I could only look at the man and wonder. He continued:

"For fully five months this was the routine. I sketched and spoke to those of the clan who came to see and watch me and talk to me. I did many little services for those who came near me which I could see pleased them. At last I was invited to eat and sleep among them though the Chief gave me some of the squaws' work to do. I knew this was the last test before they gave me their confidence. Little by little the old men came to ask advice, then at last I was admitted to their Council in the *estufa*. This was the seventh month among them. As they had seen me daily sketching, my doing so in the Councilroom did not alarm them — in fact they were pleased to see the snakes on paper; they compared them and were satisfied they were good.

"Altogether I remained nine months to make sure those Indians worship snakes. I left the clan on friendly terms."

"Thank you so much for the information."

"I understand, Sister, you have had some encounters with the Apaches and other tribes of Indians. Would you mind telling me anything that would be of interest in my research work?"

"Mr. Bandelier, contacts made by me with any Indian tribe, were, and are, of a protective type. On several occasions I gave ample reasons to prove that the government agents were defrauding the tribes they were paid for assisting. I once reconciled the Apaches — in an act of injustice toward them — convincing them that one white man doing wrong to them did not mean that all white men would do as he did. In Trinidad, Colorado, in the early seventies we were all expecting an attack from the

Utes. The whole tribe was camped a few miles from Trinidad. The citizens made full preparation for defense. Our convent was to be the fort. Meanwhile, I made some of the Indians — who came in to reconnoiter — understand that we (all of the inhabitants) were friendly. Maybe they didn't test me in their own Indian way! But they soon recognized I was friendly and sincere. Their Chief at the time was Rafael, whose son was dying of pneumonia. Rafael asked if he should bury him like a dog. I said: "No. I will send for him and bury him like a Christian.' He had been baptized. After the son's burial, the tribe moved on.

"You see, Mr. Bandelier, all of my contacts with the Indians partook of protectiveness and nothing of a scientific nature."

"Yes, I see, Sister, I see very clearly." Then he added: "I was told you had turned down taking charge of the Catholic Indian School which the Most Rev. Archbishop J. B. Salpointe established in Santa Fe."

"That is partly true. When His Grace unfolded his plans to me I saw at a glance we could not make a success of the school. His Grace had in mind the appointment (as superintendent and field worker) of a Rev. gentleman whose sympathies were not with the Indians. I wrote plain facts to our Superiors — so we were counted out. The Loretto Sisters took the school and resigned at the end of the first scholastic year. The Rev. Superintendent wrote asking me to find him a Number One secular teacher and he would find several others. I secured a No. 1 secular teacher and when answering him, I said: 'The ill success of your Indian school should not be attributed to the teachers.'

"The next step taken by His Grace was that he negotiated for Mother Drexel's Sisters. I said a fervent *Deo Gratias*, being sure the school would be successful under the new management.

"These, Mr. Bandelier, are the facts concerning the Catholic Indian School in Santa Fe.

"When a Jesuit messenger, Rev. Father Fede, was sent from

the Apache Indians to ask me to teach their squaws and papooses, I would have been delighted to do so if my superiors had appointed companions to go with me. The request came from both the Apaches and Father Stephan of the Catholic Indian Bureau, Washington, D. C. Father Stephan offered me $12,000 to work with. I replied: 'Keep the $12,000, but get the permission for me and companions and the rest of my life will be given to the betterment of the Apaches.'

"The permission was not obtained. In my opinion, only the constant living among them will ever make the gradual change that will evolve the best inherent qualities of any Indian tribe. Money will not do it — nor Government Indian Schools either. A truly Christian life, combined with personal sacrifice prolonged into years, will accomplish what millions will not do."

§ 20

May 9, 1889.

A long stretch since I put pen to this journal. The intervening periods were given to music lessons — both vocal and instrumental — Spanish classes, concerts, bazaars, and best of all, to alleviating human distress whenever it came to our notice.

Albricias!

So our good native people say when they have pleasant news to impart. The financial debt on Saint Vincent Academy, New Town, is liquidated.

You may not know, dearest Sister Justina, that the convent of Old Town took the responsibility of paying off the financial debt on the Academy. What yet remains to be paid is a small amount to Jesus and Mariano Armijo. Those two families are to take our indebtedness out in educational terms. Don Perfecto Armijo's children have the right to attend our Academy[3] (boarding school) at Cincinnati — you may remember having heard of the Misses Victoriana and Candelaria Armijo being there. One of the young ladies' uncles was to visit them. The family wired to this effect:

"St. Vincent Academy,
        Cincinnati, Ohio.
                Jesus has left Albuquerque.
                        Angelita Armijo."

When the clerk at the Western Union received the message
he was more than nonplussed, but he knew he had read the
ticks correctly, so he handed the message to the messenger boy
saying aloud: "God help Albuquerque, if Jesus has left it."

This is a case where ignorance was not bliss. We had ex-
changed the land which had been donated to us for an Industrial
School for land at the base of the Sandía Mountains. I hope to
see a hospital there some day.

June 14, 1889. — I received a letter from Mother Mary Paul
which tells me to be at Mount St. Joseph for the annual retreat.
I much regret, dear, you are not to be there. Each sacrifice
brings us nearer to the goal for which we gave ourselves to
God's service. . . .

Motherhouse, August 11, 1889. — So, dearest, you are to
replace me in Old Albuquerque and I am to resume my first
school work in the Southwest, Number One School in Trinidad.
I'm a false prophet if the Sisters of Number One public school
in Trinidad, Colorado, will not be forced to resign.

I've watched the trend of bigotry. We have set the example
of liberality and blazed the path of morality and self-sacrifice —
all that remains to us now is to be *sacrificed.*

I left the Mother House August 18 for Trinidad to be in
time for the teachers' examination.

PART

IV

Trinidad Again

WHEN Sister Blandina returned to her first Western mission after an absence of twelve years, she found a settled Trinidad, one that now boasted more than 9000 inhabitants. Many old faces had disappeared from view, but the landmark she missed most poignantly was the frontier adobe church, built in 1866, where she had first come during those cold, December days of 1872. Now a lofty, bell-towered, gray-stone structure, having a seating capacity of 2000, rose firmly from the native soil. The new Holy Trinity Church had been dedicated to the Holy Trinity on that glorious feast day, May 31, 1885, four years before the pioneer's return.

The townspeople were jubilant at Sister's return. Honors, however, sat lightly upon her shoulders. There was still so much work to be done, so many souls to win to Christ. Her rare foresight warned her that soon the Sisters of Charity who had opened Public School Number One would be asked to lay aside their religious garb. Meanwhile she worked ceaselessly among the people. Frequently she thought of the early settlers, many of whom desired only to get rich and then get out of the Territory. She thought of the hunters and trappers who took beavers and later buffalo skins, and left nothing in return. Then she reflected, "But when the Church comes, she settles down among her children, because she is above all else a Mother."

A month before Sister's return, the Sisters of Charity had formally opened a hospital, Mount San Rafael, in Trinidad, on July 26, 1889. Sister Blandina's dear Irish friend, Sister Catherine from Santa Fe, had supervised its construction and was now superior of the hospital. To defray expenses, Sister Catherine continued her begging trips through Colorado and New Mexico. Often Sister Blandina accompanied her, and they re-lived the old days, for though neither Sister was old chronologically, both had lived through an intense era in American history. Both had come to the Southwest while the buffalo were plentiful. They had watched the progress of the railroad, the "bad medicine wagon," as the Indians called it. They had seen it ascend the steep slopes of Raton Pass, and hurry down into the towns of New Mexico. Their country of the Southwest had changed but the Sisters kept their memory of it alive.

Sister Blandina's life in the Southwest was ending. Unknown to her a new labor among her own Italian people in Cincinnati, the city of her childhood, was opening. There with the gentle and loving Sister Justina she would establish the first organized Italian Welfare Center in the United States.

During the last years of her life, Sister Blandina found youth again in remembering her beloved first-love, the Southwest.

"Adios, Trinidad, of heart-pains and consolations!"

§ 1

Trinidad, Colorado, August, 1889.

August 24. Sister Justina asked me to accompany her to the School Superintendent's office to give in her annual report, etc., of School Number One, as well as to introduce me. The scene enacted in the Superintendent's office amused me beyond expression.

When we entered the Sanctorum and he saw Sister Justina, though she said: "This is the Sister who is to take my place," he ignored her words and began to lament her change.

"What will the Mexican element do? Who will control those pupils? I know your throat is perforated, but I prefer you would make use of one of the older pupils to give out the questions and you correct. If you say so, I will wire your headquarters to have you remain. I cannot see School Number One without you."

"Professor, all arrangements have been made for my transfer to Albuquerque, New Mexico."

I interposed: "Professor, I am highly pleased to note your appreciation of Sister Justina's qualifications for the position she held. I wish to call your attention to the fact that before the school board determined to build a High School, I taught the High School branches in School Number One. As for my Spanish — judge by my English — moreover, I love the Mexicans equally with Sister Justina."

"Is it possible that this is Sister Blandina?"

"It is."

"Sister, I will take pleasure in tendering you an Honorary Certificate. Your record of four years of successful teaching in School Number One entitles you to it. I apologize for my rudeness when you first came in. The trouble is, I have been so annoyed that Sister Justina had to give up school work that I could not imagine anyone else being able to adjust herself to our native element as she has done."

"Thank you, Professor. You will find School Number One in number one condition for the first day of school."

Two weeks after my arrival in Trinidad Mrs. ——, one of the daughters of the man who was to have been hanged by "Mob Law" (he had shot an innocent young Irishman) and who was saved from that tragic death by the then Sheriff accompanying me and the prisoner to the mortally wounded man's room to cause a reconciliation on condition that the "law should take its course," asked me to visit her mother who had never left their dwelling since that "melancholy day."

"You will not recognize mother. Her hair is snowy white. Presumably you know I am principal of one of the grade schools. I trust you are pleased to see how one of your pupils climbed the Teachers' ladder."

That same day I made a call on Mrs. ——'s mother. I would not have known her so sorrowfully resigned! Her two sons (now real estate agents) came in and we talked over the years they attended school and the transitional state since the time a man's life had not the value of a horse, and the present settled condition of Trinidad.

Both men retired, and presently the man saved from "mob law" stood in the center of the open folding doors, head bowed, his hands in his coat sleeves, his white beard reaching to waist line. He looked at me, bowed low and retired. Not a word was spoken among any of us as to what was uppermost in our minds. I could not help reflecting what a heavy burden the family was carrying. Were they Catholics, their minds could unburden in the confessional. Christ knew the best remedy for the perfectly moulded nature vitiated by the weakness of woman and the cowardice of man. . . .

Election time, 1891. Oh ye wise who are not hypocrites, watch the play of politics going on in the state. Two men running for State Superintendent of Schools, one sells out to the other for a certain sum and the promise of being Superintendent of Schools in a thriving town of Southwest Colorado, thus ousting its present occupant.

But the voting? Yes, the voting will take place — but the man to occupy the position has been slated and he will get there. Watch. Retribution never fails. . . .

Trinidad has lost its frontier aspect. The jail is built to hold its inmates. Billy the Kid's gang is dissolved. Dick Wootton's tollgate is no more. The remaining men who were ready at the least provocation or no provocation (except that of strong drink) to raise the trigger have settled down to domestic infelicity. Few of the latecomers would venture to read on the faces of men who at present aim at being peaceful citizens — the freaks performed in other days. Those who know thank God that conditions are partly adjusted. . . .

Mother Blanche received wires and letters from citizens of

Albuquerque to have me there for a few weeks. The reason is most laughable. A young man whom I prevented from being sent to the penitentiary by adjusting his case out of court, and who is habitually intoxicated, is leading a faction of our natives to compel the Sisters to give up the public schools of Old Town!

§ 2

Old Albuquerque, 1891. After my arrival here a member of the school board remarked: "That young inebriate counts upon the idea that the Sisters will not go to a public assembly to take the Teachers' public school examination."

"In this case I clearly see it is of vital importance for the Sisters to take the examination wherever it will be held."

The Teachers' Examination today. The Court House is filled to capacity. There are three tables in the enclosure usually occupied by Court officials and separated from the audience by a neat wooden railing. The Sisters — four of us — were assigned to one oblong table. Next to us were placed a number of young ladies — most of them our former pupils. Parallel to their table sat a goodly number of teachers and aspiring teachers. The examination papers were distributed. I had not turned one when from the exit door came an intoxicated voice: *"Allí está la Hermana Blandina — no podemos hacer nada."* (There is Sister Blandina — we can do nothing.) This was the man leading the faction.

The words were scarcely uttered when Mr. Mariano Otero (usually called the King of Bernalillo County) strode over the railing and came, as he said, "to condole with me over the difficult examination questions!"

This must have been meant in derision, for any fourth year high school pupil could answer them. Still, Mr. Otero remained, talking on topics of general interest while the Sisters with me turned their third paper. At last he said: *"Adiós,"* only to be followed by Mr. Amada Baca's younger brother. I looked at Mr. Bond, the presiding officer, but my look brought no relief. Mr. Baca must have seen I was worried and said: "Many of us want to see you when this thing is over." With those words he left me.

But, though annoyed, I was not prevented from seeing several humorous byplays at the table of teachers and would-be teachers. One gray haired old gentleman who had been teaching in a country school for thirty years looked at his first paper, rumpled it and put it in his pocket. The second and third met the same fate. The presiding spirit went to him and said: "Those questions, when answered, must be left face downward."

The old gentleman's dignity was much perturbed — he left.

One young man — recently from somewhere — drew his pencil through most of the questions — turned the papers face downward and made his exit. One of the young ladies next to our table leaned over to ask a question. The Sister nearest to her said: "This is not a schoolroom, but an individual examination."

All this I noticed while the two gentlemen took my time from my examination papers, but the instant Mr. Baca left I went to Mr. Bond and asked him to prevent anyone from interrupting me — which he did.

You must take into account, Sister Justina, that this is the first Teachers' Public Examination ever held in this Territory. This covers all territory, but does not hide from me the fact that before long all school funds will be diverted into channels dug out by politicians. The only available public school funds for nuns will be the country schools where politicians will not find persons to teach except the "Benighted Catholics."

A few days after the examinations, Mr. Bond and the other members of the examination board came to the Convent in a body to present our certificates, saying: "We want the pleasure of personally handing you the first four Number One teachers' certificates issued in Albuquerque under the new school law."

The one small faction of the inebriate having naturally died, I returned to Trinidad to find Mr. Butler — the School Superintendent — buried, and a new occupant in his place.

The new Superintendent's name is Stephen and the new State Superintendent of Public Schools is Dick, well known in Trinidad.

§ 3

Summer of 1892. I'm to meet the School Board.

We met.

The intent of the meeting was to notify me that "under no circumstances does the school board want to lose your services, but we ask you to change your mode of dress."

I looked steadily at the Chairman and replied: "The Constitution of the United States gives me the same privilege to wear this mode of dress as it gives you to wear your trousers. Good-bye. . . ."

So this is the end of twenty-two years' work in Public School Number One, opened in 1870 when Trinidad was mostly governed by the best shotmen and sheriff's lead, mobs to hang murderers, and jail birds never come to trial, and the life of a man was considered a trifle compared to the possession of a horse. Jesuits and Sisters used every effort to quell the daily storms — while School Room in School Number One exerted an influence over the pupils — grown men and women — attending Room Number One that often astonished its teacher.

Money considerations never entered the mind of her who had early in life evaluated money and eternity. We supplied the school building, janitor, and made repairs, and daily from the one story adobe building went forth cleaned hearts that had entered with murderous thoughts and designs; hearts filled to overflowing with the desire to get rich quick; hearts whose morality was fit companion to the beasts of the plains; and these spasmodically agitated hearts were quelled to calmness by her whose sole thought was peace — the path to Heaven. . . .

Within the same week I received the letter that follows:

E. Brigham   C. A. Washburn

Brigham & Washburn

Real Estate, Loans & Insurance

Trinidad, Colorado

June 17, 1892.

Sister Blandina,
Trinidad, Colorado.
Dear Madam:

I am requested by the School Board — as Secretary of the Board — to notify you and Sister Rose Alexius that your applications as teachers in the public schools of Trinidad, Colorado, for the coming year can only be accepted upon the condition that you shall lay aside your dress of black, peculiar to your church and office, and be willing to comply with all the rules of the Board and Superintendent — the same as is required of other teachers in the Trinidad Schools.

> Very Respectfully,
> Trinidad School Board
> Per E. Brigham, Secy.

P. S. Sister Blandina, you understand full well that your qualifications as a teacher are not questioned, also those of Sister Alexius are very satisfactory. But you understand full well our position and that anything in a public school that savors of sectarianism brings us into trouble and is directly in opposition to all our school laws, and the duties required of School Directors, hence there is but one course of action, and that must be in the line of our duty and you can but say that we are justified in this matter.

> Very respectfully,
> E. Brigham.

On receipt of this letter I wrote Mother Mary Blanche, telling her of meeting the School Board and the result of the meeting. No comments from that great heart except: "You foresaw this. God ever bless you. Saint Patrick's School, Pueblo, Colorado, needs a principal — fill the vacancy."[1]

When I told Father Personé, S.J., the pastor of Holy Trinity parish of my being sent to Pueblo he said: "Please, Sister, not until you have made a survey of every Mexican family who has children of school age. Register the names and hand the list to me. This will be your last act of love to our native population."

This was done in order to secure the attendance of our native children in the parish school which will open in September.

Adiós, Trinidad, of heart-pains and consolations!

Footnotes

PART I

1. Second Motherhouse of the Sisters of Charity, also called "Cedar Grove." First Motherhouse was situated on Mount Harrison in Cincinnati. This Motherhouse was also called Mt. St. Vincent. The Sisters moved to Mount Harrison in 1854, and to "Cedar Grove" in 1857; and finally to the site of the present Motherhouse, Mt. St. Joseph in 1869.

2. Mother Josephine Harvey re-elected Mother General in 1871. Died March 31, 1895, at the age of 76. Mother Regina Mattingly's term of office expired in 1871. She was then sent to Steubenville, Ohio, on mission where she was Sister Blandina's superior. She was re-elected Mother General in 1877. Mother Regina died June 4, 1883, at the age of 56. Her ancestors came from Maryland and were among the first settlers of Kentucky.

3. Former Motherhouse of the Sisters of Charity on Price Hill, Cincinnati, Ohio, called "Cedar Grove," was the home of Judge Alderson; at that time called "The Cedars." Mother Margaret Cecilia George, first Cincinnati superior of the Sisters of Charity, brought the Sisters to live there in 1857. Mother Margaret was born in Sligo, Ireland, in 1789. Her parents moved to Baltimore, Maryland, when she was five. She entered the Sisters of Charity Community at Emmitsburg, Maryland, February 2, 1812, where Mother Elizabeth Seton, foundress of the Community, received her. Sister Margaret's mother entered the Sisters of Charity Community when she was forty years old. She was known as Sister Bridget. Mother Margaret died November 11, 1868, at Cedar Grove.

4. Sister Anthony O'Connell, Civil War Nurse. Called "The Angel of the Battlefield." Died December 8, 1897, at the age of 83. Sister Anthony, also referred to as "The Florence Nightingale of America," led the first six Sisters of Charity to the Civil War battlefields. Altogether 35 Sisters of Charity of Cincinnati served as Civil War nurses.

5. Sister Gabriella Crowe, a Civil War nurse, died February 9, 1911, at the age of 80.

6. Sister Delphina Hannon died October 24, 1925, at the age of 73.

7. Sister Sophia Gilmeyer, a pupil of Mother Seton, was a native of Maryland. When she entered the Community of the Sisters of Charity in Maryland she brought her slaves, horses, musical instruments and fortune. Was a Civil War nurse. Died November 21, 1872, at the age of 65.

8. Sister Benedicta Cain died February 9, 1915, at the age of 89. She served the Civil War soldiers at St. John's Hospital, Cincinnati, conducted by the Sisters of Charity.

9. Second Archbishop of Cincinnati, Ohio. Born February 26, 1800. Died July 4, 1883.

10. Father J. F. Callaghan, editor and proprietor of the *Catholic Telegraph* from 1869–1881.

11. Sister Antonia McCaffrey entered the Sisters of Charity at Emmitsburg, Maryland, January 2, 1850. Died January 4, 1900, at the age of 73.

12. Sister Gonzaga Sheehan died January 29, 1887, at the age of 51. Was a Civil War nurse.

13. "Captain William Becknell, of Missouri, was the father of the Santa Fe Trail and the real founder of the commerce of the prairies. It was he who took the first successful trading expedition to Santa Fe. In 1821, with four companions, Captain Becknell crossed the plains. They started from the town of Franklin, Missouri, with the original purpose of trading with the Indians, but having fallen in with a party of Mexican rangers, they were prevailed upon to go to Santa Fe, where, notwithstanding the small amounts of merchandise which they carried, very handsome profits were realized."

Source — *Leading Facts of New Mexican History* by Ralph Emerson Twitchell, Vol. II (Cedar Rapids, Iowa: *The Torch Press*, 1912), p. 103.

14. Kit Carson — born in Kentucky in December, 1809. He was taken to Missouri as a child, went west at seventeen and in 1853, he herded 6,500 sheep to California. Known as "The Happy Warrior," he led the First New Mexico Volunteers during the Civil War and was made a brevet brigadier-general. As a New Mexico Indian agent, he lived in Taos where he was baptized a Catholic by Padre Martinez, Feb. 28, 1842. He married Sophia Jaramillo the following year and died May 23, 1868, at Fort Lyon, Colorado.

15. Uncle "Dick" Wootton — one of the very earliest of the pioneers, a contemporary of the Bents, St. Vrain, "Kit" Carson and others, was born in Mecklenberg County, Virginia, May 6, 1816. He was named Richens Lacy Wootton. In 1836, he went to Independence, Missouri, and joined a wagon train belonging to Bent and St. Vrain which was ready to start westward to Fort Bent located on the Arkansas River, a short distance west of what is now the line between Kansas and Colorado. In 1865, Uncle "Dick" procured a charter from the Colorado legislature, also one from the New Mexico legislature authorizing him to construct an inter-territorial highway from Trinidad into certain towns in the Territory of New Mexico. This was a toll road. Uncle "Dick" died August 21, 1893, at his home near Trinidad. Buried from Holy Trinity Catholic Church, August 25.

16. Las Animas County was created by an act of the Legislature in 1866. The origin of the name was *El Rio de Las Animas*, the river of souls, from whence issued strange, mournful cries. In 1860, the region was called El Rio Las Animas. Permanent settlement by Spanish Americans was made in 1862. There were originally 19 Plazas, and later 27, built for habitation and mutual protection from the Indians. Trinidad, in 1866, was a small but important trading center. "The western quarter of the valley is

mountainous with valleys and mountain peaks between the ranges. The ranges were covered with pine forests, the foothills with pinon and scrub oak trees."

Honora De Busk Smith: Unpublished thesis, U. of Colo., 1930, Hist. Dept., *Early Life in Trinidad and the Purgatory Valley.*

17. In 1868, Bishop J. P. Machebeuf met one of the founders of Trinidad, Don Felipe Baca, and talked to him about securing the Sisters of Charity of Mt. St. Joseph, Ohio, to open and establish a school. Mr. Baca volunteered to donate several acres of land with the buildings on said premises situated in the very center of Trinidad. February 6, 1870, on Friday morning at two o'clock, Sister Ann Mary Devine, Sister Eulalia Whitty and Sister Fidelis Millmore arrived from Cincinnati. Sisters Ann Mary and Eulalia then went on to Santa Fe to replace Sister Augustine and Sister Louise Barron who came to Trinidad. The school opened March 4, 1870.

18. Father Peter John Munnecom later returned to his homeland, Holland. The Jesuits took charge of Holy Trinity Parish, November 19, 1875.

19. The Sisters of Charity opened the first public school in the Territory.

20. Don Felipe Baca originally from Guadalupe, Mora County, New Mexico, with Don Pedro Valdez camped, 1858–1860, near the present site of Trinidad. One of original founders of Trinidad. The town was organized in 1877, and incorporated in 1879.

21. The Diocese of Denver established a Vicariate Apostolic for Colorado and Utah in 1868. The first baptism recorded in the Holy Trinity Church is recorded thus: "On the 24th day of June in the year 1866 I solemnly baptized Julian Wootton, adopted son of Richard Wootton of Raton, of the Rio de Las Animas. Godparents Antonio Frederico Lujan and Maria Paulina Lujan (Signed) Pedro Juan Munnecom, Parish Priest of the Most Holy Trinity Parish." This church was used until it was replaced by a new one in 1885. Bishop Joseph P. Machebeuf made his first pastoral visit on November 1, 1868; was Vicar Apostolic of Colorado at the time.

22. In 1877, the Sisters had their own chapel. Sister Maria Alphonsa McCabe and Sister Angela Murphy decorated the new chapel for the first time for the Feast of All Saints, November 1, 1877.

23. Sister Martha Goodin died March 18, 1884, at the age of 50.

24. Sister Eulalia Whitty died March 18, 1917, age 79.

25. Sister Fidelis Millmore.

26. Bishop Salpointe, second Bishop of Santa Fe. John Baptist Salpointe was a writer. Born in Clermont, France. Spent forty years in the missions of Arizona and New Mexico. He was the first Bishop of Arizona, and the second Archbishop of Santa Fe. He died at Tucson, Arizona, July 15, 1898.

27. Jesuits took charge of Holy Trinity Parish, November 19, 1875. Their territory included 27 villages; 47 miles east and west and 68 miles north and south. Lived in direst poverty. Fathers Charles M. Pinto and Alexander Leone were the first Jesuits there.

28. Baptized Projectus Joseph Machebeuf, he later, on coming to

America, transposed the two names. He was born August 11, 1812, at Riom in France. He entered the Seminary of Mont Ferrand in 1831. He was ordained December, 1836. On May 21, 1839, he and his lifelong friend, John Baptist Lamy, left Riom for America. Arrived in New Mexico with Bishop Lamy, in 1851, as his Vicar-General. Father Machebeuf worked in the Cincinnati diocese prior to his coming to New Mexico. Later became the first Bishop of Colorado. Died in Denver July 10, 1889. He is known as "The Apostle of Colorado." He went to Colorado from New Mexico on October 29, 1860. He is buried in Mount Olivet Cemetery, Denver, in a crypt reserved for the Bishops and Archbishops of Denver.

29. Billy was angry because Sister Blandina knew his purpose in coming to Trinidad. He felt that he and his gang had been betrayed by the sick member.

30. The Rev. L. M. Fede, S.J.

31. The newspaper, *Revista Catolica*, was started in January, 1875, at Las Vegas, New Mexico, by the Jesuit Fathers.

PART II

1. Established 1859.

2. Established 1853.

3. First Bishop of Santa Fe. Arrived in New Mexico in 1851. Created Archbishop, February 16, 1875. He and Joseph Projectus Machebeuf, first Bishop of Denver, were lifelong friends. He was born in Lengdes near Clermony in France, October, 1814. Ordained December, 1838, at Mont Ferrand. Came to United States in the following year. Worked in the Cincinnati diocese eleven years. Called "God's Gentleman" and "New Mexico's first citizen." Died February 13, 1888. He is buried in his Cathedral.

4. Sister Catherine Mallon, blue eyed and Irish, made her vows the morning she was chosen to go West with the pioneer band. She died October 27, 1906. She was 66 years of age and 44 years a Sister of Charity.

5. Sister Vincent O'Keefe, first Sister of Charity postulant received in Cincinnati. Soft voiced, small of stature, superbly courageous, yet she never overcame the loneliness and homesickness she felt in the Southwest. Died at 82, April 2, 1912. Was a Civil War nurse.

6. Sister Pauline Leo, affectionately called "Hermana Pablita." Came to Santa Fe as a young Sister. Mothered hundreds of orphans. Died May 27, 1910, at the age of 78.

7. Sister Theodosia Farn, died March 6, 1917, at the age of 84. New Mexicans said she was "the embodiment of wholesomeness and good cheer. Where she came the sunshine came." She served the sick soldiers during the Civil War at St. John's Hospital, operated by the Sisters of Charity in Cincinnati.

8. The morning after their arrival in Denver the newspapers announced, "Four Sisters of Charity are going to New Mexico to speculate."

9. *The New Mexican* (Weekly), September 15, 1865:
"In the last coach from the East arrived four Sisters of Charity, who, we are informed, design establishing a hospital in this city under the auspices of Bishop Lamy."

The New Mexican (Weekly), October 13, 1865 (ad.) Sisters Hospital:
"A small body of Sisters of Charity having arrived in this city design opening a Hospital for the sick and infirm.

"The institution will be located in the former residence of the Right Rev. Bishop Lamy. The house is exceedingly commodious, with garden and grounds of very great beauty.

"The number of poor persons they will be able to take care of depends upon the liberality and benevolence of the people of this city and Territory.

"Attached to the establishment will be several excellent rooms for the reception of sick boarders. They will receive the constant attention of trained and experienced nurses, with every comfort and convenience possible in this country.

"The rate of board will be reasonable. For particulars apply to Sister Servant Mary Vincent."

10. Mother Magdalen Hayden opened the first school under the direction of the Sisters of Loretto at Santa Fe, in January, 1853. The stairway in the Gothic Chapel of Our Lady of Light, often referred to as "St. Joseph's Stairway," was built during her superiorship. She died in 1894.

11. The Sisters of Loretto arrived in Santa Fe September 25, 1852.

12. In *The New Mexican* for October 13, 1865, there was this entry:
" . . . The Sisters of Charity are about, opening a hospital in this city for the needy and infirm. The undertaking is praiseworthy and deserves the encouragement of our citizens. We understand that they will shortly visit our citizens for the purpose of soliciting and in the way of subscriptions, and it is to be hoped that our people will contribute liberally, knowing the benevolent purpose for which it is intended."

13. The Barron sisters were cultured, highly educated women whose home was in Cincinnati. They presented a sharp contrast — Sister Augustine: dignified, reserved; Sister Louise, joyous, lighthearted.
Sister Augustine was a Civil War nurse. She died February 10, 1898, at the age of 72. Sister Louise died September 3, 1886, at the age of 57.

14. Sister Alphonsa Thompson, a native of Kentucky, 18 years old. Archbishop Lamy wrote of her to the Loretto Motherhouse, "Sister Alphonsa died at 10:00 a.m., July 24, 1867. She was well-educated and a model of virtue." Her grave has never been found.

15. Hermana Dolores entered the Community at the age of 60. She died April 13, 1887, at the age of 81.

16. Prominent citizen of Santa Fe. He and other Santa Feans prepared the city for a widespread celebration when the pallium was bestowed upon Bishop John Baptist Lamy in 1875.

17. Appointed by President Hayes, he was inaugurated October 1, 1878, at Santa Fe.

18. Original name of El Paso was Franklin, named in 1852, for Franklin Coontz, postmaster. The name was changed to El Paso in 1859.

19. The Spaniards first called it *Rio Bravo Del Norte* (The swift river of the north).

20. The river is navigable only a short distance from the sea into which it empties.

21. The firm of Browne and Manzanares was one of the largest mercantile establishments in the Southwest with branches in Las Vegas, Socorro, and Trinidad.

22. Governor Lionel A. Sheldon was appointed by President Garfield soon after his inauguration, and assumed office May 15, 1881.

23. The railroad reached Albuquerque in April, 1880.

PART III

1. Sister Mary Agnes McCann, author of *The History of Mother Seton's Daughters*, 3 vols. (New York: Longmans, 1923). Died October 12, 1931, at the age of 81.

2. Billy the Kid was killed July 14, 1881, at Maxwell's ranch.

3. The school at San Miguel opened in September, 1884, under the direction of the Sisters of Charity. Four Sisters were sent to San Miguel: Sister Ann Mary Devine, superior; Sister Lucia Gleason; Sister Angelica Ortiz; and Sister Mary Carmel Garcia. The mission remained open until 1904. Sister Renetta, superior there for some years, was doctor, nurse, and undertaker, as well as sexton. During a smallpox epidemic she visited the adobes vaccinating the well and nursing the sick.

There was another Sister on the mission at San Miguel, Sister Donata Apodaca, who died during an epidemic, shortly after the Sisters' arrival. Sister Donata, a very young Sister, is buried beneath the altar of the church at San Miguel.

4. Sister Mary de Sales Leheny studied medicine. Performed operations in Santa Fe in the early days when there was question of life or death. She was strong, tall, matter-of-fact, and known for her excellent nursing throughout the Southwest. She died November 29, 1934, at the age of 79.

5. Thomas B. Catron, born October 6, 1840, Lafayette County, Missouri. Fought in Civil War. Appointed United States Attorney by President Grant.

6. Assumed office June 15, 1885.

7. Adolph E. Bandelier, ethnologist, archeologist, writer.

8. Mt. St. Vincent Academy, Price Hill, Cincinnati, Ohio. It was opened in 1857.

PART IV

1. St. Patrick's School, Pueblo, opened September 1, 1890, under the supervision of the Jesuit Fathers. Sister Pelagia Schroeder was the first superior. She died November 8, 1932, at the age of 81.

Bibliography

Daily Journal, 1882; Albuquerque Morning Journal, 1900.

Archives, Archdiocese of Denver; Denver, Colorado.

Archives, Archdiocese of Santa Fe; Santa Fe, New Mexico.

Archives, Sisters of Charity, Mt. St. Joseph, Ohio.

Arizona and New Mexico, Business Directory, 1897.

Baedecker, Northern Italy Including Florence.

Bancroft, Hubert H., Arizona and New Mexico (San Francisco: Hubert Co., 1889).

Bandelier, Adolph, and Hewett, Edgar L., Indians of the Rio Grande Valley (Albuquerque: Univ. of New Mexico Press, 1937).

Barker, Sister Roseanna, S.C., Mother Margaret Cecilia George, unpublished thesis (St. Louis University, 1944).

Barton, George, Angels of the Battlefield (Philadelphia: Catholic Art Publishing Co., 1897).

Belloc, Hilaire, The Contrast (New York: McBride, 1924).

Beshoar, Michael, M.D., History of Trinidad and Las Animas County (Denver, Colo.: Steam Printing Co., 1882).

Bieber, Ralph P., Southwest Historical Series; Vol. 1. (Glendale, Calif.: Arthur H. Clark Co., 1931).

Bloom, Lansing B., Editor; Walter, Paul A. F., Managing Editor, New Mexico Historical Review, Vol. IV (1929). Published quarterly by the Historical Society of New Mexico and the University of New Mexico.

Burns, Walter Noble, The Saga of Billy the Kid (Garden City, N. Y.: Doubleday, Page and Co., 1926).

Catholic Telegraph, Cincinnati, Ohio, 1831–1941.

Catholic Encyclopedia, Vol. III (New York: Encyclopaedia Press, 1914).

Cincinnati City Directory, 1862–1878.

Cincinnati Enquirer, 1913–1941.

Cincinnati Times Star, 1913–1941.

Coe, George Washington, The Autobiography of, as related to Nan Hillary Harrison (Boston and New York: Houghton Mifflin Co., 1934).

Conrad, Howard Louis, "Uncle Dick" Wootton (Chicago: W. E. Dibble and Co., 1890).

Connelley, William E., Doniphan's Expedition (Kansas City, Mo.: Bryant and Douglas Book and Stationery Co., 1907).

De Fouri, Very Rev. James H., Historical Sketch of the Catholic Church in New Mexico (San Francisco: McCormick, 1887).

—— *Martyrs of New Mexico — a Brief Account of the Lives and Deaths of the Earliest Missionaries in the Territory* (Las Vegas: Revista Catolica Printing Co., 1893).

Denver Catholic Register, Dec., 1929; Jan.–Feb., 1941.

Denver Republican (Republican Publishing Co., 1893).

Dickens, Charles, *American Notes*, Vol. II (London: Chapman and Hall, Strand, 1842).

Embe (Marianna Burgess), *Stiya, a Carlisle Indian Girl at Home* (Cambridge Press, 1891).

Faure, Gabriel, *The Land of St. Francis of Assisi* (London: The Medici Society, Ltd., 1924).

French, Sister Florita, S.C., *History of St. Vincent Academy*, unpublished thesis (Albuquerque: University of New Mexico, 1942).

Garrett, Pat F., *The Authentic Life of Billy the Kid* (New York: The Macmillan Co., 1927).

Gregg, Josiah, *Commerce of the Prairies*, Vol. I and II (New York: J. and H. G. Langley, 8 Astor House, 1845).

Haines, Helen, *History of New Mexico* (New York: New Mexico Historical Publishing Co., 1891).

Hall, Frank, *History of the State of Colorado*, 4 vols. (Chicago: The Blakely Printing Co., 1891).

Howlett, Rev. W. J., *Life of the Right Reverend Joseph P. Machebeuf, D.D.* (Pueblo: The Franklin Press Co., 1908).

Hulbert–Moody, *The Highways of Commerce*, Vol. XVII; Part 1, "The Paths of Inland Commerce," Archer B. Hulbert; Part 2, "The Railroad Builders," John Moody (New Haven: Yale University Press, 1920).

Inman, Col. Henry, *Old Santa Fe Trail* (New York: The Macmillan Co., 1897).

Johnston, Edwards, *Marching With the Army of the West*, Ferguson Southwest Historical Series, edited by Ralph P. Bieber, Vol. IV (Glendale, Calif.: Arthur H. Clark Co., 1936).

Lawlor, Sister Catherine Miriam, S.C., *History of the Sisters of Charity in New Mexico, 1865–1900*, unpublished thesis (Omaha: Creighton University, 1938).

Lummis, Charles F., *My Friend Will*, second edition (Chicago: A. C. McClurg and Co., 1912).

McCann, Sister Mary Agnes, S.C., *The History of Mother Seton's Daughters*, Vols. I, II, III (New York: Longmans, Green & Co., 1923).

McGoffin, Susan Shelby, *Down the Santa Fe Trail and into Mexico* (New Haven: Yale University Press, 1926).

Meline, James F., *Two Thousand Miles on Horseback* (New York: Hurd and Houghton, 1868).

Miles, Gen. Nelson A., *Personal Recollections and Observations of General Nelson A. Miles* (Chicago and New York: The Werner Co., 1897).

Minogue, Anna C., *The Santa Maria Institute* (New York: The America Press, 1922).

Monica, Sister, O.S.U., Ph.D., *The Cross in the Wilderness* (London and New York: Longmans, Green and Co., 1930).

Murphy, Sister Leona, S.C., *The Life Story of the Sisters of Charity of Cincinnati, Ohio* (1941).

New Mexican (1865), *Santa Fe New Mexican* (1914).

New Mexico, An Illustrated History of (Chicago: The Lewis Publishing Co., 1895).

New Mexico Writers Program of the Works Projects Administration, *New Mexico: A Guide to the Colorful State*, sponsored by the American Guide Series, Coronado Cuarto Centennial Commission (New York: Hastings House Publishers, 1940).

Ohio Guide, American Guide Series, sponsored by the Ohio State Archaeological and Historical Society (New York: Oxford University Press, 1940).

O'Malley, Francis Joseph, *A Literary Addendum: Willa Cather's Archbishop Latour in Reality — John Baptist Lamy — A Presentation of His Letters, Life, and Associates During the Missionary Years in the Diocese of Santa Fe*, unpublished thesis (Notre Dame, Ind.: University of Notre Dame, 1933).

Pearce, Thomas M., and Hendon, Telfair, *America in the Southwest* (Albuquerque: The University Press, 1933).

Perrotta, Rev. Christopher, O.P., *Catholic Care of the Italian Immigrant in the United States* (Washington, D. C.: Catholic University of America, 1925).

Prince, L. Bradford, LL.D., *A Concise History of New Mexico* (Cedar Rapids, Iowa: The Torch Press, 1912).

Pueblo Chieftain, 1865–1870.

Ruxton, George, *Adventures in Mexico* (London: J. Murray, 1847).

Sabin, Edwin L., *Kit Carson Days* (Chicago: A. C. McClurg & Co., 1914).

Salpointe, Most Rev. J. B., *Soldiers of the Cross* (Banning, Calif.: St. Boniface's Industrial School, 1898).

Santa Fe New Mexican, 1915.

Segale, Sister Blandina, S.C., *At the End of the Santa Fe Trail* (Columbus: Columbia Press, 1932).

Smith, Honora BeBusk, *Early Life in Trinidad and Purgatory Valley*, unpublished thesis (Boulder: University of Colorado, 1930).

Street, George G., *Che! Wah! Wah!* (Rochester: E. R. Andrews, Printer and Bookbinder, 1883).

Symonds, John Addington; Cerf, Bennett A.; Klopfer, Donald S., *Renaissance in Italy*, Vols. I and II (New York: The Modern Library). First Modern Library Edition, by arrangement with Charles Scribner's Sons, 1935.

Thwaites, Reuben G., *Early Western Travels* (Cleveland: Clark Co., 1904–1907).

Trail, Official Organ Society of Sons of Colorado, Vol. XIX, No. 8 (1927).

Twitchell, Ralph Emerson, *Leading Facts in New Mexican History*, 5 vols. (Cedar Rapids: The Torch Press, 1911).

Veritas: The Santa Maria (Columbus: Columbia Press, 1928–1930).

Warner, Louis H., *Archbishop Lamy, an Epoch Maker* (Santa Fe: Santa Fe New Mexican Publishing Corp., 1936).

Webb, James Josiah, *Adventures in the Santa Fe Trade* (Glendale, Calif.: Arthur H. Clark, 1931).

Wehmhoff, Sister Mary Walter, S.C., *Educational Activities of the Santa Maria Institute*, unpublished thesis (Dayton: University of Dayton, 1944).

White, Owen, *Out of the Desert: The Historical Romance of El Paso* (The McMath Company, 1923).

Index

Armida F. Palladino
310 North Sixth Street
Albuquerque, New Mexico

CPSIA information can be obtained at www.ICGtesting.com
Printed in the USA
LVOW01s2359130714

393918LV00006B/240/P

9 781162 764764